Practical C++ Design

From Programming to Architecture

Second Edition

Adam B. Singer

Apress®

Practical C++ Design: From Programming to Architecture

Adam B. Singer
The Woodlands, TX, USA

ISBN-13 (pbk): 978-1-4842-7406-4   ISBN-13 (electronic): 978-1-4842-7407-1
https://doi.org/10.1007/978-1-4842-7407-1

Managing Director, Apress Media LLC: Welmoed Spahr
Acquisitions Editor: Steve Anglin
Development Editor: Matthew Moodie
Coordinating Editor: Mark Powers

Cover designed by eStudioCalamar

Cover image by Jeremy Zero on Unsplash (www.unsplash.com)

Distributed to the book trade worldwide by Apress Media, LLC, 1 New York Plaza, New York, NY 10004, U.S.A. Phone 1-800-SPRINGER, fax (201) 348-4505, e-mail orders-ny@springer-sbm.com, or visit www.springeronline.com. Apress Media, LLC is a California LLC and the sole member (owner) is Springer Science + Business Media Finance Inc (SSBM Finance Inc). SSBM Finance Inc is a **Delaware** corporation.

For information on translations, please e-mail booktranslations@springernature.com; for reprint, paperback, or audio rights, please e-mail bookpermissions@springernature.com.

Apress titles may be purchased in bulk for academic, corporate, or promotional use. eBook versions and licenses are also available for most titles. For more information, reference our Print and eBook Bulk Sales web page at http://www.apress.com/bulk-sales.

Any source code or other supplementary material referenced by the author in this book is available to readers on GitHub via the book's product page, located at www.apress.com/9781484274064. For more detailed information, please visit http://www.apress.com/source-code.

Printed on acid-free paper

For Terri, Caroline, and Rebecca.

Table of Contents

About the Author

Adam B. Singer graduated first in his class at the Georgia Institute of Technology in 1999 with a bachelor's degree in chemical engineering. He subsequently attended the Massachusetts Institute of Technology (MIT) on a National Defense Science and Engineering Graduate Fellowship. He graduated from MIT with a Ph.D. in chemical engineering in 2004 after defending his thesis titled "Global Dynamic Optimization."

Since graduation, Adam has been employed by ExxonMobil[1] in various Upstream organizations, including research, information technology, and digital transformation. He has held both technical and managerial roles in software development, design, and project management in areas such as mathematical optimization, reservoir modeling and simulation, decision support under uncertainty, basin modeling, well log modeling, process stratigraphy, geoscience platform architecture, and data science. He has also served on and chaired committees designing in-house training in the areas of technical software development and computational and applied mathematics. He is currently the Senior Principal Digital Architect for ExxonMobil.

Adam additionally held the title of adjunct assistant professor in the Department of Computational and Applied Mathematics at Rice University from 2007 to 2012. In 2006 and 2007, he taught a graduate-level course, CAAM 520, on computational science. The course focused on the design and implementation of high-performance parallel programs.

---

[1] The advice, information, and conclusions discussed in this book are those of the author and have not been endorsed by, or reflect the opinions or practices of, ExxonMobil Corporation or its affiliates.

About the Technical Reviewer

German Gonzalez-Morris is a software architect/engineer working with C/C++,
Java, and different application containers, in particular with WebLogic Server.
He has developed various applications using JEE, Spring, and Python. His areas
of expertise also include OOP, Java/JEE, Python, design patterns, algorithms, Spring
Core/MVC/security, and microservices. German has worked with performance
messaging, RESTful API, and transactional systems. For more information about him,
visit `www.linkedin.com/in/german-gonzalez-morris`.

Preface

Motivation of the Author

Throughout my career, I have mentored both students and fellow employees in programming, and many of them have suggested that I write my thoughts down in book form. However, I have typically responded with the rebuttal that I felt I had nothing novel to present. Being a largely self-taught programmer, I have always been able to rattle off a long list of books from which I have derived most of my knowledge. Therefore, what could I write about that has not already been said?

I came to realize, however, that the majority of books that I had encountered tended to focus only on pieces of design or implementation rather than taking a holistic approach. For example, if one wants to learn the C++ language, Stroustrup [30] or Lippman and Lajoie [19] are excellent references. For learning C++ best practices, one need only read the books by Sutter [31, 32, 33], Sutter and Alexandrescu [34], or Meyers [22, 21, 23]. Of course, learning to program extends well beyond C++. For data structures and algorithms, there are always the classics by Knuth [15, 16, 17] or the more accessible and concise book by Cormen et al. [10]. To learn object-oriented analysis and design, the book by Booch et al. [8] is an excellent reference. Of course, design patterns can be learned from Gamma et al. [11], and general programming practices can be learned from many books such as those by McConnell [20], Spinellis [29], or Kernighan and Pike [14].

Certainly, the deeper the specialty one seeks, the more esoteric the book one can find (and should eventually read). This book is not such a book. Rather, I have striven to write a book that operates from the premise that the reader already possesses a working knowledge of the information encased in works such as the aforementioned titles. In this book, I instead attempt to ground the reader's theoretical knowledge of design through practice using a single case study.

Target Audience

As mentioned previously, the goal of this book is not to present any specific topic but rather to explore the interrelationship of often compartmentalized subjects. The successful combination of these components to form a cohesive, maintainable, elegant piece of software is, in essence, design. As such, this book is intended to target practicing professionals, in particular those who have several years of development experience but who do not yet possess sufficient experience to architect independently a large software project.

Because my intent is to emphasize utilization of one's existing knowledge effectively to design software, I make little effort to explain individual topics in great depth. I believe too many books classified as intermediate to advanced fail because the author devotes too much content describing prerequisites. The result is a massive tome filled with unnecessary detail for the advanced reader, while the beginner is left with a long and complicated exposition that is still inaccessible because the beginner does not possess sufficient knowledge or experience to grasp the subject regardless of the amount of detail devoted to the description. I have, therefore, aimed for conciseness over completeness. Often, I simply refer the reader to relevant material rather than myself describe a background topic in great detail. While this strategy may indeed make this book difficult for beginners, I hope experienced professionals appreciate both the brevity of the book and its tone, which assumes the reader is competent at their craft.

Structure of the Book

Learning most tasks in programming requires hands-on experience and repetition; design is no exception. My opinion is that design is best learned through a combination of self-exploration and mentoring from an expert. For this reason, I have chosen to organize this book as a study in design through the detailed working of a case study. Instead of discussing design elements in the abstract, we will instead examine the concrete application of design principles as they relate to the design and construction of a simplistic (but not too simplistic) software project. Importantly, we will not only examine successful results that led to the final implementation, but we will also spend time considering alternatives, some of which are viable and others which are not. Where multiple solutions may suffice, choosing one over the other is often either a matter of context or just taste. Regardless, experience is usually the arbiter of such decisions, and hopefully this book will enable the reader to learn from the author's experiences without having to repeat his mistakes. That is, I hope I have created a book that can serve as a self-contained master class in design.

The Case Study

To this point, I have not yet mentioned the subject of the case study central to this book. In my opinion, an ideal problem would be one that is not too daunting and yet not so trivial that it needs no design. Additionally, the domain of the problem should be readily understandable to any reader. For this reason, I have chosen to implement a stack-based, Reverse Polish Notation (RPN) calculator that I named pdCalc, short for practical design calculator. Functionally, pdCalc was inspired by the HP48S calculator, an old favorite calculator of mine from high school and college (which still sits on my desk today). I cannot imagine any reader being unfamiliar with the basic operations of a calculator, and making the calculator use RPN adds a little twist that I hope will make the project interesting. If your sole objective were to code a simple calculator with basic functionality, admittedly, the design of pdCalc is overkill, and more code is written from scratch than is strictly necessary. Remember, pdCalc's primary purpose is to serve as an instructional tool – a reduced-size representation of a real project. That pdCalc happens to be a functioning RPN calculator is a secondary objective.

Language Selection

Design as an abstract concept can be taught in the absence of a particular programming language. However, once committed to a concrete example, a specific language must be chosen for the implementation. I decided to write the case study exclusively using C++. While every line of the program does not appear in the text, all of the source code is available for the reader to examine. Despite this book's primary focus on design, reading the source code is a good way to learn how implementation details in a specific language enable or, at least, facilitate a chosen design. The source code also serves as a high-quality (I hope) exemplar of a modern C++ implementation of a complete user application. I highly recommend reading and modifying the source code in conjunction with reading the text.

The decision to use C++ does not imply that C++ is the best choice for all programs, and, in fact, it may not even be the best choice for the program examined in this book. However, to ground the abstraction, a concrete language had to be selected. I chose

C++ because it is standardized, widely deployed, and available at zero cost on many platforms. Selfishly, I also chose C++ because it is my most proficient language. While I could, perhaps, have chosen another language meeting the aforementioned objective criteria (e.g., Python), the resulting code would probably have been functional but nonidiomatic due to my relative lack of expertise.

During the writing of the first edition of this book, C++0x was ratified as C++11 and then updated as C++14. C++11, with smart pointers, move semantics, lambdas, variadic templates, and a host of other new features, fundamentally changed how one could express a design in the C++ language. My objective at the time was to avoid incorporating modern C++ features where they were inappropriate just to demonstrate usage. Instead, I sought to highlight how these new language elements could be used effectively in the design of a large-scale program. Hopefully, I achieved my objective.

Design and architecture have not changed significantly since the publication of the first edition of this book, so why write a second edition? If this were an abstract design book, such an update would be unnecessary. However, since the publication of the first edition, C++17 and C++20 were both ratified. Because the book's case study is accompanied by a complete implementation, expressing a concrete design using C++ has evolved with new language developments. While C++17 added several new implementation features, none of these features substantially impacted the ability to express designs in the language. C++20, on the other hand, is different.

C++20, maybe even more so than C++11, fundamentally changes how designs may be expressed in C++. In particular, four new major language features were added: ranges, coroutines, concepts, and modules, all of which make, at least, a brief appearance in the case study. The ranges library does not fundamentally alter program design. It does, however, fundamentally change the way algorithms can be implemented, especially with the better integration of the functional programming paradigm as enabled through views. Coroutines add cooperative multitasking to the C++ language. We will see that even in a single-threaded program such as the one described in this book, coroutines can be used to express an idea from the first edition differently. Concepts change the way generic programs are constructed. This book's design does not make extensive use of templates; therefore, concepts make only the briefest of appearances. Lastly, C++20 finally brings modularization to C++ as a formal language construct. This change drastically impacts how code can be organized, including, in many instances, completely eliminating the need for header files. We will explore the usage of C++ modules, and their interaction with dynamically linked libraries, in some depth.

In the second edition, I again endeavor to illustrate the interplay between implementation and design and hence aim to demonstrate how language features enable the more natural expression of design paradigms. Where the design usage of modern C++ language or library features are generalizable beyond the case study, I have chosen to highlight these points in a sidebar. Sidebars are inclusive of all new language features since C++11.

GUI Framework, Tooling, External Dependencies, and Compilers

While graphical user interfaces (GUI) are not the primary focus of this book, our program will eventually acquire one; hence, selecting a particular GUI framework was necessary. I selected Qt for this purpose and successfully tested the code against Qt versions 5 and 6. As with C++, Qt is widely deployed, cross platform, and free. As with C++, again, selfishly, I chose Qt because I am experienced using desktop Qt and personally enjoy using it. A big advantage of using Qt is that it makes nearly all of the source code for the project platform independent. Where platform independence was not achievable, I encapsulated the platform-dependent code behind an abstract interface. We'll explore this design pattern, in depth, in Chapter 7.

In the first edition of this book, pdCalc was mostly self-contained, from both a code and tooling standpoint; Qt was the only external dependency necessary to compile, build, and test the code. For the second edition, however, a few external dependencies were necessary. First, I changed the build system from using Qt's own qmake to Kitware's CMake [1]. CMake is cross platform, free of charge, easy to obtain, and practically a de facto standard for building C++ applications. For my purposes, CMake made experimentation with different C++20 compilers easier and more efficient. Of note, CMake's C++20 tooling for modules was still immature at the time of writing, so some parts of the build scripts are more imperative than I expect will be necessary in the future. Second, while C++20 added coroutines as a new low-level language feature, the standard did not incorporate any high-level supporting libraries. In order to focus on the design aspects of using coroutines rather than their implementation mechanics, I increased the level of abstraction by using Lewis Baker's cppcoro [7] library to implement a generator (see Chapter 5). For convenience, I included the single necessary file from cppcoro into a third-party directory included with pdCalc's source code.

In general, I always strive to write standards-conforming, platform-independent code. Since any known platform-specific code is compartmentalized and encapsulated, extension to other platforms should be straightforward if you can tolerate the pain of customizing the build system. Therefore, the source code in this book should compile with any C++20-compliant compiler and on any platform where Qt is supported. Unfortunately, over a year after finalization of the standard, only one compiler, Microsoft's Visual C++ (MSVC), is sufficiently standards conforming to actually compile the full source code presented in this book. (To be fair, 2020 was a very strange year.) GCC is close, but it lacks two key features. First, GCC's C++ standard library implementation is missing the C++20 formatting library. This problem can be easily remedied by substituting the MIT licensed fmt library [2] in its place. The bigger problem is the immaturity of C++ modules support in GCC. Specifically, pdCalc's source code, at the time of writing, causes GCC to produce internal compiler errors; I have submitted multiple bug reports. Clang's support of C++20, while laudable, is behind both GCC and MSVC. At the current pace of development, I expect GCC to reach sufficient standards conformance to compile this book's source code ahead of clang.

The Source Code

The source code (and supporting unit tests) for pdCalc is available, in its entirety, from Apress's GitHub repository (`https://github.com/Apress/practical-cplusplus-design-2e`). Appendix A describes, in detail, how to download and build the source code. Although most readers will likely prefer to download the source using a git client, the entire source code is also available from GitHub as a single zip file.

The source code itself is licensed under the GNU Public License (GPL) version 3. I hope you find the source code useful for learning about design and implementation. Beyond its use as an educational aid for this book, you are, of course, free to do anything you like with the source code within the rights granted to you by the GPL.

For the first edition of this book, I wrote the source code for pdCalc from scratch specifically targeting new language features of C++11; the source code was updated for C++14 shortly before publication. For the second edition of this book, I updated and refactored the source code to use C++17 and C++20 features instead of performing a complete rewrite. This strategy has two implications. First, not every line of code was touched, although more lines were touched than I originally anticipated. Nevertheless,

I likely missed places where newer features of the language could have been used but weren't. In other instances, newer features were intentionally not used because of compiler or language support. For example, while most of pdCalc was upgraded to extensively use modules, the GUI was not because, at the time of writing, modules and Qt's meta object compiler (MOC) did not interoperate well. Second, because I was literally refactoring the source code for the sole purpose of incorporating new language features, I was able to identify specifically where new language features enabled different design paradigms. Where these changes were significant, I contrasted the original version of the source code and its design to the updated version directly in the book's text.

This book uses two distinct fonts: the standard font you are reading now and a fixed width font used for source code. The fixed width font is demonstrated in the following list of standard library containers: vector, list, and map. When clear from context, to save space, I often omit namespaces and template arguments. When the discussion requires a block of source code, it will be offset from the rest of the text as follows:

```
class ExampleClass
{
public:
  // your implementation here
};
```

In general, I tried to reproduce the code in the text identically to the code in the repository. However, in some cases, parts of the source were deliberately omitted in the text either for brevity or clarity. I tried to note instances where the differences are significant. Where the two differ, assume the code in the repository is the more correct and complete version.

Contacting the Author

I suspect that as you read this book and explore the source code, you will invariably have questions. Please feel free to contact me with questions about the content of the book, questions about the source code, errors, or improvements to my design or implementation. I can be contacted at PracticalDesignBook@gmail.com. I will make my best effort to reply to all reasonable email related to pdCalc, but without knowing the volume of email I'll receive, I can make no ironclad guarantee that I will be able to respond to every request. With respect to the first edition of this book, I can proudly state that I responded to each and every email that I received in great detail. Unfortunately, the previous statement is true by vacuous argument as no one emailed me. Nonetheless, I reiterate that anyone should feel free to ask me questions, and I will make my best effort to respond in a timely manner.

Parting Advice

Finally, in addition to learning something, I hope that you, the reader, have fun with the subject. My personal suggestion is to try to think about the design decisions yourself before reading my solutions. If you are truly industrious, you may even want to implement your own calculator using a completely different, possibly better design. After all, as I said before, design is ultimately about both experience and taste, and your experience and taste may differ significantly from mine. Enjoy!

CHAPTER 1

Defining the Case Study

1.1 A Brief Introduction

This book is about programming design. However, unlike many books on this topic, this book teaches design by exploration rather than design by instruction. Typically, most authors writing about some aspect of design establish principles they wish to convey, lay out these principles in the abstract, and then proceed to give examples supporting the current points. This is not such a book. Rather, this book defines a practical problem to be solved and proceeds to examine its solution in detail. That is, instead of deciding on a topic and creating trivial examples to support its teaching, I have defined a hard problem and then let the solution of this problem dictate what topics should be discussed.

Interestingly enough, the preceding approach is exactly how I would tell someone *not* to learn a subject. I always stress that people should learn broad fundamentals first and subsequently apply these principles to solving problems. However, this is not a book meant to teach the principles of design. Rather, this is a book meant for someone who already knows the fundamentals but wishes to deepen their knowledge of practice. This is a book meant to teach someone the craft of designing and implementing a realistic, albeit small, program from start to finish. This process involves more than knowing elements of design. It involves understanding when and how to use what you know, understanding how to decide between seemingly equivalent approaches, and understanding the long-term implications of various decisions. This book is not comprehensive in its coverage of data structures, algorithms, design patterns, or C++ best practices; volumes of books exist to cover these topics. This is a book about learning how to apply this knowledge to write code that is organized, cohesive, sensible, purposeful, and pragmatic. In other words, this book is about learning to write code that both gets the job done now (development) and allows others to continue to get the job done in the future (maintenance). This, I have termed practical design.

© Adam Singer 2022
A. B. Singer, *Practical C++ Design*, https://doi.org/10.1007/978-1-4842-7407-1_1

In order to explore practical design, we need a case study. Ideally, the case study problem should be

- Large enough to be more than trivial

- Small enough to be tractable

- Familiar enough to not require domain-specific expertise

- Interesting enough to maintain the reader's attention for the duration of the book

After taking the preceding criteria into consideration, I decided to select a stack-based, Reverse Polish Notation (RPN) calculator as the case study. The details of the calculator's requirements will be defined in the following. I believe that the code for a fully functioning calculator is significant enough that the detailed study of its design provides sufficient material to cover a book. Yet the project is small enough that the book can be a reasonable length. Certainly, specialized domain expertise is not required. I suspect every reader of this book has used a calculator and is well versed in its basic functionality. Finally, I hope that making the calculator RPN provides a suitable twist to stave off boredom.

1.2 A Few Words About Requirements

No matter how big or how small, all programs have requirements. Requirements are those features, whether explicit or implicit, functional or nonfunctional, to which the program must comply. Entire books have been written on gathering and managing software requirements (see, e.g., [36] or [28]). Typically, despite one's best efforts, it is practically impossible to gather all of the requirements up front. Sometimes, the effort required is economically infeasible. Sometimes, domain experts overlook what seem like obvious requirements to them, and they simply neglect to relate all of their requirements to the development team. Sometimes, requirements only become apparent after the program begins to take shape. Sometimes, the customer does not understand their own requirements well enough to articulate them to the development team. While some of these dilemmas may be mitigated using agile development methods, the fact remains that many design decisions, some of which may have far-reaching implications, must occur before all of the requirements are known.

In this book, we will not study techniques for gathering requirements; rather, our requirements are simply given up front. Well, most of them will be given up front. A few of the requirements have been explicitly reserved until a later chapter so that we can study how our design might change to accommodate unknown future expansion. Certainly, one could justly argue that since the author knows how the requirements will change, the initial design will correctly "predict" the unforeseen features. While this criticism is fair, I nonetheless argue that the thought process and discussion behind the design decisions are still relevant. As a software architect, part of your job will be to anticipate future requests. Although any request is possible, incorporating too much flexibility at the outset is not economical. Designing for future expansion must always be considered as a trade-off between the cost difference for expressly accommodating expandability up front vs. modifying the code later if a change is requested. Where a design should land in the spectrum between simplicity and flexibility must ultimately be measured against the likelihood of a feature request materializing and the feasibility of adding a new feature if its incorporation is not considered at the beginning.

1.3 Reverse Polish Notation (RPN)

I presume that anyone reading this book is familiar with the typical operation of a calculator. However, unless you grew up using a Hewlett-Packard calculator, you may be unfamiliar with how a stack-based RPN calculator functions (see [10] if you are unfamiliar with how a stack works). Simply stated, input numbers are pushed onto a stack, and operations are performed on the numbers already on the stack. A binary operator, such as addition, pops the top two numbers from the stack, adds the two numbers, and then pushes the result onto the stack. A unary operator, such as the sine function, pops one number from the top of the stack, uses this number as the operand, and pushes the result onto the stack. For those familiar with basic compiler lingo, RPN functions as the postfix notation of the operation (see [4] for a detailed discussion of postfix notation). The following list describes my opinion of just a few of the advantages of Reverse Polish Notation over conventional syntax:

- All operations can be expressed parentheses-free.

- Multiple inputs and outputs can be visualized simultaneously.

- Large calculations can be trivially decomposed into multiple, simple operations.

- Intermediate results can be trivially retained and reused.

While RPN will likely seem incredibly awkward at first, once you've become accustomed to it, you will curse every calculator that does not employ it when you are tasked with performing anything more complicated than simple arithmetic.

To ensure that the operation of an RPN calculator is clear, let's examine a short example. Suppose we wish to evaluate the following expression:

$$\frac{(4+7)*3+2}{7}$$

On a typical, non-RPN calculator, we would type $((4+7)*3+2)/7$ and then press the = key. On an RPN calculator, we would instead type $4\ 7 + 3 * 2 + 7\ /$, where there is an enter command following each number in order to push the input onto the stack. Note that for many calculators, to reduce key entry, operations such as + may also function to implicitly enter the previous number on the stack. Figure 1-1 shows the preceding calculation performed step by step on an RPN calculator.

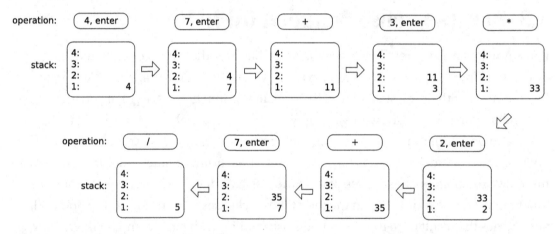

Figure 1-1. *An example calculation performed on an RPN calculator showing intermediate steps. Counterintuitively, the top of the stack is at the bottom of the screen*

1.4 The Calculator's Requirements

Once you understand the nature of Reverse Polish Notation, the rest of the calculator's functionality should be straightforward from the requirements description. If RPN is still unclear, I recommend spending some time clarifying this concept before proceeding. Given that caveat, the requirements of the calculator are now defined as follows:

- The calculator will be stack based; the stack size should not be hard-coded.

- The calculator will use RPN to perform operations.

- The calculator will exclusively operate on floating-point numbers; a technique for entering input numbers (including scientific notation) should be implemented.

- The calculator will have the ability to undo and redo operations; the undo/redo stack sizes should be conceptually unlimited.

- The calculator will have the ability to swap the top two elements of the stack.

- The calculator will be able to drop (erase) an element from the top of the stack.

- The calculator will be able to clear the entire stack.

- The calculator will be able to duplicate the element from the top of the stack.

- The calculator will be able to negate the element from the top of the stack.

- The calculator will implement the four basic arithmetic operations: addition, subtraction, multiplication, and division. Division by 0 is impermissible.

- The calculator will implement the three basic trigonometric functions and their inverses: sin, cos, tan, arcsin, arccos, and arctan. Arguments to the trigonometric functions will be given in radians.

- The calculator will implement functions for y^x and $\sqrt[x]{y}$.

- The calculator will implement a runtime plugin structure to expand the operations the calculator can perform.

- The calculator will implement both a command line interface (CLI) and a graphical user interface (GUI).

- The calculator will not support infinity or imaginary numbers.

- The calculator will be fault tolerant (i.e., it will not crash if the user gives bad input) but does not need to handle floating-point exceptions.

Now that the calculator has requirements, it deserves a name. I chose to call the calculator pdCalc, short for practical design calculator. Please accept my apologies to you for my lack of naming creativity.

The remainder of this book will examine, in detail, the complete design of a calculator that satisfies the preceding requirements. In addition to describing the decisions made for the final design, we will also discuss alternatives to understand why the final decisions were made and what could have been the consequences of different decisions. I'll note that the final design presented in this book is not the only design that will meet the requirements, and it may not even be the best design that meets the requirements. I encourage the ambitious reader to experiment with alternate designs and extend the calculator to meet their own needs and interests.

1.5 The Source Code

Throughout the text of this book, we will be examining a lot of code snippets as we design our calculator. Most of these code snippets are taken directly from pdCalc's GitHub source repository (see Appendix A for instruction for downloading the source code). I will point out any significant differences between the code in the text and the code in the repository. Occasionally, code snippets are comprised of small, contrived examples. These code snippets are not part of pdCalc's source repository. All of the code is made available under the GPL version 3 [12]. I highly encourage you to experiment with the source code and modify it in any way you see fit.

In order to build pdCalc, you will need access to a C++20-compliant compiler, Qt (version 5 or 6), and CMake. In order to not introduce additional dependencies, the unit tests are performed with Qt's QtTest. At the time this edition was written, Microsoft's Visual C++ (MSVC) was the only compiler with sufficient C++20 conformance to build pdCalc. Hopefully, GCC and clang will reach C++20 maturity soon. However, due to the inability of GCC or clang to build pdCalc, I have only built and tested the program in Windows using MSVC. However, as additional compilers reach a sufficient level of C++20 maturity, the code should also build and execute on additional systems with little or no source code modification. Some tweaks to the CMake project files will be necessary for porting to a different platform, although I have at least provided hooks to get one started with Linux using either GCC or clang. Because I expect that the audience for this book leans toward developers with years of experience, I suspect that building the code from source will be a fairly trivial task. However, for completeness, I have included build guidance in Appendix A. Additionally, I have included Appendix B to explain the organization of pdCalc's source code, libraries, and executables. Although these two appendices appear at the end of the book, you may wish to read them first if you intend to build pdCalc and explore its full implementation while reading the text.

CHAPTER 2

Decomposition

Software is complex, one of the most complex endeavors humankind has ever undertaken. When you first read the requirements document for a large-scale programming project, you may feel overwhelmed. That's expected; the task is overwhelming! For this reason, large-scale programming projects typically begin with analysis.

The analysis phase of a project consists of the time spent exploring the problem domain in order to understand the problem completely, clarify the requirements, and resolve any ambiguities between the client's and developer's domains. Without fully understanding the problem, you, as the architect or developer, have absolutely no chance of developing a maintainable design. For the case study chosen for this book, however, the domain should be familiar (if not, you may wish to pause here and partake in an analysis exercise). Therefore, we skip a formal, separate analysis phase. That said, aspects of analysis can never be skipped entirely, and we will explore several analysis techniques during the construction of our design. This intentional coupling of analysis and design emphasizes the interplay between these two activities to demonstrate that even for the simplest of problem domains, producing a good design requires some formal techniques for analyzing the problem.

One of the most important techniques we have as software designers for addressing inherent problem complexity is hierarchical decomposition. Most people tend to decompose a problem in one of two ways: top-down or bottom-up. A top-down approach starts by looking at the whole picture and subsequently subdividing the problem until reaching the bottom-most level. In software design, the absolute bottom-most level would be individual function implementations. However, a top-down design might stop short of implementation and conclude by designing objects and their public interfaces. A bottom-up approach would start at the individual function or object level and combine components repeatedly until eventually encompassing the entire design.

© Adam Singer 2022
A. B. Singer, *Practical C++ Design*, https://doi.org/10.1007/978-1-4842-7407-1_2

For our case study, both top-down and bottom-up approaches will be used at various stages of the design. I find it practical to begin decomposition in a top-down fashion until bulk modules and their interfaces are defined and then actually design these modules from the bottom-up. Before tackling the decomposition of our calculator, let's first begin by examining the elements of a good decomposition.

2.1 The Elements of a Good Decomposition

What makes a decomposition good? Obviously, we could just randomly split functionality into different modules and group completely unconnected components. Using the calculator as an example, we could place arithmetic operators and the GUI in one module while placing trigonometric functions with the stack and error handling in another module. This is a decomposition, just not a very useful one.

In general, a good design will display attributes of modularity, encapsulation, cohesion, and low coupling. Many developers will have already seen many of the principles of a good decomposition in the context of object-oriented design. After all, breaking code into objects is, itself, a decomposition process. Let's first examine these principles in an abstract context. Subsequently, we'll ground the discussion by applying these principles to pdCalc.

Modularity, or breaking components into independently interacting parts (modules), is important for several reasons. First, it immediately allows one to partition a large, complex problem into multiple, smaller, more tractable components. While trying to implement code for the entire calculator at once would be difficult, implementing an independently functioning stack is quite reasonable. Second, once components are split into distinct modules, tests can be defined that validate individual modules instead of requiring the entire program to be completed before integration testing commences. Third, for large projects, if modules with clear boundaries and interfaces are defined, the development effort can be divided between multiple programmers (or teams of programmers) preventing them from constantly interfering with one another's progress by needing to modify the same source files.

The remaining principles of good design, encapsulation, cohesion, and low coupling all describe characteristics that modules should possess. Basically, they prevent spaghetti code. Encapsulation, or information hiding, refers to the idea that once a module is defined, its internal implementation (data structures and algorithms) remains hidden from other modules. Correspondingly, a module should not make use of the private implementation of any other module. That is not to say that modules should not interact with one another. Rather, encapsulation insists that modules interact with one another only through clearly defined and, preferably, limited interfaces. This distinct separation ensures that internal module implementation can be independently modified without concern for breaking external, dependent code, provided the interfaces remain fixed and the contracts guaranteed by the interfaces are met.

Cohesion refers to the idea that the code inside a module should be self-consistent or, as the name implies, cohesive. That is, all of the code within a module should logically fit together. Returning to our example of a poor calculator design, a module mixing arithmetic code with user interface code would lack cohesion. No logical ties bind the two concepts together (other than that they are both components of a calculator). While a small code, like our calculator, would not be completely impenetrable if it lacked cohesion, in general, a large, noncohesive code base is very difficult to understand, maintain, and extend.

Poor cohesion can manifest in one of two ways: either code that should not be together is crammed together or code that should be together is split apart. In the first instance, code functionality is almost impossible to decompose into mentally manageable abstractions because no clear boundaries exist between logical subcomponents. In the latter situation, reading or debugging unfamiliar code (especially for the first time) can be very frustrating because a typical execution path through the code jumps from file to file in a seemingly random fashion. Either manifestation is counterproductive, and we thus prefer cohesive code.

Finally, we examine coupling. Coupling represents the interconnectedness of components, be it functional coupling or data coupling. Functional coupling occurs when the logical flow of one module requires calling another module to complete its action. Conversely, data coupling is when data is shared between individual modules either via direct sharing (e.g., one or more modules point to some set of shared data) or via passing of data (e.g., one module returning a pointer to an internal data structure to another module). To argue for zero coupling is clearly absurd because this state would imply that no module could communicate in any way with any other module. However, in good design, we do strive for low coupling. How low should low be? The glib answer is as low as possible while still maintaining the ability to function as necessary. The reality is that minimizing coupling without detrimentally complicating code is a skill acquired with experience. As with encapsulation, low coupling is enabled by ensuring that modules communicate with one another only through cleanly defined, limited interfaces. Code that is highly coupled is difficult to maintain because small changes in one module's design may lead to many unforeseen, cascading changes through seemingly unrelated modules. Note that whereas encapsulation protects module A from internal implementation changes to module B, low coupling protects module A from changes to the interface of module B.

2.2 Selecting an Architecture

Although it is now tempting to follow our preceding guidelines and simply start decomposing our calculator into what seem like sensible constituent components, it's best to first see if someone else has already solved our problem. Because similar problems tend to arise frequently in programming, software architects have created a catalog of templates for solving these problems; these archetypes are called patterns. Patterns typically come in multiple varieties. Two categories of patterns that will be examined in this book are design patterns [11] and architectural patterns.

Design patterns are conceptual templates used to solve similar problems that arise during software design; they are typically applied to local decisions. We will encounter design patterns repeatedly throughout this book during the detailed design of our calculator. Our first top level of decomposition, however, requires a pattern of global scope that will define the overarching design strategy, or software architecture. Such patterns are naturally referred to as architectural patterns.

Architectural patterns are conceptually similar to design patterns; the two differ primarily in their domains of applicability. Whereas design patterns are typically applied to particular classes or sets of related classes, architectural patterns typically outline the design for an entire software system. Note that I refer to a software system rather than a program because architectural patterns can extend beyond simple program boundaries to include interfaces to hardware, networking, security, databases, the coupling of multiple independent programs, etc. Complex architectural patterns for entire systems are prevalent in modern, cloud-deployed solutions.

Two architectural patterns of particular interest for our case study are the multitiered architecture and the model-view-controller (MVC) architecture. We'll examine each of these two patterns in the abstract before applying them to pdCalc. The successful application of an architectural pattern to our case study will represent the first level of decomposition for the calculator.

2.2.1 Multitiered Architecture

In a multitiered, or n-tiered, architecture, components are arranged sequentially in tiers. Communication is bidirectional via adjacent tiers, but nonadjacent tiers are not permitted to communicate directly. An n-tiered architecture is depicted in Figure 2-1.

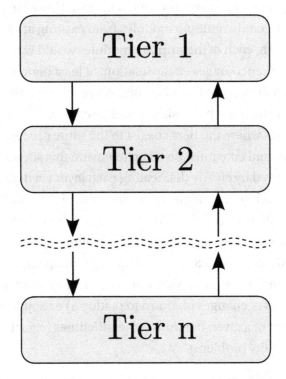

Figure 2-1. *A multitiered architecture with arrows indicating communication*

The most common form of the multitiered architecture is the three-tiered architecture. The first tier is the presentation layer, which consists of all of the user interface code. The second tier is the logic layer, which captures the so-called business logic of the application. The third tier is the data layer, which, as the name implies, encapsulates the data for the system. Very often, the three-tiered architecture is applied as a simplistic enterprise-level platform, where each tier could represent not only a different local process but also possibly a different process operating on a different machine. In such a system, the presentation layer would be the client interface, whether it be a traditional desktop application or a browser-based interface. The logic layer of the program could run on either the client or server side of the application or, possibly, on both. Finally, the data layer would be represented by a database that could be running locally or remotely. However, as we shall see with pdCalc, the three-tiered architecture can also be applied to a single desktop application.

Let's examine how the three-tiered architecture obeys our general decomposition principles. First and foremost, at the highest level of decomposition, the architecture is modular. At least three modules, one for each tier, exist. However, the three-tiered architecture does not preclude multiple modules from existing at each tier. If the system were large enough, each of the primary modules would warrant subdivision. Second, this architecture encourages encapsulation, at least between tiers. While one could foolishly design a three-tiered architecture where adjacent tiers accessed private methods of neighboring tiers, such a design would be counterintuitive and very brittle. That said, in applications where the tiers coexist in the same process space, it is very easy to intertwine the layers, and care must be taken to ensure this situation does not arise. This separation is achieved by clearly delineating each layer via definitive interfaces. Third, the three-tiered architecture is cohesive. Each tier of the architecture has a distinct task, which is not commingled with the tasks of the other tiers. Finally, the three-tiered architecture truly shines as an example of limited coupling. By separating each of the tiers via clearly defined interfaces, each tier can change independently of the others. This feature is particularly important for applications that must execute on multiple platforms (only the presentation layer changes platform to platform) or applications that undergo unforeseen replacement of a given tier during their lifetimes (e.g., the database must be changed due to a scalability problem).

2.2.2 Model-View-Controller (MVC) Architecture

In the model-view-controller (MVC) architecture, components are decomposed into three distinct elements aptly named the model, the view, and the controller. The model abstracts the domain data, the view abstracts the user interface, and the controller manages the interaction between the model and the view. Often, the MVC pattern is applied locally to individual GUI widgets at the framework level where the design goal is to separate the data from the user interface in situations where multiple distinct views may be associated with the same data. For example, consider a scheduling application with the requirement that the application must be able to store dates and times for appointments, but the user may view these appointments in a calendar that can be viewed by day, week, or month. Applying MVC, the appointment data would be abstracted by a model module (likely, a class in an object-oriented framework), and each calendar style would be abstracted by a distinct view (likely, three separate classes). A controller would be introduced to handle user events generated by the views and to manipulate the data in the model.

At first glance, MVC seems no different than the three-tiered architecture with the model replacing the data layer, the view replacing the presentation layer, and the controller replacing the business logic layer. The two architectural patterns are different, however, in their interaction pattern. In the three-tiered architecture, the communication between layers is rigidly linear. That is, the presentation and data layers talk only bidirectionally to the logic layer, never to each other. In MVC, the communication is triangular. While different MVC implementations differ in their exact communication patterns, a typical implementation is depicted in Figure 2-2. In this figure, the view can both generate events to be handled by the controller and get the data to be displayed directly from the model. The controller handles events from the view, but it can also directly manipulate either the model or the controller. Finally, the model can be acted upon directly by either the view or the controller, but it can also generate events to be handled by the view. A typical such event would be a state change event that would cause the view to update its presentation to the user.

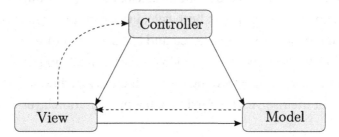

Figure 2-2. *An MVC architecture with arrows indicating communication. Solid lines indicate direct communication. Dashed lines indicate indirect communication (e.g., via eventing) [38]*

As we did with the three-tiered architecture, let's now examine how MVC obeys our general decomposition principles. First, an MVC architecture will usually be broken into at least three modules: model, view, and controller. However, as with the three-tiered architecture, a larger system will admit more modules because each of the model, view, and controller will require subdivision. Second, this architecture also encourages encapsulation. The model, view, and controller should only interact with one another through clearly defined interfaces, where events and event handling are defined as part of an interface. Third, the MVC architecture is cohesive. Each component has a distinct, well-defined task. Finally, we ask if the MVC architecture is loosely coupled. By inspection, this architectural pattern is more tightly coupled than the three-tiered architecture because the presentation layer and the data layer are permitted to have direct dependencies. In practice, these dependencies are often limited either through loosely coupled event handling or via polymorphism with abstract base classes. Typically, however, this added coupling does usually relegate the MVC pattern to applications in one memory space. This limitation directly contrasts with the flexibility of the three-tiered architecture, which may span applications over multiple memory spaces.

2.2.3 Architectural Patterns Applied to the Calculator

Let's now return to our case study and apply the two architectural patterns discussed previously to pdCalc. Ultimately we'll select one as the architecture for our application. As previously described, a three-tiered architecture consists of a presentation layer, a logic layer, and a data layer. For the calculator, these tiers are clearly identified as entering commands and viewing results (via either a graphical or command line user interface), the execution of the commands, and the stack, respectively. For the MVC architecture, we have the stack as the model, the user interface as the view, and the command dispatcher as the controller. Both calculator architectures are depicted in Figure 2-3. Note that in both the three-tiered and MVC architectures, the input aspects of the presentation layer or view are responsible only for accepting the commands, not interpreting or executing them. Enforcing this distinction alleviates a common problem developers create for themselves, the mixing of the presentation layer with the logic layer.

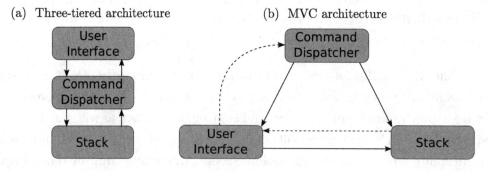

Figure 2-3. *Calculator architecture options*

2.2.4 Choosing the Calculator's Architecture

From Figure 2-3, one quickly identifies that the two architectures partition the calculator into identical modules. In fact, at the architectural level, these two competing architectures differ only in their coupling. Therefore, in selecting between these two architectures, we only need to consider the design trade-offs between their two communication patterns.

Obviously, the main difference between the three-tiered architecture and the MVC architecture is the communication pattern between the user interface (UI) and the stack. In the three-tiered architecture, the UI and stack are only allowed to communicate indirectly through the command dispatcher. The biggest benefit of this separation is a decrease in coupling in the system. The UI and the stack need to know nothing about the interface of the other. The disadvantage, of course, is that if the program requires significant direct UI and stack communication, the command dispatcher will be required to broker this communication, which decreases the cohesion of the command dispatcher module. The MVC architecture has the exact opposite trade-off. That is, at the expense of additional coupling, the UI can directly exchange messages with the stack, avoiding the awkwardness of the command dispatcher performing added functionality unrelated to its primary purpose. Therefore, the architecture decision reduces to examining whether or not the UI frequently needs a direct connection to the stack.

In an RPN calculator, the stack acts as the repository for both the input and output for the program. Frequently, the user will wish to see both the input and output exactly as it appears on the stack. This situation favors the MVC architecture with its direct interaction between the view and the data. That is, the calculator's view does not require the command dispatcher to translate the communication between the data and the user because no transformation of the data is required. Therefore, I selected the model-view-controller as the architecture for pdCalc. The advantages of the MVC architecture over the three-tiered architecture are, admittedly, small for our case study. Had I instead chosen to use the three-tiered architecture, pdCalc still would have had a perfectly valid design.

2.3 Interfaces

Although it might be tempting to declare our first level of decomposition complete with the selection of the MVC architecture, we cannot yet declare victory. While we have defined our three highest-level modules, we must also define their public interfaces. However, without utilizing some formal method for capturing all the data flows in our problem, we are very likely to miss key necessary elements of our interface. We therefore turn to an object-oriented analysis technique, the use case.

A use case is an analysis technique that generates a description of a specific action a user has with a system. Essentially, a use case defines a workflow. Importantly, a use case does not specify an implementation. The customer should be consulted during use case generation, particularly in instances where a use case uncovers an ambiguity in the requirements. Details concerning use cases and use case diagrams can be found in Booch et al. [9].

For the purpose of designing interfaces for pdCalc's high-level modules, we will first define the use cases for an end user interacting with the calculator. Each use case should define a single workflow, and we should provide enough use cases to satisfy all of the technical requirements for the calculator. These use cases can then be studied to discover the minimal interactions required between the modules. These communication patterns will define the modules' public interfaces. An added benefit of this use case analysis is that if our existing modules are insufficient to implement all of the workflows, we will have uncovered the need for additional modules in our top-level design.

2.3.1 Calculator Use Cases

Let's create the use cases for our requirements. For consistency, use cases are created in the order in which they appear in the requirements.

Use Case: User enters a floating-point number onto the stack

Scenario: The user enters a floating-point number onto the stack. After entry, the user can see the number on the stack.

Exception: The user enters an invalid floating-point number. An error condition is displayed.

Use Case: User undoes last operation

Scenario: The user enters the command to undo the last operation. The system undoes the last operation and displays the previous stack.

Exception: There is no command to undo. An error condition is displayed.

Use Case: User redoes last operation

Scenario: The user enters the command to redo the last operation. The system redoes the last operation and displays the new stack.

Exception: There is no command to redo. An error condition is displayed.

Use Case: User swaps top stack elements

Scenario: The user enters the command to swap the top two elements on the stack. The system swaps the top two elements on the stack and displays the new stack.

Exception: The stack does not have at least two numbers. An error condition is displayed.

Use Case: User drops the top stack element

Scenario: The user enters the command to drop the top element from the stack. The system drops the top element from the stack and displays the new stack.

Exception: The stack is empty. An error condition is displayed.

Use Case: User clears the stack

Scenario: The user enters the command to clear the stack. The system clears the stack and displays the empty stack.

Exception: None. Let clear succeed even for an empty stack (by doing nothing).

Use Case: User duplicates the top stack element

Scenario: The user enters the command to duplicate the top element on the stack. The system duplicates the top element on the stack and displays the new stack.

Exception: The stack is empty. An error condition is displayed.

Use Case: User negates the top stack element

Scenario: The user enters the command to negate the top element on the stack. The system negates the top element on the stack and displays the new stack.

Exception: The stack is empty. An error condition is displayed.

Use Case: User performs an arithmetic operation

Scenario: The user enters the command to add, subtract, multiply, or divide. The system performs the operation and displays the new stack.

Exception: The stack size is insufficient to support the operation. An error condition is displayed.

Exception: Division by zero is detected. An error condition is displayed.

Use Case: User performs a trigonometric operation

Scenario: The user enters the command for sin, cos, tan, arcsin, arccos, or arctan. The system performs the operation and displays the new stack.

Exception: The stack size is insufficient to support the operation. An error condition is displayed.

Exception: The input for the operation is invalid (e.g., arcsin(-50) would produce an imaginary result). An error condition is displayed.

Use Case: User performs y^x

Scenario: The user enters the command for y^x. The system performs the operation and displays the new stack.

Exception: The stack size is insufficient to support the operation. An error condition is displayed.

Exception: The input for the operation is invalid (e.g., $-1^{0.5}$ would produce an imaginary result). An error condition is displayed.

Use Case: User performs $\sqrt[x]{y}$

Scenario: The user enters the command for $\sqrt[x]{y}$. The system performs the operation and displays the new stack.

Exception: The stack size is insufficient to support the operation. An error condition is displayed.

Exception: The input for the operation is invalid (e.g., $\sqrt[4]{-1}$ would produce an imaginary result). An error condition is displayed.

Use Case: User loads a plugin

Scenario: The user places a plugin into the plugin directory. The system loads the plugin on startup, making the plugin functionality available.

Exception: The plugin cannot be loaded. An error condition is displayed.

2.3.2 Analysis of Use Cases

We will now analyze the use cases for the purpose of developing C++ interfaces for pdCalc's modules. For the moment, we will simply consider these interfaces abstractly as the publicly facing function signatures to a collection of classes and functions grouped logically to define a module. We will translate these informal concepts into C++20 modules in Section 2.5. For the sake of brevity, the std namespace prefix is omitted in the text.

Let's examine the use cases in order. As the public interface is developed, it will be entered into Table 2-2. The exception will be for the first use case, whose interface will be described in Table 2-1. By using a separate table for the first use case, we'll be able to preserve the errors we'll make on the first pass for comparison to our final product. By the end of this section, the entire public interface for all of the MVC modules will have been developed and cataloged.

We begin with the first use case, entering a floating-point number. The implementation of the user interface will take care of getting the number from the user into the calculator. Here, we are concerned with the interface required to get the number from the UI onto the stack.

Regardless of the path the number takes from the UI to the stack, we must eventually have a function call for pushing numbers onto the stack. Therefore, the first part of our interface is simply a function on the stack module, push(), for pushing a double-precision number onto the stack. We enter this function into Table 2-1. Note that the table contains the complete function signature, while the return type and argument types are omitted in the text.

Now, we must explore our options for getting the number from the user interface module to the stack module. From Figure 2-3b, we see that the UI has a direct link to the stack. Therefore, the simplest option would be to push the floating-point number onto the stack directly from the UI using the push() function we just defined. Is this a good idea?

By definition, the command dispatcher module, or the controller, exists to process commands the user enters. Should entering a number be treated differently than, for example, the addition command? Having the UI bypass the command dispatcher and directly enter a number onto the stack module violates the principle of least surprise (also referred to as the principle of least astonishment). Essentially, this principle states that when a designer is presented with multiple valid design options, the correct choice is the one that conforms to the user's intuition. In the context of interface design, the user is another programmer or designer. Here, any programmer working on our system would expect all commands to be handled identically, so a good design will obey this principle.

To avoid violating the principle of least surprise, we must build an interface that routes a newly entered number from the UI through the command dispatcher. We again refer to Figure 2-3b. Unfortunately, the UI does not have a direct connection to the command dispatcher, making direct communication impossible. It does, however, have an indirect pathway. Thus, our only option is for the UI to raise an event (we'll study events in detail in Chapter 3). Specifically, the UI must raise an event indicating that a number has been entered, and the command dispatcher must be able to receive this event (eventually, via a function call in its public interface). Let's add two more functions to Table 2-1, one for the numberEntered() event raised by the UI and one for the numberEntered() event handling function in the command dispatcher.

Once the number has been accepted, the UI must display the revised stack. This is accomplished by the stack signaling that it has changed and the view requesting n elements from the stack and displaying them to the user. We must use this pathway as the stack only has an indirect communication channel to the UI. We add three more functions to Table 2-1, a stackChanged() event on the stack module, a stackChanged() event handler on the UI, and a getElements() function on the stack module (see the modern C++ sidebar on move semantics to see options for the getElements() function signature). Unlike the entering of the number itself, it is reasonable to have the UI directly call the stack's function for getting elements in response to the stackChanged() event. This is, in fact, precisely how we want a view to interact with its data in the MVC pattern.

Of course, the aforementioned workflow assumes the user entered a valid number. For completeness, however, the use case also specifies that error checking must be performed on number entry. Therefore, the command dispatcher should actually check the validity of the number before pushing it onto the stack, and it should signal the user interface if an error has occurred. The UI should correspondingly be able to handle error events. That's two more functions for Table 2-1, an error() event on the command dispatcher and a function, displayError(), on the UI, for handling the error event. Note that we could have selected an alternative error handling design by leaving the UI to perform its own error checking and only raise a number entered event for valid numbers. However, for improved cohesion, we prefer placing the "business logic" of error checking in the controller rather than in the interface.

Phew! That completes our analysis of the first use case. In case you got lost, remember that all of the functions and events just described are summarized in Table 2-1. Now just 12 more exciting use cases to go to complete our interface analysis! Don't worry, the drudgery will end shortly. We will soon derive a design that can consolidate almost all of the use cases into a unified interface.

Before proceeding immediately to the next use case, let's pause for a moment and discuss two decisions we just implicitly made about error handling. First, the user interface handles errors by catching events rather than by catching exceptions. Because the user interface cannot directly send messages to the command dispatcher, the UI can never wrap a call to the command dispatcher in a try block. This communication pattern immediately eliminates using C++ exceptions for intermodule error handling (note that it does not preclude using exceptions internally within a single module). In this case, since number entry errors are trapped in the command dispatcher, we could have notified the UI directly using a callback. However, this convention is not sufficiently general, for it would break down for errors detected in the stack since the stack has no direct communication with the UI. Second, we have decided that all errors, regardless of cause, will be handled by passing a string to the UI describing the error rather than making a class hierarchy of error types. This decision is justified because the UI never tries to differentiate between errors. Instead, the UI simply serves as a conduit to display error messages verbatim from other modules.

MODERN C++ DESIGN NOTE: MOVE SEMANTICS

In Table 2-1, the stack has the function void getElements(size_t, vector<double>&), which enables callers to fill a vector with the top *n* elements from the stack. However, the interface of the function tells us nothing about how the elements are actually added to the vector. Are they added at the front? Are they added at the back? Is it presumed that the vector is already sized correctly and the new elements are entered using operator[]? Are old elements erased from the vector before the new ones are added? Hopefully, this ambiguity would be resolved by developer documentation (good luck with that one). In the absence of further information, one would likely conclude that new elements were simply pushed to the back of the vector.

Beginning with C++11, however, the preceding interface ambiguity can be resolved semantically by the language itself. Rvalue references and move semantics allow us to make this interface decision very explicit. We can now efficiently (i.e., without copying the vector or relying on the compiler to implement the return value optimization) implement the function vector<double> getElements(size_t). A temporary vector is created internally in the function, and its contents are moved into the caller on function return. The interface contract is now explicit: a new vector of size *n* will be returned and filled with the top *n* elements on the stack.

To not bloat the interface in the text, both variants of the function do not explicitly appear in the tables defining the interface. However, both variants do appear in the source code. This convention will often be used in this book. Where multiple helper calls performing the same operation are useful in the implementation, both appear there, but only one variant appears in the text. This omission is acceptable for the illustrative purposes of this book, but this omission would not be acceptable for a detailed design specification for a real project.

The next two use cases, undo and redo of operations, are sufficiently similar that we can analyze them simultaneously. First, we must add two new events to the user interface: one for undo and one for redo. Correspondingly, we must add two event handling functions in the command dispatcher for undo and redo. Before simply adding these functions to Table 2-2, let's take a step back and see if we can simplify.

At this point, you should begin to see a pattern emerging from the user interface events being added to the table. Each use case adds a new event of the form xCommandEntered(), where x has thus far been replaced by number, undo, or redo. In subsequent use cases, x might be replaced with operations such as swap, add, sin, and exp. Rather than continue to bloat the interface by giving each command a new event in the UI and a corresponding event handler in the command dispatcher, we instead replace this family of commands with the rather generic sounding UI event commandEntered() and the partner event handler commandEntered() in the command dispatcher. The single argument for this event/handler pair is a string, which encodes the given command. By using the ASCII representation of a number as the string argument, commandEntered() additionally replaces numberEntered() in Table 2-1.

Table 2-1. *Public interfaces derived from the analysis of the use case for entering a floating-point number onto the stack*

Module	Functions	Events
User interface	void displayError(const string&) void stackChanged()	numberEntered(double)
Command dispatcher	void numberEntered(double)	error(string)
Stack	void push(double) void getElements(size_t, vector<double>&)	stackChanged()

Combining all of the UI command events into one event with a string argument instead of issuing each command as an individual event serves several design purposes. First, and most immediately evident, this choice declutters the interface. Rather than needing individual pairs of functions in the UI and the command dispatcher for each individual command, we now need only one pair of functions for handling events from all commands. This includes the known commands from the requirements and any unknown commands that might derive from future extensions. The runtime flexibility needed to accommodate unknown commands drives using a string parameter instead of, say, using an enumerated type. However, more importantly, this design promotes cohesion because now the UI does not need to understand anything about any of the events it triggers. Instead, the deciphering of the command events is placed in the command dispatcher, where this logic naturally belongs. Creating one commandEntered() event for commands even has direct implications on the implementations of commands, graphical user interface buttons, and plugins. We will reserve those discussions for when we encounter those topics in Chapters 4, 6, and 7.

We now return to our analysis of the undo and redo use cases. As described previously, we will forgo adding new command events in Table 2-2 for each new command we encounter. Instead, we add the commandEntered() event to the UI and the commandEntered() event handler to the command dispatcher. This event/handler pair will suffice for all commands in all use cases. The stack, however, does not yet possess all of the necessary functionality to implement every command. For example, in order to undo pushes onto the stack, we will need to be able to pop numbers from the stack. Let's add a pop() function to the stack in Table 2-2. Finally, we note that a stack error could occur if we attempted to pop an empty stack. We, therefore, add a generic error() event to the stack to mirror the error event on the command dispatcher.

We move to our next use case, swapping the top of the stack. Obviously, this command will reuse the commandEntered() and error() patterns from the previous use cases, so we only need to determine if a new function needs to be added to the stack's interface. Obviously, swapping the top two elements of the stack could either be implemented via a swapTop() function on the stack or via the existing push() and pop() functions. Somewhat arbitrarily, I chose to implement a separate swapTop() function, so I added it to Table 2-2. This decision was probably subconsciously rooted in my natural design tendency to maximize efficiency (the majority of my professional projects are high-performance numerical simulations) at the expense of reuse. In hindsight, that might not be the better design decision, but this example demonstrates that sometimes, design decisions are based on nothing more than the instincts of a designer as colored by their individual experiences.

At this point, a quick scan of the remaining use cases shows that, other than loading a plugin, the existing module interfaces defined by Table 2-2 are sufficient to handle all user interactions with the calculator. Each new command only adds new functionality internal to the command dispatcher, the logic of which will be detailed in Chapter 4. Therefore, the only remaining use case to examine concerns loading plugins for pdCalc. The loading of plugins, while complex, is minimally invasive to the other modules in the calculator. Other than command and user interface injection (we'll encounter these topics in Chapter 7), the plugin loader is a stand-alone component. We therefore defer the design of its interface (and the necessary corresponding changes to the other interfaces) until we are ready to implement plugins.

Deferring the design of a significant portion of the top-level interface is a somewhat risky proposition and one to which design purists might object. Pragmatically, however, I have found that when enough of the major elements have been designed, you need to start coding. The design will change as the implementation progresses anyway, so seeking perfection by overworking the initial design is mostly futile. Of course, neither should one completely abandon all upfront design in an agile frenzy!

This said, a few caveats exist for adopting a strategy of delaying the design of a major component. First, if the delayed portion of the design will materially impact the architecture, the delay may potentially cause significant rework later. Second, delaying parts of the design prolongs the stabilization of the interfaces. Such delays may or may not be problematic on large teams working independently on connected components. Knowing what can and what cannot be deferred comes only with experience. If you are uncertain as to whether the design of a component can be safely deferred or not, you are much better off erring on the side of caution and performing a little extra design and analysis work up front to minimize the impact on the overall architecture. Poor designs impacting the architecture of a program will impact development for the duration of a project. They cause much more significant rework than poor implementations, and in the worst-case scenario, poor design decisions become economically infeasible to fix. Sometimes, they can only be fixed in a major rewrite, which may never occur.

Table 2-2. *Public interfaces for the entire first-level decomposition*

Module	Functions	Events
User interface	void postMessage(const string&) void stackChanged()	commandEntered(string)
Command dispatcher	void commandEntered(const string&)	error(string)
Stack	void push(double) void getElements(size_t, vector<double>&) double pop() void swapTop()	stackChanged() error(string)

Before completing the analysis of the use cases, let's compare the interface developed in Table 2-1 for the first use case with the interface developed in Table 2-2 encompassing all of the use cases. Surprisingly, Table 2-2 is only marginally longer than Table 2-1. This is a testament to the design decision to abstract commanding into one generic function instead of individual functions for each command. Such simplifications in the communication patterns between modules is one of the many time-saving advantages of designing code instead of just hacking away. The only other differences between the first interface and the complete interface are the addition of a few stack functions and the modification of a few function names (e.g., renaming the `displayError()` function to `postMessage()` to increase the generality of the operation).

2.3.3 A Quick Note on Actual Implementation

For the purposes of this text, the interfaces developed, as exemplified by Table 2-2, represent idealizations of the actual interfaces deployed in the code. The actual code may differ somewhat in the syntax, but the semantic intent of the interface will always be preserved. For example, in Table 2-2, we have defined the interface to get n elements as `void getElements(size_t, vector<double>&)`, which is a perfectly serviceable interface. However, using new features of modern C++ (see the sidebar on move semantics), the implementation makes use of rvalue references and move construction by also providing `vector<double> getElements(size_t)` as a logically equivalent, overloaded interface.

Defining good C++ interfaces is a highly nontrivial task; I know of at least one excellent book dedicated entirely to this subject [27]. Here, in this book, I only provide a sufficient level of detail about the interfaces needed to clearly explain the design. The available source code demonstrates the intricacies necessary for developing efficient C++ interfaces. In a very small project, allowing developers some latitude in adapting the interface can usually be tolerated and is often beneficial as it allows implementation details to be delayed until they can be practically determined. However, in a large-scale development, in order to prevent absolute chaos between independent teams, it is wise to finalize the interfaces as soon as practical before implementation begins. Critically, external interfaces must be finalized before they are exposed to clients. Client facing interfaces should be treated like contracts.

2.4 Assessment of Our Current Design

Before beginning the detailed design of our three major components, let's stop and assess our current design against the criteria we identified in the beginning of this chapter. First, having defined three distinct modules, our design is clearly modular. Second, each module acts as a cohesive unit, with each module dedicated to one specific task. User interface code belongs to one module, operational logic belongs to another, and data management belongs to yet another, separate module. Additionally, each module encapsulates all its own features. Finally, the modules are loosely coupled, and where coupling is necessary, it is through a set of clearly defined, concise, public interfaces. Not only does our top-level architecture meet our good design criteria, but it also conforms to a well-known and well-studied architectural design pattern that has been successfully used for decades. At this point, we have reaffirmed the quality of our design and should feel very comfortable when we proceed to the next step in our decomposition, the design of the individual components.

2.5 Implementing Our Design Using C++20 Modules

Beginning with C++20, modules have become a formal part of the C++ language. In this section, we'll discuss the general advantages of modules over header files, the source code and tooling changes required to support modules, and how we will implement pdCalc using modules. Despite the newness of this language feature, in keeping with the ethos of this book, I will refrain from introducing the syntax of modules and focus instead on using C++20 modules from a design perspective. I refer readers unfamiliar with modules to the excellent three-part blog post about modules on vector-of-bool [3]. We begin by describing the C++ problems that modules solve.

2.5.1 Why Modules?

Much of the motivation for modules stems from the shortcomings of the header file inclusion model. Prior to C++20, the source file served as the sole input for a translation unit (TU). Essentially, a translation unit consists of all of the source code required to generate a single object file. Of course, as experienced C++ programmers, we know that most programs rely upon interacting components from multiple translation units that are ultimately combined by linking.

Consider the compilation of TU A that is dependent on functions or classes from TU B. The pre-C++20 language model requires the dependent interfaces from B be textually visible during the translation of A. This textual inclusion and assembly of "foreign" source code into a currently compiling TU is conventionally performed by the preprocessor, as directed by programmers via the omnipresent #include statement.

Textually including header files has been causing C++ programmers problems for decades. Essentially, these problems derive from three primary sources: repeated compilation of identical code, preprocessor macros, and one-definition-rule violations. We'll examine each problem in turn to understand why using modules is an improvement over using header files.

First, consider build times. Everyone has written the following first C++ program (or some variant):

```
#include <iostream>

int main(int argc, char* argv[])
{
  std::cout << "hello, world!" << std::endl;
  return 0;
}
```

Counting whitespace and lines containing only brackets, the source code listing for the preceding "hello world" program is seven lines long, or is it? After the preprocessor executes, the generated translation unit in GCC version 10.2.0 is 30,012 lines long, and that was from (directly) including only one standard header file used solely to emit command line output! Every time you include <vector> in a file, you've added another 14,000 lines to your TU. Want a smart pointer (<memory>)? That will cost you a little more than 23,000 lines. Given that header files can be very large and reused across many TUs in any given program, wouldn't it be nice if the language provided a mechanism to reuse them without textually including them everywhere? How much faster would "hello, world" compile if it truly were only seven lines long?

Modules indeed address the textual header inclusion problem (or will once they become pervasive). Modules introduce a new type of translation unit, the module unit, which, unlike traditional header files, can be used via the language import statement rather than preprocessor textual inclusion. Now, in addition to object files, compilers implement modules by producing compiled module interface (CMI) units, which carry the necessary symbolic information for other TUs to compile against interfaces when a

CMI is imported without the need to textually include source code. Therefore, modules can be compiled once and reused, thereby reducing overall compile time by removing the need to recompile module interfaces. Speedup is, at least, a theoretical promise. In practice, the textual inclusion model permits embarrassingly parallel compiles, while modules imply compile time source code dependencies that may partially eliminate parallel compiling. The severity of this problem will hopefully be lessened when tooling catches up to the new compilation model. Whether modules lead to faster build times than traditional header inclusion for complex builds remains to be seen. My bet is that modules will eventually decrease build times for most complex builds after compiler and tool writers obtain a few years of practical experience with the model.

The second problem with the header inclusion model derives from the hoisting of macros from header files into translation units. This problem manifests itself in one of two ways, either as an errant, unexpected symbol definition or the even more surprising behavior, that the order of header file inclusion may change the behavior of the code. Consider the following (very) contrived example:

```
// File A.h
#define FOO_IS_FOO

inline void foo() { cout << "foo" << endl; }

// File B.h
#ifdef FOO_IS_FOO
  #define FOO foo
#else
  #define FOO bar
#endif

inline void bar() { cout << "bar" << endl; }

// File exec1.cpp
#include "A.h"
#include "B.h"
void exec1()
{
  FOO(); // prints: foo - great, FOO is foo
}
```

```
// File exec2.cpp
#include "B.h"
#include "A.h"
void exec2()
{
  FOO(); // prints: bar - what, FOO is bar?!
}
```

The preceding insidious error is rarely this straightforward to diagnose. Often, the error arises when another developer defines a temporary symbol in a header (say, while debugging) and accidentally checks the code in before removing the macro. When the macro is a commonly used symbol such as DEBUG or FLAG, your code may change behavior if you change the order of inclusion (maybe while refactoring).

Modules fix the problems caused by macro definitions because modules, in general, do not export preprocessor macros into importing translation units. Macros are implemented by the preprocessor via text replacement. Since modules are imported rather than textually included into consuming translation units, any macros defined in a module remain local to the module's implementation. This behavior is unlike header files, which export macros merely by text visibility, implicitly, irrespective of intention.

The third problem caused by including header files derives from C++'s one definition rule (ODR). The ODR states that a noninline function may only be defined once in a given translation unit and once in a program. Inline functions with external linkage can be defined multiple times provided all definitions are identical. How does the ODR problem arise when using the header inclusion model? Consider a program that must be assembled by linking the separately compiled object code generated from foo.cpp and bar.cpp as defined in the following code listing:

```
// File A.h
#ifndef A_H
#define A_H
void baz() { /* cool stuff */ }
#endif

// File foo.cpp
#include "A.h"
// bunch of foo-y functions
```

```
// File bar.cpp
#include "A.h"
// bunch of bar-y functions
```

At first glance, you might think that the include guard in A.h saves us from an ODR violation. However, the include guard only prevents the contents of A.h from being textually included twice into one translation unit (avoiding circular includes). Here, A.h is correctly included once in two distinct translation units, which each compile into separate object code. Of course, because baz() was not inlined, the inclusion of its definition in each of foo.o and bar.o, respectively, causes an ODR violation if foo.o and bar.o are linked together in one program.

Honestly, I find the preceding problem rarely occurring in practice. Experienced programmers know to either inline baz() or declare baz() in A.h and define it in a separate source file. Regardless, modules eliminate this type of ODR violation since function declarations are made visible to consumers by import statements rather than textual inclusion.

There you have it – modules are simply better header files. While the previous statement is true, I would be extremely disappointed if programmers used modules only as improved header files. While I suspect modules will indeed be used for this purpose, especially as programmers transition to using modules in legacy software, I believe the primary role of modules should be to provide a language mechanism to formally implement the design concept of modularity. We'll see how C++20 modules support pdCalc's modularity shortly, but first, we need to consider those times when legacy header files must still be used.

2.5.2 Using Legacy Headers

Ideally, all code could be ported to modules, and the import statement could quickly replace header file inclusion. However, certainly during the transition, you will likely need to mix modules and header files. That said, realistically, because header files have been around for decades, you'll likely be dealing with mixing modules and header files for a long time. Let's examine how this is done.

First, in non-module code, nothing prevents you from using header files the way they've always been used. If that were not true, every bit of legacy code would immediately cease to work. Additionally, if you are not authoring a named module, you are free to mix and match imports and #includes. However, if you are writing a module, special syntactic rules exist for including header files.

To be precise, all C++ code now exists in some module *purview*. A module purview is simply all of the code contained inside a module. When you author a named module, that is, your file begins with the declaration of a module name, such as

```
export module myMod;
```

the rest of the file is in myMod's module purview. All code not in a named module resides in the global module. To include a header file, which resides in the global module, into a named module would inject all of the header file's symbols into the named module's purview. This action is not likely to have the desired effect. Instead, we have two options.

The first option for using a header file in a module is to import the header instead of to #include it. For a header file named MyCoolHeader.h, we would use the following code:

```
import <MyCoolHeader.h>;
```

Double quotes can also be used instead of the angle brackets. A header-unit import, to which it is more properly referred, basically treats the header file as if it were a module, and the header file's code is imported like a module import rather than included textually like a traditional header #include statement. Unfortunately, there is an edge case where this does not work as expected, which is when the header file itself expects some preprocessor state to preexist before the include statement. Consider the following implementation outline for MyCoolheader.h:

```
// MyCoolHeader.h
#ifdef OPTION_A
// cool option A stuff...
#elif OPTION_B
// cool option B stuff...
#else
#error Must specify an option
// uh oh, not cool stuff...
#endif
```

MyCoolHeader.h cannot be imported and used because importing a module, even if it's really a header file masquerading as a module, does not see any macros from the importing code's purview. Additionally, while not required by the standard, many compilers require separate compilation of header units before use. To remedy these problems, enter the second option for using legacy headers in a module purview.

The second option for using legacy header files in a named module is to simply include the header file in a specially defined region of the named module file that precedes the module's purview. This special region is referred to as the global module fragment. It is accessed as follows:

```
module;
// The global module fragment
#define OPTION_A // or B, if you prefer
#include <MyCoolheader.h>
export module mod;
// mod's purview begins now...
```

The preceding syntax can be employed in module interfaces or module implementation files. For simplicity, in pdCalc, where it is necessary to use legacy header files (e.g., currently, the standard library), I have chosen to use the direct inclusion of legacy headers into the global module fragment rather than precompiling and importing header files.

We are almost ready to examine how pdCalc itself is modularized. However, because modules are such a new feature, we'll first take a quick detour to examine how they impact source code organization.

2.5.3 Source Code Organization Prior to C++20

The design concept of modularity is not new. Prior to C++20, however, no language mechanism existed to implement modules. Given the lack of direct language support, developers employed one of three mechanisms to "imitate" modules logically: source code hiding, dynamically linked library (DLL) hiding, or implicit hiding. We'll briefly discuss each one.

Prior to C++20, modules could be constructed from a single source file and a single header file by exploiting the header inclusion model. The header file listed only the public interfaces for the module, and the implementation of the module would reside in a single source file; language visibility rules enforced privacy of the implementation. While this technique worked for small modules, source code management became unwieldy for large modules because many different functions and classes needed to be grouped into a single source file, creating a lack of source file level cohesion.

I have personally seen the source code hiding strategy employed in at least one open source package. While this project did accomplish module interface hiding from a technical perspective, the result was an entire library distributed as a single header file and a single source file. The header file was over 3,000 lines long, and the source file was nearly 20,000 lines long. While some programmers may not object to this style, I do not believe this solution was optimally designed for readability or maintainability. This open source package, to the best of my knowledge, had a single author. Readability and maintainability for a team of developers were, therefore, unlikely to have been his primary objectives.

The second technique used prior to C++20 to create modules was to rely on the operating system and compiler's ability to selectively export symbols from dynamically linked libraries. While DLL hiding is a true form of modularity, employing this option was, of course, outside the scope of the C++ language itself. DLL hiding was based on the operating system's library format and implemented via compiler directives. Essentially, the programmer decorated classes or functions with special compiler directives to indicate whether a function was to be imported or exported from a DLL. The compiler then created a DLL that only publicly exported the appropriately marked symbols, and code linking to the DLL specified which symbols it intended to import. Since the same header had to be marked as an export while compiling the DLL and as an import while compiling code using the DLL, the implementation was typically accomplished by using compiler/OS-specific preprocessor directives.

While DLL hiding indeed created true module encapsulation, it suffered from three significant problems. First and foremost, because DLL hiding was derived from the operating system and compiler rather than the language itself, its implementation was not portable. In addition to requiring that code be augmented with preprocessor directives, system-specific nonportability always complicated build scripts, creating a maintenance problem for code needing to compile on distinct systems. The second problem with DLL hiding was that one was essentially forced to align modules along DLL boundaries. While more than one module could be placed in one shared library, DLL hiding only defined modules at the external DLL interface. Therefore, nothing prevented two modules sharing one shared library from seeing each other's internal interfaces. Finally, DLL hiding required the construction of a DLL, which is obviously not applicable to, for example, a module defined in a header-only library.

Interestingly enough, because C++ modules are a language construct and dynamically linked libraries are an operating system construct, we now have the added complication that C++ modules must coexist and interact with DLLs despite both being completely independent syntactically. For example, a DLL could contain one or more C++ modules, and programmers could be free to set each C++ module's DLL visibility independently. That is, a DLL that contains three C++ modules might expose zero (albeit a somewhat useless DLL), one, two, or three separate C++ modules. Even stranger, although I have not verified it myself, one might be able to spread one module across multiple DLLs. Regardless, organization of modules across library boundaries is now yet another issue programmers must consider and a decision we will address when discussing pdCalc's source code organization.

The final legacy modularity technique, which I have termed implicit hiding, was nothing more than hiding the interface by not documenting it. What did this mean in practice? Since the C++ language did not directly support modules, implicit hiding simply drew a logical construct around a group of classes and functions and declared those classes to compose a module. Often, code not intended to be used by a consumer would be placed in a separate namespace, frequently named `detail`. This style was seen frequently in header-only libraries. The language allowed any public function of any class to be called from code external to the module. Therefore, the module's public interface was "declared" by only documenting those functions that should be called from the outside. From a purely technical perspective, implicit hiding was no hiding at all!

Why would anyone have chosen implicit hiding over either source code hiding or DLL hiding? Quite simply, the choice was made either for expedience or from necessity (header-only modules). Using implicit hiding allowed developers to organize classes and source code in a logical, readable, and maintainable style. Each class (or group of closely related classes) could be grouped into its own header and source file pair. This enabled minimal inclusion of only necessary code, which led to faster compile times. Implicit hiding also did not force the boundary definitions for inclusion into a particular shared library, which could be important if there were a design goal of minimizing the number of individual shared libraries shipped with a package. The problem with implicit hiding was, of course, that no language mechanism existed to prevent the misuse of functions and classes not intended by the designer to be used outside of a logical module.

Now that modules are a part of C++20, will you continue to see the three "imitation" module techniques described previously? Absolutely. First, C++20 modules are neither fully implemented nor robust. Attempting to adopt modules today for a cross platform, commercial code base would actually be an impediment. It was, by a wide margin, *the* biggest obstacle that I encountered trying to update pdCalc for the second version of this book. Second, for the foreseeable future, legacy code will continue to dominate. While new projects may adopt C++20 modules from the outset, older projects will continue to use their existing techniques unless major refactoring efforts are undertaken. Generally, adopting new language features is an insufficiently compelling reason to warrant refactoring. Therefore, in practice, any refactoring to modules in legacy code will, at best, be piecemeal. Finally, old habits die hard. Never underestimate the unwillingness of people to learn new techniques or refuse to abandon entrenched positions. I have no doubt that you will even encounter programmers strongly advocating against using modules for a whole host of reasons.

2.5.4 Source Code Organization Using C++20 Modules

Despite significant language evolution over the preceding decades, modules bring the first change that fundamentally impacts how source code is organized and compiled. Legacy code issues aside, beginning with C++20, we no longer need to rely on the "hacks" previously mentioned to organize our code into modules – the language now supports modularity directly. Where we formerly had only the organizational concept of a translation unit, C++20 adds the module unit, which, very loosely, is a source file that declares the source to be part of a module. We will now examine how module units change the way C++20 source code is organized.

First, we must understand how modules themselves are constructed. Module units are syntactically divided between module interface units and module implementation units. Module interface units are those module units that export the module and its interface. Only a module interface unit is required for a compiler to generate an importable CMI. Conversely, a module implementation unit is any module unit that does not export a module or its interface. As is obvious from its name, a module implementation unit implements a module's functionality. A module's interface and its implementation may appear in the same file or in separate files.

Where possible, I prefer to organize module units in a single file; I find the simplicity appealing. However, achieving this simple file structure is not always possible. First, CMIs are not distributable artifacts. Therefore, any binary module that is distributed is required to also provide the source code for its module interface for recompilation by the consumer (e.g., the interface for a plugin system). Assuming you do not want to provide implementation details to binary module consumers, you'll want to place these module interfaces and implementations in different files and only distribute the former.

Second, because CMIs must exist before a module can be imported, modules with cyclic dependencies require splitting interfaces from implementations. The cyclic compilation dependency can then be broken by using incomplete types declared with forward declarations in the interfaces. These interfaces can then be independently compiled to CMIs, which can subsequently be imported during separate module implementation compilations.

Knowing we will encounter both module interface unit and implementation unit files, let's briefly discuss file naming conventions. While not standardized, a few common conventions exist for C++ header and implementation file extensions (e.g., .cpp, .cxx, .h, .hpp, etc.). However, module interface unit files are neither header files nor implementation files (whereas implementation units very clearly are implementation files), so what file extension should we use for them? At present, compiler implementers have not adopted a uniform standard. MSVC and clang have adopted the file extensions .ixx and .cppm, respectively, for module interface units, while GCC's primary module implementer has not adopted any different file extension for module interface units. Programmers are, of course, free to choose whatever file extension they want for module interface units, but MSVC and clang require setting a compiler flag to indicate translation of a module interface unit if deviating from the compiler's specific expected file extensions. Fortunately, no one has adopted a new file extension for module implementation units. pdCalc uses the convention that any file exporting a module interface uses the .m.cpp file extension, implementation files (module or otherwise) use the .cpp file extension, and legacy header files use the .h file extension. Adopting a convention for pdCalc that does not introduce a new file extension ensures that source files will be recognized as C++ files by any existing code editor.

From the preceding explanation, one might conclude that modules, with their interface and implementation file pairs, seem organizationally no better than header files and their associated implementation files. Where we formerly used header files to define interfaces, we now use module interface files. Where we formerly used implementation files, we now use module implementation files. Of course, we gain all of the advantages of modules as better header files, but we are still stuck with modules being defined in a single interface/implementation file pair, which is only an incremental improvement over our legacy approach. Enter module partitions.

A module partition is exactly what you would expect it to be from its name, a mechanism for partitioning a module into separate components. Specifically, partitions provide a means to reduce a module's complexity by dividing it into any number of logical subunits of classes, functions, and source files while still maintaining module-level encapsulation. Syntactically, a module partition is defined by a parent module name and a partition name separated by a colon. For example, module A could be composed of partitions A:part1 and A:part2. As with a plain module, a module partition is divided between a module partition interface unit and a module partition implementation unit. These two pieces may appear in the same file or in different files. Each module partition behaves like its own module with the exception that it cannot be externally accessed as a separate unit. That is, only a component of a module, either the primary module or another partition, can import a module partition. If a module partition is intended to form part of a module's interface, then the primary module interface must export import the partition. Note that while a module can contain any number of module partitions and their associated module partition interfaces, a module itself can have only one primary module interface, which is the single definition of its exportable interface.

Module partitions are significantly more relatable when explained through an example, so let's examine one directly from pdCalc. Consider three classes: Publisher, Observer, and Tokenizer. We'll discuss the function of each class in depth later in the book. For now, just note that each class provides utility functionality to pdCalc. We have several options for making these classes available. At one extreme, we could make each class into its own module. For example:

```
export module pdCalc.Publisher;

export class Publisher{...};
```

Note that the period separating pdCalc and Publisher bears no semantic meaning. The period is merely a syntactic convention for classifying modules to avoid module name conflicts. Unfortunately, due to a linker bug in MSVC, pdCalc's source code uses underscores rather than periods to separate module names. However, the period is retained for the book's text.

Any code needing to consume Publisher does so with the following command:

```
import pdCalc.Publisher;

// use Publisher like any other class:
Publisher p;
```

Analogously, we would define modules `pdCalc.Observer` and `pdCalc.Tokenizer`, which would be imported by `import pdCalc.Observer` and `import pdCalc.Tokenizer`, respectively. Essentially, the preceding strategy is an adoption of modules as better header files. Recall, however, that we started this example by stating that `Publisher`, `Observer`, and `Tokenizer` together provided utility services to pdCalc. Logically, therefore, we might instead want to provide a `Utilities` module that, when imported, provided access to all three classes, `Publisher`, `Observer`, and `Tokenizer` at once. We can achieve this objective without having to mash all of the classes into a single module interface by using module partitions:

```
// Utilities.m.cpp (or .cppm or .ixx)
export module pdCalc.Utilities;

export import :Observer;
export import :Publisher;
export import :Tokenizer;

// Observer.m.cpp (or .cppm or .ixx)
export module pdCalc.Utilities:Observer;

export class Observer{...};

// Analogous implementations for Publisher and Tokenizer...
```

The `export import` syntax simply means that a module partition interface unit is being imported into the primary module interface unit and subsequently reexported by the module. Now, the three classes can be used:

```
import pdCalc.Utilities;

// use classes from any of the partitions:
Publisher p;
Tokenizer t;
```

For convenience, modules can export other modules using the same syntax even if those other modules are not partitions. We'll see this alternative strategy shortly.

The primary advantage of using module partitions is that each partition can be written as a module, but the partitions cannot be accessed individually as separate modules. Instead, the partitions separate the module into cohesive, logical components, while the interface to the module is centralized and controlled through the single primary module interface. The interface of any particular partition can optionally be reexported directly via an `export import` statement in the primary module interface.

A middle ground does exist between making each class its own separately importable module and making each class a module partition of a `Utilities` module. Specifically, each class can be written as its own module:

```
export module pdCalc.Observer;

export class Observer{...};
```

However, we can provide a convenience `Utilities` module interface that `export imports` each individual module:

```
// Utilities.m.cpp (or .cppm or .ixx)
export module pdCalc.Utilities;

export import pdCalc.Observer;
export import pdCalc.Publisher;
export import pdCalc.Tokenizer;
```

As with using module partitions, all of the classes can then be used by importing the `Utilities` class:

```
import pdCalc.Utilities;

// use classes from any of the partitions:
Publisher p;
Tokenizer t;
```

The preceding model is akin to creating a single header file that contains nothing but includes statements for other header files.

Given that we can essentially achieve the same functionality using any of the module techniques described previously, how do we choose the right design? Making each class its own module gives the end user the greatest amount of granularity because each class can be imported separately, as needed. However, this usage of C++ modules ignores the developer's intent to provide a logically cohesive `Utilities` module. Again, it's using C++ modules solely as better header files. Conversely, by using partitions, we provide a true, cohesive `Utilities` module, but we force end users to import all or nothing. Finally, we have the compromise solution, where end users can import individual classes or import all of them together through a single module interface. The compromise design is less about modularity and more about convenience and flexibility.

Having described the trade-offs for several different module strategies, how do we choose the right one for any given design? In many respects, constructing a module is analogous to constructing a class, but at a different scale. Not coincidentally, we can use the exact same design criteria: encapsulation, high cohesion, and low coupling. However, as with designing classes, many of the choices reduce to granularity, intent, and personal opinion. As with many aspects of design, no single right answer exists. Trial and error, taste, and experience go a long way.

2.5.5 Modules and pdCalc

We now return to the concrete modularization of pdCalc. In Section 2.2, we decomposed pdCalc according to the MVC architectural pattern into three high-level modules: a stack module, a user interface module, and a command dispatcher module. In Section 2.3, we employed use case analysis to assist in defining these modules' interfaces, subsequently cataloging them in Table 2-2. We also indicated that at least one additional module would be needed for plugin management. We now ask, are any additional modules needed, how are these modules represented in code, and how should these C++ modules be distributed into dynamically linked libraries? We'll answer these questions in sequence.

Refining pdCalc's Modules

As you might expect, the real-world implementation of pdCalc's modules is not quite as straightforward as the design's idealization. This discrepancy arises for several reasons. Let's consider each of these reasons in detail.

First, the preceding analysis that defined pdCalc's modules only considered the functional requirements of the calculator. We did not consider the infrastructure need for utility classes, as alluded to in Section 2.5.4, that might be reusable by multiple modules. As just a single example, consider the need for a generalized error handling class that could be used by both the stack and the command dispatcher modules. Programmatically, we could just implement these utility classes and functions in one of the existing modules. However, this strategy would decrease modular cohesion and potentially increase unnecessary coupling between modules. Instead, we'll provide an independent, cohesive utilities module that can be used by multiple other modules.

The second reason to provide additional modules is not about the conceptual design of pdCalc but is instead about the C++ language mechanics of modules. As previously mentioned, compiled module interfaces are not designed to be distributed artifacts. Calling into a distributed binary module requires access to the module interface's source code. Therefore, when only a small part of a large module's interface needs to be called externally, it is advantageous to factor this large module into independent modules to avoid unnecessary module interface distribution. This is particularly true for modules constructed from partitions. Consider a large module composed of six partitions with the following interface:

```
// BigModule.m.cpp
export module BigModule;

export import :PartOne;
export import :PartTwo;
export import :PartThree;
export import :PartFour;
export import :PartFive;
export import :PartSix;
```

Suppose all of BigModule is used by the main program, but only the classes defined in the PartFive partition are needed to construct plugins. Where the CMI can be reused within the main program, BigModule.m.cpp would need to be distributed to plugin writers. However, because BigModule.m.cpp exports its partitions' interfaces, it cannot be compiled without the files containing these six partition interfaces. Rather than distributing all of these source files, it is preferred to factor PartFive into an independent module and distribute only its interface file to plugin writers. Of course, if desired for convenience, this new stand-alone module can still be added to BigModule's interface via an export import while simultaneously maintaining its independence for distribution purposes. We'll see this pattern in pdCalc when we encounter the Command interface in Chapter 4.

The third reason that pdCalc's implemented modules do not exactly match the modules defined in Table 2-2 is that at present, not all legacy code can be modularized. This situation is expected and encountered frequently in real-world projects. Some existing projects will take time to adopt new features, and some existing projects will never adopt new features because the benefits of adoption are not justified relative to their costs. With respect specifically to pdCalc, the graphical user interface cannot be modularized as a partition of the user interface module because at the time of writing, Qt's meta object compiler (MOC) is incompatible with C++ modules. Therefore, while I originally intended pdCalc's GUI to appear as a partition of the user interface module, instead, the GUI is designed using a legacy header file interface. Essentially, this design implies that the GUI is a stand-alone, legacy, "logical-only" module.

The final reason that pdCalc's modularization deviates slightly from Table 2-2 is that Table 2-2 is not inclusive of the entire interface. Some minor functionality was omitted intentionally from the table (e.g., constructors, test harness code), and, of course, some necessary functionality cannot yet be anticipated at this stage of the design. The module interfaces defined in Table 2-2 will expand as we design pdCalc.

Code Representation of Modules in pdCalc

We are now prepared to list the final modules for pdCalc and explain at a superficial level why each one exists. Chapters 3 through 7 will explore these modules in detail.

First, we defined three modules in Table 2-2 that derive from pdCalc's implementation of the model-view-controller architecture. These modules are named `stack` (model, Chapter 3), `userInterface` (view, Chapters 5 and 6), and `commandDispatcher` (controller, Chapter 4). Each module is broken into numerous partitions comprising the internal classes and functionality to implement these modules, thereby allowing the logic of the module to be distributed into cohesive subunits while still preserving module-level encapsulation. As discussed previously, while pdCalc's GUI cannot be formally modularized using C++20 syntax due to Qt incompatibilities, it logically belongs to the `userInterface` module. The GUI portion of the `userInterface` module is accessed via including the appropriate header files rather than through an `import` statement. Obviously, the GUI component of the `userInterface` module does not benefit from the new language support in C++20 for modules.

Second, as previously discussed, pdCalc requires a `utilities` module. The `utilities` module consists of an `Exception` class, a `Publisher` class, an `Observer` class, and a `Tokenizer` class. Each of these classes is contained within a module partition. The `Publisher` and `Observer` classes are described in detail in Chapter 3, where they are used as the foundational building blocks for implementing events. The `Tokenizer` class, which breaks streams of character input into distinct lexical tokens, is introduced in Chapter 5.

The next family of modules is those modules that are required to be independently distributable artifacts. pdCalc contains three such modules: the `command`, `plugin`, and `stackInterface` modules. These modules need to be independently distributable because each module interface must be distributed to plugin implementers. The `command` module contains the abstract classes required for implementing commands (e.g., addition, subtraction, entering a number, undo, etc.). We'll encounter these command classes when we discuss the command pattern in Chapter 4. The `plugin` module contains the abstract class required to define a pdCalc consumable plugin. Plugins are discussed in depth in Chapter 7. The `stackInterface` module transforms the C++ style interface of the `Stack` class into a plain C style interface. Why this step is necessary for plugins is also described in Chapter 7.

The next module to which we previously alluded is the module for managing plugins. Specifically, the `pluginManagement` module finds plugins, loads plugins, unloads plugins, and injects the functionality of plugins into pdCalc. The implementation of the `pluginManagement` module is discussed in Chapter 7.

Modules and DLLs for pdCalc

In Section 2.5.5, we defined eight distinct C++ modules. However, eight modules do not immediately imply the need for eight DLLs. So what's the right number?

Realistically, pdCalc is small enough that one could very easily justify bundling the entire code into a single library. Nevertheless, for instructive purposes, I chose to subdivide pdCalc into several distinct DLLs, some containing only one module and some containing multiple. Originally, I intended to create five DLLs, one each for the model, the view, the controller, the utilities, and the plugin management. These five modules represent the logical architecture of pdCalc's highest-level decomposition. The remaining three modules only exist separately due to the syntactical rules required to create independently distributable artifacts; they do not warrant independent DLLs. However, the `stack` module is only a single module interface file. The overhead to create a DLL for this module felt more onerous than valuable. Once I realized lumping was necessary, I decided to combine the controller, plugin management, and stack modules into a unified backend DLL. The final result is that pdCalc is divided into three DLLs: a utilities DLL, a backend DLL, and a user interface DLL. Of course, by definition, any plugins themselves must be contained in separate DLLs. The main routine for the application is compiled into its own executable.

Is three DLLs the right number of shared libraries for pdCalc? Not really. I think any number of DLLs between one and five is justifiable. As frequently occurs in design, there is often not a right or a wrong answer, only trade-offs. Here, we are weighing the pros and cons between simplicity and DLL cohesion. Sometimes, no compelling advantages or disadvantages distinguish alternatives. At these junctions, you just need to make a decision, document it, and move on to the next task. Architecture is not the science of choosing right from wrong, for the expert discards wrong immediately. Rather, architecture is the art of selecting, from the collection of good alternatives, the decisions that optimize the design for the given requirements. Good architecture isn't always "right," but it should always be intentional.

2.6 Next Steps

Where do we go from here? We have now established the overall architecture of our calculator, but how do we tackle the task of choosing which component to design and implement first? In a corporate setting, with a large-scale project, the likelihood would be that many modules would be designed and coded simultaneously. After all, isn't that one of the primary reasons for creating distinct modules separated cleanly by interfaces? Of course, for our project, the modules will be handled sequentially, with some level of iteration to make a posteriori improvements. Therefore, we must choose one module to design and build first.

Of the three main modules comprising the model-view-controller design, the most logical starting point is the module with the fewest dependencies on the other modules. From Figure 2-3, we see that, in fact, the stack is the only module that has no dependencies on the interfaces of the other modules. The only outward pointing arrow from the stack is dashed, which means that the communication is indirect via eventing. Although the figure makes this decision pictorially obvious, one would likely reach the same conclusion without the architecture diagram. The stack is essentially an independent data structure that is easy to implement and test in isolation. Once the stack has been completed and tested, it can be integrated into the design and testing of the remaining modules. We therefore begin our next level of decomposition by designing and implementing the stack.

The Stack

The stack is the first module of the calculator that we will design and implement. While we defined the module's public interface in Chapter 2, we said very little about its implementation. We now need to decompose the stack into the functions and classes that provide the module's functionality. Hence, this is where we begin. If you're a little rusty on the mechanics of the stack data structure, now would be a great time to consult your favorite data structures and algorithms book. My personal favorite is the one by Cormen et al. [10].

3.1 Decomposition of the Stack Module

The first question to ask in decomposing the stack module is, "Into how many pieces should the stack be divided?" In object-oriented parlance, we ask, "How many objects do we need, and what are they?" In this case, the answer is fairly obvious: one, the stack itself. Essentially, the entire stack module is the manifestation of a single data structure, which can easily be encapsulated by a single class. The public interface for this class was already described in Chapter 2.

The second question one might ask is, "Do I even need to build a class at all or can I just use the Standard Template Library (STL) `stack` class directly?" This is actually a very good question. All design books preach that you should never write your own data structure when you can use one from a library, especially when the data structure can be found in the STL, which is guaranteed to be a part of a standards-conforming C++ distribution. Indeed, this is sage advice, and we should not rewrite the mechanics of the stack data structure. However, neither should we use the STL `stack` directly as the stack in our system. Instead, we will write our own stack class that encapsulates an STL container as a private member.

© Adam Singer 2022
A. B. Singer, *Practical C++ Design*, https://doi.org/10.1007/978-1-4842-7407-1_3

Suppose we chose to implement our stack module using an STL `stack`. Several reasons exist for preferring encapsulating an STL container (or a data structure from any vendor) vs. direct utilization. First, by wrapping the STL `stack`, we put in an interface guard for the rest of the calculator. That is, we are insulating the other calculator modules from potential changes to the underlying stack implementation by separating the stack's interface from its implementation (remember encapsulation?). This precaution can be particularly important when using vendor software because this design decision localizes changes to the wrapper's implementation rather than to the stack module's interface. In the event that the vendor modifies its product's interface (vendors are sneaky like that) or you decide to exchange one vendor's product for another's, these changes will only locally impact your stack module's implementation and not affect the stack module's callers. Even when the underlying implementation is standardized, such as the ISO standardized STL `stack`, the interface guard enables one to change the underlying implementation without impacting dependent modules. For example, what if you changed your mind and later decided to reimplement your stack class using, for example, a `vector` instead of a `stack`?

The second reason to wrap an STL container instead of using it directly is that this decision allows us to limit the interface to exactly match our requirements. In Chapter 2, we expended a significant amount of effort designing a limited, minimal interface for the stack module capable of satisfying all of pdCalc's use cases. Often, an underlying implementation may provide more functionality than you actually wish to expose. If we were to choose the STL `stack` directly as our stack module, this problem would not be severe because the STL `stack`'s interface is, not surprisingly, very similar to the interface we have defined for the calculator's stack. However, suppose we selected Acme Corporation's `RichStack` class with its 67 public member functions to be used unwrapped as our stack module. A junior developer, who neglected to read the design spec, may unknowingly violate some implicit design contract of our stack module by calling a `RichStack` function that should not have been publicly exposed in the application's context. While such abuse may be inconsistent with the module's documented interface, one should never rely on other developers actually reading or obeying the documentation (sad, but true). If you can forcibly prevent a misuse from occurring via a language construct that the compiler can enforce (e.g., access limitation), do so.

The third reason to wrap an STL container is to expand or modify the functionality of an underlying data structure. For example, for pdCalc, we need to add two functions (`getElements()` and `swapTop()`) not present on the STL `stack` class and transform the error handling from standard exceptions to our custom error events. Thus, the wrapper class enables us to modify the STL's standard container interface so that we can conform to our own internally designed interface rather than being bound by the functionality provided to us by the STL.

As one might expect, the encapsulation scenario described previously occurs quite frequently and has therefore been codified as a design pattern, the adapter (wrapper) pattern [11]. As described by Gamma et al., the adapter pattern is used to convert the interface of a class into another interface that clients expect. Often, the adapter provides some form of transformational capabilities, thereby also serving as a broker between otherwise incompatible classes.

In their original description of the pattern, the adapter is abstracted to allow a single message to wrap multiple distinct adaptees via polymorphism using an adapter class hierarchy. For the needs of pdCalc's stack module, one simple concrete adapter class suffices. Remember, design patterns exist to assist in design and communication. Try not to get caught in the trap of implementing patterns exactly as they are prescribed in texts. Use the literature as a guide to help clarify your design, but, ultimately, prefer to implement the simplest solution that fits your application rather than the solution that most closely resembles the academic ideal.

A final question we should ask is, "Should my stack be generic (i.e., templated)?" The answer here is a resounding maybe. In theory, designing an abstract data structure to encapsulate any data type is sound practice. If the end goal of the data structure is to appear in a library or to be shared by multiple projects, the data structure should be generalized. However, in the context of a single project, I do not recommend making data structures generic, at least not at first. Generic code is harder to write, more difficult to maintain, and more difficult to test. Unless multiple type usage scenarios exist up front, I find writing generic code to not be worth the bother. I've finished too many projects where I spent extra time designing, implementing, and testing a generic data structure only to use it for one type. Realistically, if you have a nongeneric data structure and suddenly discover you do need to use it for a different type, the refactoring necessary is not usually more difficult than had the class been designed to be generic from the outset. Furthermore, the existing tests will be easily adapted to the generic interface providing a baseline for correctness established by a single type. We will, therefore, design our stack to be double specific.

3.2 The Stack Class

Now that we have established that our module will consist of one class, an adapter for an underlying stack data structure, we set out to design it. One of the first questions to be asked when designing a class is, "How will this class be used?" For example, are you designing an abstract base class to be inherited and thus be used polymorphically? Are you designing a class primarily as a plain old data (POD) repository? Will many different instances of this class exist at any given time? What is the lifetime of any given instance? Who will typically own instances of these classes? Will instances be shared? Will this class be used concurrently? By asking these and other similar questions, we uncover the following list of functional requirements for our stack:

- Only one stack should exist in the system.

- The stack's lifetime is the lifetime of the application.

- Both the UI and the command dispatcher need to access the stack; neither should own the stack.

- Stack access is not concurrent.

Anytime the first three criteria previously mentioned are met, the class is an excellent candidate for the singleton pattern [11].

3.2.1 The Singleton Pattern

The singleton pattern is used to create a class where only one instance should ever exist in the system. The singleton class is not owned by any of its consumers, but neither is the single instance of the class a global variable (some do, however, argue that the singleton pattern is global data in disguise). In order to not rely on the honor system, language mechanics are employed to ensure only a single instantiation can ever exist.

Additionally, in the singleton pattern, the lifetime of the instance is often from the time of first instantiation until program termination. Depending on the implementation, singletons can be created either to be thread safe or suitable for single-threaded applications only. An excellent discussion concerning different C++ singleton implementations can be found in Alexandrescu [5]. For our calculator, we'll prefer the simplest implementation that satisfies our goals.

In order to derive a simple singleton implementation, we refer to our knowledge of the C++ language. First, as previously discussed, no other class owns a singleton instance nor is the singleton's instance a global object. This implies that the singleton class needs to own its single instance, and the ownership access should be private. In order to prevent other classes from instantiating our singleton, we will also need to make its constructors and assignment operators either private or deleted. Second, knowing that only one instance of the singleton should exist in the system immediately implies that our class should hold its instance statically. Finally, other classes will need access to this single instance, which we can provide via a public static function. Combining the aforementioned points, we construct the following shell for the singleton class:

```cpp
class Singleton
{
public:
  static Singleton& Instance
  {
    static Singleton instance;
    return instance;
  }

  void foo(){ /* does foo things */ }

private:
  // prevent public instantiation, copying, assignment, movement,
  // & destruction
  Singleton() { /* constructor */ }
  Singleton(const Singleton&) = delete;
  Singleton& operator=(const Singleton&) = delete;
  Singleton(Singleton&&) = delete;
  Singleton&& operator=(Singleton&&) = delete;
  ~Singleton() { /* destructor */ }
};
```

The static instance of the Singleton class is held at function scope instead of class scope to prevent uncontrollable instantiation order conflicts in the event that one singleton class's constructor depends on another singleton. The details of C++'s instantiation ordering rules are beyond the scope of this book, but a detailed discussion in the context of singletons can be found in Alexandrescu [5].

Note that due to the lack of locking surrounding the access to the one instance, our model singleton is currently only suitable for a single-threaded environment. In this age of multicore processors, is such a limitation wise? For pdCalc, absolutely! Our simple calculator has no need for multithreading. Programming is hard. Multithreaded programming is much harder. Never turn a simpler design problem into a harder one unless it's absolutely necessary.

Now that we have the shell of a `Singleton` class, let's see how to use it. In order to access the instance and call the `foo()` function, we simply use the following code:

```
Singleton::Instance().foo();
```

On the first function call to the `Instance()` function, the `instance` variable is statically instantiated, and a reference to this object is returned. Because objects statically allocated at function scope remain in memory until program termination, the `instance` object is not destructed at the end of the `Instance()` function's scope. On future calls to `Instance()`, instantiation of the `instance` variable is skipped (it's already constructed and in memory from the previous function call), and a reference to the `instance` variable is simply returned. Note that while the underlying singleton instance is held statically, the `foo()` function itself is not static.

The inquisitive reader may now question, "Why bother holding an instance of the class at all? Why not instead simply make all data and all functions of the `Singleton` class static?" The reason is because the singleton pattern allows us to use the `Singleton` class where instance semantics are required. One particular important usage of these semantics is in the implementation of callbacks. For example, take Qt's signals and slots mechanism (we'll encounter signals and slots in Chapter 6), which can be loosely interpreted as a powerful callback system. In order to connect a signal in one class to a slot in another, we must provide pointers to both class instances. If we had implemented our singleton without a private instantiation of the `Singleton` class (i.e., utilizing only static data and static functions), using our `Singleton` class with Qt's signals and slots would be impossible.

3.2.2 The Stack Module As a Singleton Class

We now possess the basic design for our stack module. We have decided that the entire module will be encapsulated in one class, which essentially acts as an adapter for an STL container. We have decided that our one class fits the model criteria for a singleton, and this singleton class will have the public interface designed in Chapter 2. Combining each of these design elements gives us the initial declaration for our class.

Listing 3-1. The stack as a singleton

```
// All module names in the repository source code are separated by
// underscores instead of periods due to a Visual Studio compiler bug.
// The book text uses the more conventional period as the module name
// separator (i.e., pdCalc_stack in source code).
export module pdCalc.stack;

export class Stack
{
public:
  static Stack& Instance();
  void push(double);
  double pop();
  void getElements(int, vector<double>&) const;
  void swapTop();

private:
  Stack();
  ~Stack();
  // appropriate blocking of copying, assigning, moving...
  deque<double> stack_;
};
```

Because the focus of this book is on design, the implementation for each member function is not provided in the text unless the details are particularly instructive or highlight a key element of the design. As a reminder, the complete implementation for pdCalc can be downloaded from the GitHub repository. Occasionally, the repository source code will be a more sophisticated variant of the idealized interfaces appearing in the text. This will be the general format for the remainder of this book.

You probably noticed that, despite the STL providing a stack container, our Stack class was implemented using a deque; that's odd. Let's take a brief detour to discuss this relevant implementation detail. We spent a lot of time reviewing the importance of using the adapter pattern in the Stack's design to hide the underlying data structure. One of the justifications for this decision was that it enabled the ability to seamlessly alter the underlying implementation without impacting classes dependent upon the Stack's interface. The question is, "Why might the underlying implementation of the Stack change?"

In my first version of the Stack's implementation, I selected the obvious choice for the underlying data structure, the STL stack. However, I quickly encountered an efficiency problem using the STL stack. Our Stack class's interface provides a getElements() function that enables the user interface to view the contents of the calculator's stack. Unfortunately, the STL stack's interface provides no similar function. The only way to see an element other than the top element of an STL stack is to successively pop the stack until the element of interest is reached. Obviously, because we are only trying to see the elements of the stack and not alter the stack itself, we'll need to immediately push all the entries back onto the stack. Interestingly enough, for our purposes, the STL stack turns out to be an unsuitable data structure to implement a stack! There must be a better solution.

Fortunately, the STL provides another data structure suitable for our task, the double-ended queue, or deque. The deque is an STL data structure that behaves similarly to a vector, except the deque permits pushing elements onto both its front and its back. Whereas the vector is optimized to grow while still providing a contiguity guarantee, the deque is optimized to grow and shrink rapidly by sacrificing contiguity. This feature is precisely the design trade-off necessary to implement a stack efficiently. In fact, the most common method to implement an STL stack is simply to wrap an STL deque (yes, just like our Stack, the STL's stack is also an example of the adapter pattern). Fortuitously, the STL deque also admits nondestructive iteration, the additional missing requirement from the STL stack that we needed to implement our Stack's getElements() method. It's good that I used encapsulation to hide the Stack's implementation from its interface. After realizing the limitations of visualizing an STL stack, I was able to change the Stack class's implementation to use an STL deque with no impact on any of pdCalc's other modules.

3.3 Adding Events

The final element necessary to build a Stack conforming to the stack interface from Chapter 2 is the implementation of events. Eventing is a form of weak coupling that enables one object, the notifier or publisher, to signal any number of other objects, the listeners or subscribers, that something interesting has occurred. The coupling is weak because neither the notifier nor the listener needs to know directly about the other's interface. How events are implemented is both language and library dependent, and even within a given language, multiple options may exist. For example, in C#, events are part of the core language, and event handling is relatively easy. In C++, we are not so lucky and must implement our own eventing system or rely on a library providing this facility.

The C++ programmer has several published library options for handling events; prominent among these choices are boost and Qt. The boost library supports signals and slots, a statically typed mechanism for a publisher to signal events to subscribers via callbacks. Qt, on the other hand, provides both a full event system and a dynamically typed event callback mechanism, which, coincidentally, is also referred to as signals and slots. Both libraries are well documented, well tested, well respected, and available for open source and commercial use. Either library would be a viable option for implementing events in our calculator. However, for both instructive purposes and to minimize the dependency of our calculator's backend on external libraries, we will instead implement our own eventing system. The appropriate decision to make when designing your own software is very situationally dependent, and you should examine the pros and cons of using a library vs. building custom event handling for your individual application. That said, the default position, unless you have a compelling reason to do otherwise, should be to use a library.

3.3.1 The Observer Pattern

Because eventing is such a commonly implemented C++ feature, you can rest assured that a design pattern describing eventing exists; this pattern is the observer. The observer pattern is a standard method for the abstract implementation of publishers and listeners. As the name of the pattern implies, here, the listeners are referred to as observers.

In the pattern as described by Gamma et al. [11], a concrete publisher implements an abstract publisher interface, and concrete observers implement an abstract observer interface. Notionally, the implementation is via public inheritance. Each publisher owns a container of its observers, and the publisher's interface permits attaching and detaching observers. When an event occurs (is raised), the publisher iterates over its collection of observers and notifies each one that an event has occurred. Via virtual dispatch, each concrete observer handles this notify message according to its own implementation.

Observers can receive state information from publishers in one of two ways. First, a concrete observer can have a pointer to the concrete publisher it is observing. Through this pointer, the observer can query the publisher's state at the time the event occurred. This mechanism is known as pull semantics. Alternatively, push semantics can be implemented, whereby the publisher pushes state information to the observer along with the event notification. A simplified class diagram for the observer pattern exhibiting push semantics is found in Figure 3-1.

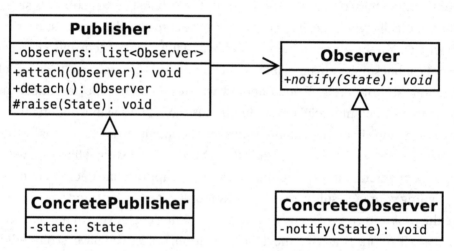

Figure 3-1. *A simplified version of the class diagram for the observer pattern as it is implemented for pdCalc. The diagram illustrates push semantics for event data*

Enhancing the Observer Pattern Implementation

In the actual implementation for our calculator, several additional features have been added beyond the abstraction depicted in Figure 3-1. First, in the figure, each publisher owns a single list of observers that are all notified when an event occurs. However, this implementation implies either that publishers have only one event or that publishers have multiple events, but no way of disambiguating which observers get called for each event. A better publisher implementation instead holds an associative array to lists of observers. In this manner, each publisher can have multiple distinct events, each of which only notifies observers interested in watching that particular event. While the key in the associative array can technically be any suitable data type that the designer chooses, I chose to use strings for the calculator. That is, the publisher distinguishes individual events by a name. This choice enhances readability and enables runtime flexibility to add events (vs., say, choosing enumeration values as keys).

Once the publisher class can contain multiple events, the programmer needs the ability to specify the event by name when `attach()` or `detach()` is called. These method signatures must therefore be modified appropriately from how they appear in Figure 3-1 to include an event name. For attachment, the method signature is completed by adding the name of the event. The caller simply calls the `attach()` method with the concrete observer instance and the name of the event to which this observer is attaching. Detaching an observer from a publisher, however, requires slightly more sophisticated mechanics. Since each event within a publisher can contain multiple observers, the programmer requires the ability to differentiate observers for detachment. Naturally, this requirement leads to naming observers as well, and the `detach()` function signature must be modified to accommodate both the observer's and event's names.

In order to facilitate detaching observers, observers on each event should be stored indirectly and referenced by their names. Thus, rather than storing an associative array of lists of observers, we instead choose to use an associative array of associative arrays of observers.

In modern C++, the programmer has a choice of using either a `map` or an `unordered_map` for a standard library implementation of an associative array. The canonical implementation of these two data structures are the red-black tree and the hash table, respectively. Since the ordering of the elements in the associative array is not important, I selected the `unordered_map` for pdCalc's `Publisher` class. However, for the likely small number of observers subscribing to each event, either data structure would have been an equally valid choice.

To this point, we have not specified precisely how observers are stored in the publisher, only that they are somehow stored in associative arrays. Because observers are used polymorphically, language rules require them to be held by either pointer or reference. The question then becomes, should publishers own the observers or simply refer to observers owned by some other class? If we choose the reference route (by either reference or raw pointer), a class other than the publisher would be required to own the memory for the observers. This situation is problematic because it is not clear who should own the observers in any particular instance. Therefore, every developer would probably choose a different option, and the maintenance of the observers over the long term would descend into chaos. Even worse, if the owner of an observer released the observer's memory without also detaching the observer from the publisher, triggering the publisher's event would cause a crash because the publisher would hold an invalid reference to the observer. For these reasons, I prefer having the publisher own the memory for its observers.

Having eschewed referencing, we must use owning semantics, and, because of the C++ mechanics of polymorphism, we must implement ownership via pointers. In modern C++, unique ownership of a pointer type is achieved via the unique_ptr (see the modern C++ sidebar on owning semantics to understand the design implications). Putting all of the preceding advice together, we are able to design the final public interface for the Publisher class:

```
// Publisher.m.cpp
export module pdCalc.utilities:Publisher;

import :Observer;

export class Publisher
{
  using ObserversList = unordered_map<string, unique_ptr<Observer>>;
  using Events = unordered_map<string, ObserversList>;
public:
  void attach(const string& eventName,
              unique_ptr<Observer> observer);
  unique_ptr<Observer> detach(const string& eventName,
                              const string& observerName);
  // ...
private:
  Events events_;
};
```

Notice that the Publisher is exported from the Publisher partition of the utilities module. The Observer partition of the utilities module is imported to provide the definition of the Observer class. At first glance, you might wonder why the Observer module partition is imported instead of simply forward declaring the Observer class. After all, only the incomplete Observer type is used in declaring Observer smart pointers in Publisher's declaration. However, the Publisher.m.cpp file contains both the partition interface unit and its implementation. Therefore, the full definition of the Observer class is needed in this file for the Publisher's definition. Had the Publisher partition been split into separate interface and implementation files, the interface would have only needed a forward declaration of Observer.

The interface for the Observer class is quite a bit simpler than the interface for the Publisher class. However, because we have not yet described how to handle event data, we are not yet ready to design the Observer's interface. We will address both event data and the Observer class's interface in the "Handling Event Data" section.

MODERN C++ DESIGN NOTE: OWNING SEMANTICS AND UNIQUE_PTR

In C++, the notion of owning an object implies the responsibility for deleting its memory when the object is no longer required. Prior to C++11, although anyone could implement his own smart pointer (and many did), the language itself expressed no standard semantics for pointer ownership (excepting auto_ptr, which was deprecated in C++11 and fully removed in C++17). Passing memory by native pointers was more of a trust issue. That is, if you "newed" a pointer and passed it via raw pointer to a library, you hoped the library deleted the memory when it was finished with it. Alternatively, the documentation for the library might inform you to delete the memory after certain operations were performed. Without a standard smart pointer, in the worst-case scenario, your program leaked memory. In the best-case scenario, you had to interface to a library using a nonstandard smart pointer.

C++11 corrected the problem of unknown pointer ownership by standardizing a set of smart pointers largely borrowed from the boost libraries. The unique_ptr finally allows programmers to implement unique ownership correctly (hence the deprecation of auto_ptr). Essentially, the unique_ptr ensures that only one instance of a pointer exists at any one time. For the language to enforce these rules, copy and nonmoving assignment for unique_ptrs are not implemented. Instead, move semantics are employed to ensure transfer of ownership (explicit function calls can also be used to manage the memory manually). Josuttis [13] provides an excellent detailed description of the mechanics of using the unique_ptr. An important point to remember is not to mix pointer types between unique_ptrs and raw pointers.

From a design perspective, the unique_ptr implies that we can write interfaces, using standard C++, that unequivocally express unique ownership semantics. As was seen in the discussion of the observer pattern, unique ownership semantics are important in any design where one class creates memory to be owned by another class. For example, in the calculator's eventing system, while the publisher of an event should own its observers, a publisher will rarely have enough information to create its observers. It is therefore important to be able to create the memory for the observers in one location but be able to pass ownership of that memory to another location, the publisher. The `unique_ptr` provides that service. Because the observers are passed to the publisher via a `unique_ptr`, ownership is transferred to the publisher, and the observer's memory is deleted by the smart pointer when the publisher no longer needs the observer. Alternatively, any class may reclaim an observer from the publisher. Since the `detach()` method returns the observer in a `unique_ptr`, the publisher clearly relinquishes ownership of the observer's memory by transferring it back to the caller.

The preceding implementation of the observer pattern explicitly enforces a design where the `Publisher` owns its `Observers`. The most natural way to use this implementation involves creating small, dedicated, intermediary `Observer` classes that themselves hold pointers or references to the actual classes that should respond to an event. For example, from Chapter 2, we know that pdCalc's user interface is an observer of the `Stack` class. However, do we really want the user interface to be an (publicly inherit from) `Observer` that is owned by the `Stack` as depicted in Figure 3-2a? No. A better solution is depicted in Figure 3-2c. Here, the `Stack` owns a stack `ChangeEvent` observer, which in turn notifies the `UserInterface` when the stack changes. This pattern enables the `Stack` and the `UserInterface` to remain truly independent. More will be said about this topic when we study our first user interface in Chapter 5.

(a) Publisher owns observer.   (b) Publisher shares observer.

(c) Publisher owns intermediary to observer.

Figure 3-2. *Different ownership strategies for the observer pattern*

Modern C++ does admit yet another sensible alternative for the ownership semantics of the observer pattern: shared ownership. As we stated previously, it is unreasonable for the `Stack` to own the user interface. Some, however, might consider it equally unreasonable to create an extra `ChangeEvent` intermediary class instead of directly making the user interface an observer. The only middle ground option available seems to be for the `Stack` to refer to the user interface. Previously, though, we stated that having a publisher refer to its observers is unsafe because the observers could disappear from under the publisher leaving a dangling reference. What if we could solve this dangling reference problem?

Fortunately, modern C++ once again comes to the rescue with shared semantics (as depicted in Figure 3-2b). In this scenario, observers would be shared using a `shared_ptr` (see the sidebar on `shared_ptrs`), while the publisher would retain a reference to observers with a `weak_ptr` (a relative of the `shared_ptr`). `weak_ptrs` are designed specifically to mitigate the problem of dangling references to shared objects. This design for shared observer ownership by publishers is described by Meyers [24] in Item 20. Personally, I prefer the design that uses owning semantics and a lightweight, dedicated observer class.

Handling Event Data

In describing the observer pattern, we mentioned that two distinct paradigms exist for handling event data: pull and push semantics. In pull semantics, the observer is simply notified that an event has occurred. The observer then has the additional responsibility of acquiring any additional data that might be required. The implementation is quite simple. The observer maintains a reference to any object from which it might need to acquire state information, and the observer calls member functions to acquire this state in response to the event.

Pull semantics have several advantages. First, the observer can choose at the time of handling the event exactly what state it wants to acquire. Second, no unnecessary resources are consumed in passing potentially unused arguments to observers. Third, pull semantics are easy to implement because events do not need to carry data. However, pull semantics also have disadvantages. First, pull semantics increase coupling because observers need to hold references to and understand the state acquisition interfaces of publishers. Second, observers only have access to the public interfaces of publishers. This access restriction precludes observers from obtaining private data from publishers.

In contrast to pull semantics, push semantics are implemented by having the publisher send state data relevant to an event when that event is raised. Observers then receive this state data as the arguments to the notify callback. The interface enforces push semantics by making the notify function pure virtual in the abstract `Observer` base class.

Push semantics for event handling also have both advantages and disadvantages. The first advantage is that push semantics decrease coupling. Neither publishers nor observers need to know about one another's interfaces. They need only obey the abstract eventing interface. Second, the publisher can send private information to the observers when it pushes state. Third, the publisher, as the object raising the event, can send precisely the data needed to handle the event. The main disadvantages of push semantics are that they are slightly more difficult to implement and potentially carry unnecessary overhead in situations where the observer does not require the state data that the publisher pushes. Finally, we note that a design that uses push semantics can always be trivially augmented with pull semantics for special cases by adding a callback reference to the pushed data. The reverse is not true since push semantics require dedicated infrastructure within the event handling mechanism.

Based on the trade-offs between push and pull semantics described previously, I chose to implement push semantics for the event handling for pdCalc. The main disadvantage of push semantics is the potential computational overhead of the implementation. However, since our application is not performance intensive, the decreased coupling this pattern exhibits and the argument control the publisher maintains outweigh the slight performance overhead. Our task now becomes designing an implementation for passing event data via push semantics.

In order to implement push semantics for event handling, one must standardize the interface for passing arguments from publisher to observer when an event is raised. Ideally, each publisher/observer pair would agree on the types of the arguments to be passed, and the publisher would call the appropriate member function on the observer when an event was raised. However, this ideal situation is effectively impossible within our publisher/observer class hierarchy because concrete publishers are not aware of the interfaces of concrete observers. Concrete publishers can only raise events generically by calling the `raise()` function in the `Publisher` base class. The `raise()` function, in turn, polymorphically notifies a concrete observer through the `Observer` base class's virtual `notify()` function. We, therefore, seek a generic technique for passing customized data via the abstract raise/notify interface.

Essentially, our problem reduces to defining an interface to `notify(T)` such that `T` can contain any type of data, including the case where the data may be null. I present two similar techniques for accomplishing this task; only the second is implemented in pdCalc. The first technique is more of a "classical" solution based on a polymorphic design. It is the only design I presented in the first edition. The second solution is based on a more modern technique called type erasure. If you were willing to write a lot of boiler plate code, type erasure was possible before C++17. However, the any class, introduced in C++17, makes applying this technique for objects trivial. The technique is called type erasure because an object's type is "erased" when passing it into the any class and only "recreated" by an any_cast when the object is extracted. Let's examine each solution sequentially.

To apply the polymorphic solution to the event data problem, we create a parallel object hierarchy for event data and pass the event data from publisher to observer via this abstract state interface. The base class in this hierarchy, EventData, is an empty class that contains only a virtual destructor. Each event that requires arguments then subclasses this base class and implements whatever data handling scheme is deemed appropriate. When an event is raised, the publisher passes the data to the observer through an EventData base class pointer. Upon receipt of the data, the concrete observer downcasts the state data to the concrete data class and subsequently extracts the necessary data via the derived class's concrete interface. While the concrete publisher and concrete observer do have to agree on the interface for the data object, neither concrete publisher nor concrete observer is required to know the interface of the other. Thus, we maintain loose coupling.

The type erasure solution to the event data problem is conceptually similar to the polymorphic approach, except we do not need an EventData base class. Instead, the standard any class replaces the abstract base class in the interface (see the sidebar discussing any, variant, and optional). Provided the concrete publisher and concrete observer implicitly agree on what is contained within this class, any object, including built-in types, can be passed as data. The agreement is enforced by the publisher passing a concrete type through an any object and the observer recreating the appropriate concrete type by any_casting the event data payload. As before, while an implicit agreement about the data must exist between concrete publisher and concrete observer, neither is required to know the interface of the other.

MODERN C++ DESIGN NOTE: USING STD::ANY, STD::VARIANT, STD::OPTIONAL, AND STRUCTURED BINDINGS

The C++17 standard library introduced three new, useful types: std::any, std::variant, and std::optional. any is designed to hold any type – the logical equivalent to a type-safe void pointer. It is a generic embodiment of type erasure for objects. variant provides a type-safe union. optional implements nullable types. Let's look at a quick example of how each is used.

any is used exactly the way you might expect given its name. That is, any is an object that can hold any value without specifying the contained value's type beforehand. For example:

```
any a = 7; // assign an int
a = "hello"; // now assign a const char*
cout << any_cast<int>(a); // a not an int; throws std::bad_any_cast
cout << any_cast<const char*>(a); // works as expected
```

A more practical example using any to pass arbitrary data between events is shown in the main text.

A union is used when you need a container capable of holding any one of a particular set of preknown types. unions are very memory efficient because they simply hold sufficient memory to hold the largest type. Consider the following language supported union:

```
union
{
  int i;
  double d;
} w;

w.i = 102; // ok, assign an int
cout << w.i; // no problem
cout << w.d; // oops, this "works" but results in nonsense
w.d = 107.3; // no problem
```

The standard library variant is a type-safe improvement upon the same concept. Using a variant, we can write the same code like the one described previously in a type-safe manner:

```
variant<int, double> v;
v = 102; // ok, assign an int
cout << std::get<int>(v); // no problem
cout << std::get<double>(v); // throws std::bad_variant_access
v = 107.3; // no problem
```

Personally, I use unions infrequently. However, when a union is needed, I strongly prefer the standard library variant over the native language union.

Now let's examine how `optional` is used. Have you ever seen code similar to the following:

```
pair<bool, double> maybeReturnsDouble(); // function declaration
```

```
// ok, but tedious:
auto [flag, val] = maybeReturnsDouble();
if(flag) { /* ok to use val */ }
```

```
// downright dreadful (and common in computational code!):
const double NullDouble = -999999999.0
double d = maybeReturnsDouble();
if(d != NullDouble) { /* ok to use d */ }
```

The preceding hacks are necessary because C++ built-in types (other than pointers) cannot express a null state, nor does the language support a facility for checking if d is uninitialized. If you choose not to initialize d, d is guaranteed to be a valid double, but there is no guarantee that its value will be anything other than whatever bit pattern happens to be sitting in the bytes assigned to d by the compiler. This behavior frequently leads to difficult-to-decipher bugs that manifest in release builds but not in debug builds since debug mode often initializes uninitialized numbers to 0, while release mode does not initialize uninitialized numbers. Thus, the following code behaves differently between release and debug mode:

```
int flag; // uh oh, forgot to initialize
// flag == 0 for debug but probably not 0 for release
```

```
if(flag) {/* will likely execute this path for release */}
else {/* will execute this path for debug */}
```

I have spent many hours explaining to junior programmers that no, they did not just find a compiler bug but rather the compiler found their bug.

The standard library `optional` class enables programmers to avoid the preceding problems. Consider the following code:

```
optional<double> maybeReturnsDouble(); // new function declaration
```

```
auto d = maybeReturnsDouble();
if(d) { /* ok to use d */ }
```

Ah, much better! Clearly, d converts to a bool, which returns true if d is nonnull. If you prefer a more verbose syntax, you can instead call the has_value() member function. Accessing the value of d can be performed by either dereferencing (i.e., *d) or through the value() member function. An optional is considered null if it is not initialized, initialized with an empty constructor (i.e., {}), or explicitly initialized with nullopt.

Did you notice anything syntactically strange in the previous code? Let's repeat a line that may have looked foreign:

```
auto [flag, val] = maybeReturnsDouble();
```

The preceding syntax is called a structured binding. Structured bindings, introduced in C++17, are a syntactic convenience to provide names to elements of an expression. Recall our original version of maybeReturnsDouble() that returned a pair<bool, double> indicating first if the double was defined and second the value of the double itself. Before structured bindings, we had a few options for using the return value: directly use pair's first and second members (opaque and confusing), create new variables and assign them to pair's first and second members (clear, but verbose), or use std::tie (now unnecessary). While the example shows a structured binding in the context of binding to accessible class members, structured bindings can also be used to bind to tuple-like objects and arrays. Additionally, structured bindings can be declared to be const or of reference type if the underlying element must be modifiable through the bound name. Although structured bindings do not fundamentally allow you to do anything you couldn't before, they are really convenient and better express the programmer's intent through a compact syntax. I find I use them a lot.

To solidify the aforementioned ideas, let's examine how the calculator's Stack implements state data. Recall from Chapter 2 that the Stack implements two events: the stackChanged() event and the error(string) event. The stackChanged() event is uninteresting in this context since the event carries no data. The error event, however, does carry data. Consider the following code that explains how to implement Stack's error condition for either the polymorphic or type erasure technique:

```
// Polymorphic event data strategy:
// Publisher.m.cpp
export class EventData
```

```
{
public:
    virtual ~EventData();
};

// Stack.m.cpp
// export to become part of the stack module's interface
export class StackErrorData : public EventData
{
public:
  enum class ErrorConditions { Empty, TooFewArguments };
  StackErrorData(ErrorConditions e) : err_(e) { }

  static const char* Message(ErrorConditions ec);
  const char* message() const;
  ErrorConditions error() const { return err_; }

private:
  ErrorConditions err_;
};

// Type erasure event data strategy:
// Publisher.m.cpp - no code necessary in this file

// Stack.m.cpp
export public StackErrorData
{
  // Same implementation as above, but no inheritance needed
};
```

The StackErrorData class defines how the Stack's event data is packaged and sent to classes observing the Stack. When an error occurs within the stack module, the Stack class raises an event and pushes information about that event to its observers. In this instance, the Stack creates an instance of StackErrorData specifying the type of error in the constructor. This enumerated type comprising the finite set of error conditions can be converted to a string using the message() function. The observers are then free to use or ignore this information when they are notified about the event's occurrence. If you were paying attention, yes, I subtly just changed the signature for the error() interface.

As a concrete example, suppose an error is triggered because an empty stack is popped. In order to raise this event, the Stack calls the following code:

```
// Polymorphic strategy:
raise(Stack::StackError(), make_shared<StackErrorData>(
  StackErrorData::ErrorConditions::Empty));
```

```
// Type erasure strategy:
raise(Stack::StackError(),
  StackErrorData{StackErrorData::ErrorConditions::Empty});
```

For both strategies, the first argument to the raise() function is a static function that returns a string that resolves to "error". Recall that in order to handle multiple events, the publisher names each event. Here, the Stack::StackError() returns the name of this event. A function is used instead of directly using the string to prevent runtime errors caused by mistyping the event name in the source code. The second argument to the raise() function creates the StackErrorData instance and initializes it with the empty stack error condition. For the polymorphic strategy, the implementation clearly passes event data using a shared_ptr. This decision is discussed in the sidebar concerning sharing semantics. For the type erasure strategy, a StackErrorData class is constructed and implicitly passed as the constructor argument to the any class in the raise() function's interface. Although the StackObserver class has not yet been introduced, we note for completeness that an event can be interpreted with code typified by the following:

```
// Polymorphic strategy:
void StackObserver::notify(shared_ptr<EventData> d)
{
  shared_ptr<StackErrorData> p = dynamic_pointer_cast<StackErrorData>(d);

  if(p)
  {
    // do something with the data
  }
  else
  {
    // uh oh, what event did we just catch?!
  }
}
```

```
// Type erasure strategy:
void StackObserver::notify(const any& d)
{
  try
  {
    const auto& d = any_cast<StackErrorData>(data);
    // do something with the data
  }
  catch(const std::bad_any_cast&)
  {
    // uh oh, what event did we just catch?!
  }
}
```

Why choose one strategy over the other? Personally, I find the type erasure approach cleaner and simpler than the polymorphic approach; in many cases, it may also be more efficient. First, using the any class requires less code than requiring a polymorphic hierarchy. Second, using the any class is less restrictive. While the aforementioned example shows an instance using a StackErrorData class in both cases, any could be used to store a simple type like a double or string, completely obviating the need for a user-defined class. Finally, depending upon the implementation of any, the type erasure method may be more efficient than the polymorphic approach. Where the polymorphic approach always requires heap allocation using a shared_ptr, a high-quality implementation of any will avoid heap allocation for objects that fit in a small memory footprint. Of course, the polymorphic approach does have one distinct advantage. It should be used in cases where polymorphism is desired (e.g., in an interface that uses virtual functions instead of type casting) or where a forced, consistent interface is desired via an abstract interface. As previously stated, the polymorphic interface was implemented for the first edition of this book. Now that C++17 includes the any class in the standard library, the implementation of pdCalc in the second edition of this book implements the type erasure strategy.

MODERN C++ DESIGN NOTE: SHARING SEMANTICS AND SHARED_PTR

Whereas `unique_ptr` enables the programmer to express, safely, unique ownership, `shared_ptr` enables the programmer to express, safely, shared ownership. Prior to the C++11 standard, C++ enabled data sharing by either raw pointer or reference. Because references for class data could only be initialized during construction, for late binding data, only raw pointers could be used. Therefore, often, two classes shared a single piece of data by each containing a raw pointer to a common object. The problem with that scenario is, of course, that it is unclear which object owns the shared object. In particular, this ambiguity implies uncertainty about when such a shared object can safely be deleted and which owning object ultimately should free the memory. `shared_ptr`s rectify this dilemma at the standard library level.

`shared_ptr` implements sharing semantics via reference counting. As new objects point to a `shared_ptr`, the internal reference count increases (enforced via constructors and assignment). When a `shared_ptr` goes out of scope, its destructor is called, which decrements the internal reference count. When the count goes to zero, the destruction of the final `shared_ptr` triggers reclamation of the underlying memory. As with `unique_ptr`, explicit member function calls can also be used to manage memory manually. Josuttis [13] provides an excellent detailed description of the mechanics of using `shared_ptr`. As with `unique_ptr`, one must be careful not to mix pointer types. The exception to this rule, of course, is mixed usage with `weak_ptr`. Additionally, reference counting carries both time and space overhead, so the reader should familiarize himself with these trade-offs before deploying shared pointers.

In terms of design considerations, the `shared_ptr` construct enables the programmer to share heap memory without directly tracking the ownership of the objects. Passing objects by value for polymorphic types is not an option, because for objects existing in a hierarchy, passing objects by value causes slicing. However, using raw pointers (or references) to pass event data is also problematic because the lifetime of these data objects cannot be known among the classes sharing them. Consider pdCalc's need to use a `shared_ptr` when using the polymorphic event data strategy. Naturally, the publisher allocates the memory when it raises an event. Since an observer may wish to retain the memory after completion of event handling, the publisher cannot simply deallocate the memory after the event has been handled. Moreover, because multiple observers can be called for any given event, neither can the publisher transfer unique ownership of the data to any given observer. For event data in pdCalc, we saw that C++17 admits an alternative design using std::any. However, type erasure cannot always be substituted for shared ownership. Where shared ownership is desired, the shared_ptr standardized in C++11 offers the ideal semantics.

Now that we understand event data, we are finally ready to write the abstract Observer interface. It is, unsurprisingly, exactly what you might have been expecting.

```cpp
export module pdCalc.utilities:Observer;
export class Observer
{
public:
  explicit Observer(std::string_view name);
  virtual ~Observer();

  virtual void notify(const any& data) = 0;
};
```

Maybe the interface is not exactly what you might have expected, particularly because the constructor to the Observer class uses a new feature of the C++ standard library introduced in C++17, the string_view. We'll pause momentarily to discuss the string_view in the following sidebar. After that brief diversion, we'll conclude the design of the Stack class's interface by demonstrating how the Stack publishes events.

MODERN C++ DESIGN NOTE: REFERRING TO STD::STRINGS WITH STD::STRING_VIEW

Before C++17, when referring to an immutable string (specifically, a sequence of characters), we typically used either a const char* or a const string&, depending on the underlying type. Why did we need a new container to refer to strings?

Using the aforementioned two types to refer to strings can be problematic. First, to use a const char*, we either need to know the underlying type is a char*, or we need to convert a string to a const char*. Additionally, const char*s do not store the length of the underlying string. Instead, it is assumed that the character sequence is null terminated (i.e., ends with '\0'). Conversely, if we instead use a const string&, this works well if the underlying type was already a string, but if the underlying type was a const char*, we need to construct a temporary string unnecessarily. The string_view class addresses these problems.

The `string_view` class is essentially a container that holds a constant pointer to a character type and an integer specifying the length of the contiguous sequence of characters that comprise the string. The implications of its implementation lead to both its strengths and its caveats. Let's start with the strengths.

The biggest strength of the `string_view` class is that it is very efficient and can point to most string types expressed in C++. Relative to a plain `const char*`, a `string_view` is safer because the `string_view` knows the length of the embedded string it represents. Being a class, a `string_view` also has a much richer interface (although one might argue `const char*`s have rich library support). Relative to a `const string&`, a `string_view` will never implicitly make a temporary copy of `const char*`, and because a `string_view` is nonowning, it has very efficient member functions for functionality like creating substrings. This efficiency arises because calls to `string_view`'s `substr()` function return a new `string_view`, which requires no construction of a new `string`, only the assignment of a character pointer (the new start) and an integer (the new length) to the same referenced original string.

`string_view`s also have a few shortcomings. While it is beneficial that a `string_view` knows its own size, this is disadvantageous for library calls expecting a null terminated string. The easiest way to produce a null terminated string from a `string_view` is to construct a `string` and use its `c_str()` function. At this point, using a `const string&` would have been the better choice. Another two instances where a `const string&` is preferred over a `string_view` are where it is known that a `string` already exists and where an existing interface requires a `string` or `const char*`.

Finally, we must be careful in managing the lifetime of a `string_view`. Importantly, a `string_view` is nonowning and is hence only "viewing" a separately owned string. If a string is destroyed before a referring `string_view`, the `string_view` will be left in an invalid state (identically to a dangling pointer). Therefore, you must always ensure that the lifetime of a string is equal to or exceeds the lifetime of any `string_view`s pointing to it.

In conclusion, `string_view` is a modern, nonowning improvement to passing strings by `const char*` and `const string&`. `string_view` should generally be preferred except in cases where we need a null terminated string, we need a `string` for a subsequent function call, or we already have a `string`. When using `string_view`, be careful about object lifetimes, ensuring that the underlying string storage outlives the `string_view`.

3.3.2 The Stack As an Event Publisher

The final step in constructing the Stack is simply to put all of the pieces together. Listing 3-1 shows the Stack as a singleton. In order to implement events, we simply modify this code to inherit from the Publisher base class. We now must ask ourselves, should this inheritance be public or private?

Typically, in object-oriented programming, one uses public inheritance to indicate the *is-a* relationship. That is, public inheritance expresses the relationship that a derived class is a type of or specialization of a base class. More precisely, the *is-a* relationship obeys the Liskov Substitution Principle (LSP) [37], which states that (via polymorphism) a function which takes a base class pointer (reference) as an argument must be able to accept a derived class pointer (reference) without knowing it. Succinctly, a derived class must be usable wherever a base class can be used, interchangeably. When people refer to inheritance, they are generally referring to public inheritance.

Private inheritance is used to express the *implements-a* relationship. Private inheritance, simply, is used to embed the implementation of one class into the private implementation of another. It does not obey the LSP, and in fact, the C++ language does not permit substitution of a derived class for a base class if the inheritance relationship is private. For completeness, the closely related protected inheritance is semantically the same as private inheritance. The only difference is that in private inheritance, the base class implementation becomes private in the derived class while in protected inheritance, the base class implementation becomes protected in the derived class.

Our question has now been refined to, "*Is* the Stack *a* Publisher or does the Stack *implement a* Publisher? The answer is yes and yes. That was unhelpful, so how do we choose?

In order to disambiguate whether we should use public or private inheritance in this instance, we must delve deeper into the usage of the Stack class. Public inheritance, or the *is-a* relationship, would indicate our intent to use the stack polymorphically as a publisher. However, this is not the case. While the Stack class is a publisher, it is not a publisher in the context that it could be substituted for a Publisher in an LSP sense. Therefore, we conclude that we should use private inheritance to indicate the intent to use the implementation of the Publisher within the Stack. Equivalently, we can state that the Stack provides the Publisher service. If you've been following along with the repository source code, you might have noticed a big hint that private inheritance was the answer. The Publisher class was implemented with a nonvirtual, protected destructor, making it unusable for public inheritance.

Readers familiar with object-oriented design may wonder why we didn't ask the ubiquitous *has-a* question, which indicates ownership or the aggregation relationship. That is, why shouldn't the Stack simply own a Publisher and reuse its implementation instead of privately inheriting from it? Many designers prefer almost exclusively to use aggregation in place of private inheritance arguing that when given an equivalent choice between these two, one should always prefer the language feature leading to looser coupling (inheritance is a stronger relationship than aggregation). This opinion has merit. Personally, though, I simply prefer to accept the technique that trades off stronger coupling for greater clarity. I believe that private inheritance more clearly states the design intent of implementing the Publisher service than does aggregation. This decision has no right or wrong answer. In your code, you should prefer the style that suits your tastes.

An additional consequence of privately inheriting from the Publisher class is that the attach() and detach() methods of the Publisher become private. However, they need to be part of the public interface for the Stack if any other class intends to subscribe to the Stack's events. Thus, the implementer must choose to utilize either using statements or forwarding member functions to hoist attach() and detach() into the public interface of the Stack. Either approach is acceptable in this context, and the implementer is free to use their personal preference.

3.3.3 The Complete Stack Module Interface

We are finally ready to write the complete Stack public interface, inclusive of both the Stack and StackErrorData classes. In the following code listing, include statements, imports, namespace using declarations, and any private portions of the classes are all omitted for brevity. All of these implementation details are, of course, included in the accompanying source code from the GitHub repository.

```
export module pdCalc.stack;

export namespace pdCalc {

class StackErrorData
{
public:
  enum class ErrorConditions { Empty, TooFewArguments };
  explicit StackErrorData(ErrorConditions e);
```

```
  static const char* Message(ErrorConditions ec);
  const char* message() const;
  ErrorConditions error() const;
};

class Stack : private Publisher
{
public:
  static Stack& Instance();

  void push(double, bool suppressChangeEvent = false);
  double pop(bool suppressChangeEvent = false);
  void swapTop();

  vector<double> getElements(size_t n) const;

  using Publisher::attach;
  using Publisher::detach;

  static string StackChanged();
  static string StackError();
};

} // namespace pdCalc
```

As described in this chapter, the Stack is a singleton class (note the Instance() method) that implements the Publisher service (note the private inheritance of the Publisher class and the hoisting of the attach() and detach() methods into the public interface). The Stack class's public section, in conjunction with the StackErrorData class, encompasses the complete interface of the stack module introduced in Table 2-2 in Chapter 2. While we have not yet described any concrete observers for the Stack, we have fully defined our event system for pdCalc, which is based on the tried and true observer pattern. At this point, we are ready to design pdCalc's next component, the command dispatcher module.

3.4 A Quick Note on Testing

Before concluding our first chapter that introduced the source code for pdCalc, we should pause a moment and say a few words about testing. Testing is by no means a central exploratory topic of this book, and trying to cover both design and testing in depth would certainly break the cohesion of this text. Instead, the reader interested in a thorough exploration of developer testing is referred to the excellent book by Tarlinder [35]. Nonetheless, testing is an integral part of any high-quality implementation.

Alongside the source code for the calculator found on GitHub, I have also included all of my automated unit testing code. Because I chose to use Qt for the graphical user interface framework for pdCalc (see Chapter 6), the QtTest framework was a natural choice on which to build pdCalc's unit test suite. Primarily, this choice does not add any additional library dependencies on the project, and the test framework is guaranteed to work on all platforms to which Qt has been ported. That said, any one of the many high-quality C++ unit test frameworks would have sufficed equally well.

Personally, I find unit testing to be indispensable when programming even small projects. First and foremost, unit tests provide a means to ensure your code functions as expected (verification). Second, unit testing enables you to see a module working correctly long before a user interface is developed. Early testing enables early bug detection, and a well-known fact of software engineering is that earlier bug detection leads to exponentially cheaper bug fixing costs. I also find that seeing modules fully working early in the development cycle is oddly motivational. Finally, unit tests also enable you to know that your code functions the same before and after code changes (regression testing). As iteration is an essential element of design and implementation, your code will change numerous times, even after you think you've completed it. Running comprehensive unit tests automatically at every build will ensure that new changes have not unpredictably broken any existing functioning units.

Because I value testing very highly (it's one of the first lessons I try to teach to new professional developers), I strove to ensure completeness in the testing of pdCalc's code. While I hope that the test code is of high quality, I admit that my testing nomenclature sometimes gets a little sloppy and, in some instances, I probably severely blurred the lines between unit, integration, and system testing. Nevertheless, all of the tests run very quickly, and they assured me that my code was verified throughout the code development portion of writing this book. However, despite my best intentions to write error-free code, and even after an irrational number of reviews of the source code, I am certain that bugs still exist in the final product. Please feel free to email me any and all errors that you find. I will make my best effort to incorporate corrections to the code in the GitHub repository and any future editions of this book, giving proper attribution to the first reader who reports any of my bugs to me.

The Command Dispatcher

The command dispatcher is the centerpiece of the calculator. As the controller in the MVC framework, the command dispatcher is responsible for the entire business logic of the application. This chapter addresses not only the specific design of the command dispatcher module for the calculator but also, more broadly, the flexible design of a loosely coupled command infrastructure.

4.1 Decomposition of the Command Dispatcher

The first question we asked when decomposing the stack was, "Into how many components should the stack be divided?" We ask the same question now for the command dispatcher. To answer this question, let's consider the functionality that the command dispatcher must encapsulate. The function of the command dispatcher is to

1. Store a collection of known commands

2. Receive and interpret requests for these commands

3. Dispatch command requests (including the ability to undo and redo)

4. Perform the actual operation (including updating the calculator's state)

In Chapter 2, we discussed the principle of cohesion. At the topmost decomposition level, the command dispatcher indeed does only one thing: it interprets commands, which is the appropriate abstraction level for the command dispatcher module. At the implementation level, however, from our list of functionality previously mentioned, the module clearly must execute multiple tasks. Therefore, we decompose the command dispatcher into several distinct classes, one for each major task it must perform, because,

© Adam Singer 2022
A. B. Singer, *Practical C++ Design*, https://doi.org/10.1007/978-1-4842-7407-1_4

at the class level, designing for cohesion implies that each class should only do one thing and, presumably, do it well. Hence, we define the following classes:

1. CommandFactory: Creates available commands

2. CommandInterpreter: Receives and interprets requests to execute commands

3. CommandManager: Dispatches commands and manages undo and redo

4. Command hierarchy: Executes commands

The CommandFactory, CommandInterpreter, and CommandManager classes are all components of the command dispatcher module. While the Command class hierarchy logically belongs to the command dispatcher module, as discussed in Chapter 2, the Command hierarchy of classes are contained in a separate command module because these classes must be independently exportable for plugin implementers. The remainder of this chapter is devoted to describing the design and salient implementation details for the aforementioned list of classes and class hierarchies.

4.2 The Command Class

At this stage in the decomposition, I find it more useful to switch to a bottom-up approach to design. In a strictly top-down approach, we would probably start with the CommandInterpreter, the class that receives and interprets command requests, and work our way down to the commands. However, in this bottom-up approach, we will begin by studying the design of the commands themselves. We begin with the abstraction known as the command pattern.

4.2.1 The Command Pattern

The command pattern is a simple, but very powerful, behavioral pattern that encapsulates a request in the form of an object. Structurally, the pattern is implemented as an abstract command base class that provides an interface for executing a request. Concrete commands simply implement the interface. In the most trivial case, the abstract interface consists solely of a command to execute the request that the command encapsulates. The class diagram for the trivial implementation is shown in Figure 4-1.

Essentially, the pattern does two things. First, it decouples the requester of a command from the dispatcher of the command. Second, it encapsulates the request for an action, which might otherwise be implemented by a function call, into an object. This object can carry state and possess an extended lifetime beyond the immediate lifetime of the request itself.

Practically, what do these two features give us? First, because the requester is decoupled from the dispatcher, the logic for executing a command does not need to reside in the same class or even the same module as the class responsible for executing the command. This obviously decreases coupling, but it also increases cohesion since a unique class can be created for each unique command the system must implement. Second, because requests are now encapsulated in command objects with a lifetime distinct from the lifetime of the action, commands can be both delayed in time (e.g., queuing commands) and undone. The undo operation is made possible because already executed commands can be retained with sufficient data to restore the state to the instant before the command was executed. Of course, combining the queuing ability with the undo ability permits the creation of an unlimited undo/redo for all requests implementing the command pattern.

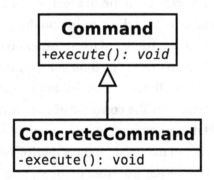

Figure 4-1. *The simplest hierarchy for the command pattern*

4.2.2 More on Implementing Undo/Redo

One of the requirements for pdCalc is to implement unlimited undo and redo operations. Most books state that undo can be implemented via the command pattern by merely augmenting the abstract command interface with an undo command. However, this simplistic treatment glosses over the actual details necessary to properly implement the undo feature.

Implementing undo and redo involves two distinct steps. First (and obviously), undo and redo must be implemented correctly in the concrete command classes. Second, a data structure must be implemented to track and store the command objects as they are dispatched. Naturally, this data structure must preserve the order in which the commands were executed and be capable of dispatching a request to undo, redo, or execute a new command. This undo/redo data structure is described in detail in Section 4.4. The implementation of undo and redo is discussed presently.

Implementing undo and redo operations themselves is usually straightforward. The redo operation is the same as the command's execute function. Provided that the state of the system is the same before the first time a command is executed and after undo has been called, then implementing the redo command is essentially free. This, of course, immediately implies that implementing undo is really about reverting the state of the system to immediately before the command was first executed.

Undo can be implemented by two similar but slightly distinct mechanisms, each responsible for restoring the system's state in different ways. The first mechanism does exactly what the name undo implies: it takes the current state of the system and literally reverses the process of the forward command. Mathematically, that is, undo is implemented as the inverse operation to execute. For example, if the forward operation were to take the square root of the number on the top of the stack, then the undo operation would be to take the square of the number on the top of the stack. The advantage of this method is that no extra state information needs to be stored in order to be able to implement undo. The disadvantage is that the method does not work for all possible commands. Let's examine the converse of our previous example. That is, consider taking the square of the number on the stop of the stack. The undo operation would be to take the square root of the result of the squaring operation. However, was the original number the positive or negative root of the square? Without retaining additional state information, the inversion method breaks down.

The alternative to implementing undo as an inverse operation is to preserve the state of the system before the command is first executed and then implement the undo as a reversion to this prior state. Returning to our example of squaring a number, the forward operation would both compute the square and save the top number on the stack. The undo operation would then be implemented by dropping the result from the stack and pushing the saved state from before the forward operation was performed. This procedure is enabled by the command pattern since all commands are implemented as instantiations of concrete command classes that are permitted to carry state.

An interesting feature of this method of implementing undo is that the operation itself need not have a mathematical inverse. Notice that in our example, the undo did not even need to know what the forward operation was. It simply needed to know how to replace the top element from the stack with the saved state.

Which mechanism to use in your application really depends on the distinct operations your application performs. When operations have no inverses, storing the state is the only option. When the inverse operation is overly expensive to compute, storing the state is usually the better implementation. When storage of the state is expensive, implementing undo via inversion is preferred, assuming an inverse operation exists. Of course, since each command is implemented as a separate class, a global decision for how undo is implemented need not be made for the entire system. The designer of a given command is free to choose the method most appropriate for that particular operation on a command-by-command basis. In some cases, even a hybrid approach (both storing and inverting separate parts of the operation) may be optimal. In the next section, we will examine the choices that I made for pdCalc.

4.2.3 The Command Pattern Applied to the Calculator

In order to execute, undo, and redo all of the operations in the calculator, we will implement the command pattern, and each calculator operation will be encapsulated by its own concrete class deriving from an abstract Command class. From the previous discussion concerning the command pattern, we can see that two decisions must be made in order to apply the pattern to the calculator. First, we must decide what operations must be supported by every command. This collection of operations will define the abstract interface of the Command base class. Second, we must choose a strategy for how undo will be supported. To be precise, this decision is always deferred to the implementer of a particular concrete command. However, by choosing either state reconstruction or command inversion up front, we can implement some infrastructure to simplify undo for command implementers. We'll tackle these two issues consecutively.

The Command Interface

Choosing what public functions to include in the abstract Command class is identical to defining the interface for all commands in the calculator. Therefore, this decision must not be taken lightly. While each concrete command will perform a distinct function, all concrete commands must be substitutable for each other (recall the LSP). Because we want interfaces to be minimal but complete, we must determine the fewest number of functions that can abstractly express the operations needed for all commands.

The first two commands to be included are the most obvious and easiest to define. They are execute() and undo(), the functions for performing the forward and inverse operations of the command, respectively. These two functions return void and require no arguments. No arguments are needed because all of the data for the calculator is handled via the Stack class, which is globally accessible via the singleton pattern. Additionally, the Command class will need a constructor and a destructor. Because the class is intended to be an interface class with virtual functions, the destructor should be virtual. The following code snippet illustrates our first attempt at an interface:

```
export module pdCalc.command;

export class Command
{
public:
  virtual ~Command();
  void execute();
  void undo();

protected:
  Command();

private:
  virtual void executeImpl() = 0;
  virtual void undoImpl() = 0;
};
```

Note the omission of the pdCalc namespace, as will generally be done throughout the text. Although explicitly listed earlier, I will also frequently omit from the text the module export line and the export keyword preceding a class name or namespace declaration if their presence can be implied from context.

In the preceding listing, the reader will immediately notice that the constructor is protected, both execute() and undo() are public and nonvirtual, and separate executeImpl() and undoImpl() virtual functions exist. The reason the constructor is protected is to signal to an implementer that the Command class cannot be directly instantiated. Of course, because the class contains pure virtual functions, the compiler prevents direct instantiation of the Command class, anyway. Making the constructor protected is, somewhat, superfluous. Defining the public interface using a combination of virtual and nonvirtual functions, on the other hand, deserves a more detailed explanation.

Defining the public interface for a class via a mixture of public nonvirtual functions and private virtual functions is a design principle known as the nonvirtual interface (NVI) pattern. The NVI pattern states that polymorphic interfaces should always be defined using nonvirtual public functions that forward calls to private virtual functions. The reasoning behind this pattern is quite simple. Since a base class with virtual functions acts as an interface class, clients should be accessing derived class functionality only through the base class's interface via polymorphism. By making the public interface nonvirtual, the base class implementer reserves the ability to intercept virtual function calls before dispatch in order to add preconditions or postconditions to the execution of all derived class implementations. Making the virtual functions private forces consumers to use the nonvirtual interface. In the trivial case where no precondition or postcondition is needed, the implementation of the nonvirtual function reduces to a forwarding call to the virtual function. The additional verbosity of insisting on the NVI pattern even in the trivial case is warranted because it preserves design flexibility for future expansion at zero computational overhead since the forwarding function call can be inlined. A more in-depth rationale behind the NVI pattern is discussed in detail in Sutter [34].

Let's now consider if either execute() or undo() requires preconditions or postconditions; we start with execute(). From a quick scan of the use cases in Chapter 2, we can see that many of the actions pdCalc must complete can only be performed if a set of preconditions are first satisfied. For example, to add two numbers, we must have two numbers on the stack. Clearly, addition has a precondition. From a design perspective, if we trap this precondition before the command is executed, we can handle precondition errors before they cause execution problems. We'll definitely want to check preconditions as part of our base class execute() implementation before calling executeImpl().

What precondition or preconditions must be checked for all commands? Maybe, as with addition, all commands must have at least two numbers on the stack? Let's examine another use case. Consider taking the sine of a number. This command only requires one number to be on the stack. Ah, preconditions are command specific. The correct answer to our question concerning the general handling of preconditions is to ask derived classes to check their own preconditions by having execute() first call a checkPreconditionsImpl() virtual function.

What about postconditions for execute()? It turns out that if the preconditions for each command are satisfied, then all of the commands are mathematically well defined. Great, no postcondition checks are necessary! Unfortunately, mathematical correctness is insufficient to ensure error-free computations with floating-point numbers. For example, floating-point addition can result in positive overflow when using the double-precision numbers required by pdCalc even when the addition is mathematically defined. Fortunately, however, our requirements from Chapter 1 stated that floating-point errors can be ignored. Therefore, we are technically excepted from needing to handle floating-point errors and do not need a postcondition check after all.

To keep the code relatively simple, I chose to adhere to the requirements and ignore floating-point exceptions in pdCalc. If I had instead wanted to be proactive in the design and trap floating-point errors, a checkPostconditions() function could have been used. Because floating-point errors are generic to all commands, the postcondition check could have been handled at the base class level.

Understanding our precondition and postcondition needs, using the NVI pattern, we are able to write the following simple implementation for execute():

```
void Command::execute()
{
  checkPreconditionsImpl();
  executeImpl();
  return;
}
```

Given that checkPreconditionsImpl() and executeImpl() must both be consecutively called and handled by the derived class, couldn't we just lump both of these operations into one function call? We could, but that decision would lead to a suboptimal design. First, by lumping these two operations into one executeImpl() function call, we would lose cohesion by asking one function to perform two distinct operations. Second, by using a separate checkPreconditionsImpl() call, we could choose either to force derived class implementers to check for preconditions (by making checkPreconditionsImpl() pure virtual) or to provide, optionally, a default implementation for precondition checks. Finally, who is to say that checkPreconditionsImpl() and executeImpl() will dispatch to the same derived class? Remember, hierarchies can be multiple levels deep.

Analogously to the execute() function, one might assume that precondition checks are needed for undoing commands. However, it turns out that we never actually have to check for undo preconditions because they will always be true by construction. That is, since an undo command can only be called after an execute command has successfully completed, the precondition for undo() is guaranteed to be satisfied (assuming, of course, a correct implementation of execute()). As with forward execution, no postcondition checks are necessary for undo().

The analysis of preconditions and postconditions for execute() and undo() resulted in the addition of only one function to the virtual interface, checkPreconditionsImpl(). However, in order for the implementation of this function to be complete, we must determine the correct signature of this function. First, what should be the return value for the function? Either we could choose to make the return value void and handle failure of the precondition via an exception or make the return value a type that could indicate that the precondition was not met (e.g., a boolean returning false on precondition failure or an enumeration indicating the type of failure that occurred). For pdCalc, I chose to handle precondition failures via exceptions. This strategy enables a greater degree of flexibility because the error does not need to be handled by the immediate caller, the execute() function. Additionally, the exception can be designed to carry a customized, descriptive error message that can be extended by a derived command. This contrasts with using an enumerated type, which would have to be completely defined by the base class implementer.

The second item we must address in specifying the signature of checkPreconditionsImpl() is to choose whether the function should be pure virtual or have a default implementation. While it is true that most commands will require some precondition to be satisfied, this is not true of every command. For example, entering a new number onto the stack does not require a precondition. Therefore, checkPreconditionsImpl() should not be a pure virtual function. Instead, it is given a default implementation of doing nothing, which is equivalent to stating that preconditions are satisfied.

Because errors in commands are checked via the checkPreconditionsImpl() function, a proper implementation of any command should not throw an exception except from checkPreconditionsImpl(). Therefore, for added interface protection, each pure virtual function in the Command class should be marked noexcept. For brevity, I often skip this keyword in the text; however, noexcept does appear in the implementation. This specifier is really only important in the implementation of plugin commands, which are discussed in Chapter 7.

The next set of functions to be added to the Command class are functions for copying objects polymorphically. This set includes a protected copy constructor, a public nonvirtual clone() function, and a private cloneImpl() function. At this point in the design, the rationale for why commands must be copyable cannot be adequately justified. However, the reasoning will become clear when we examine the implementation of the CommandFactory. For continuity's sake, however, we'll discuss the implementation of the copy interface presently.

For class hierarchies designed for polymorphic usage, a simple copy constructor is insufficient, and copies of objects must be performed by a cloning virtual function. Consider the following abbreviated command hierarchy showing only the copy constructors:

```cpp
class Command
{
protected:
  Command(const Command&);
};

class Add : public Command
{
public:
  Add(const Add&);
};
```

Our objective is to copy Commands that are used polymorphically. Let's take the following example where we hold an Add object via a Command pointer:

```cpp
Command* p = new Add;
```

By definition, a copy constructor takes a reference to its own class type as its argument. Because in a polymorphic setting we do not know the underlying type, we must attempt to call the copy constructor as follows:

```cpp
auto p2 = new Command{*p};
```

The preceding construction is illegal and will not compile. Because the Command class is abstract (and its copy constructor is protected), the compiler will not allow the creation of a Command object. However, not all hierarchies have abstract base classes, so one might be tempted to try this construction in those cases where it is legal. Beware.

This construction would slice the hierarchy. That is, p2 would be constructed as a Command instance, not an Add instance, and any Add state from p would be lost in the copy.

Given that we cannot directly use a copy constructor, how do we copy classes in a polymorphic setting? The solution is to provide a virtual clone operation that can be used as follows:

```
Command* p2 = p->clone();
```

Here, the nonvirtual clone() function dispatches the cloning operation to the derived class's cloneImpl() function, whose implementation is simply to call its own copy constructor with a dereferenced this pointer as its argument. For the preceding example, the expanded interface and implementation would be as follows:

```
class Command
{
public:
  Command* clone() const { return cloneImpl(); }

protected:
  Command(const Command&) = default;

private:
  virtual Command* cloneImpl() const = 0;
};

class Add : public Command
{
public:
  Add(const Add& rhs) : Command{rhs} { }

private:
  Add* cloneImpl() const { return new Add{*this}; }
};
```

The only interesting implementation feature here is the return type for the cloneImpl() function. Notice that the base class specifies the return type as Command*, while the derived class specifies the return type as Add*. This construction is called return type covariance, a rule which states that an overriding function in a derived class may return a type of greater specificity than the return type in the virtual interface.

Covariance allows a cloning function to always return the specific type appropriate to the hierarchy level from which cloning was called. This feature is important for implementations that have public cloning functions and allow cloning calls to be made from all levels in the hierarchy.

I chose to round out the command interface with a help message function and a corresponding virtual implementation function. The intent of this help function is to enforce that individual command implementers provide brief documentation for the commands that can be queried through a help command in the user interface. The help function is not essential to the functionality of the commands, and its inclusion as part of the design is optional. However, it's always nice to provide some internal documentation for command usage, even in a program as simplistic as a calculator.

Combining all of the aforementioned information, we can finally write the complete abstract interface for our Command class:

```
class Command
{
public:
  virtual ~Command();
  void execute();
  void undo();
  Command* clone() const;
  const char* helpMessage() const;

protected:
  Command();
  Command(const Command&);

private:
  virtual void checkPreconditionsImpl() const;
  virtual void executeImpl() noexcept = 0;
  virtual void undoImpl() noexcept = 0;
  virtual Command* cloneImpl() const = 0;
  virtual const char* helpMessageImpl() const noexcept = 0;
};
```

If you look at the source code in Command.m.cpp, you will also see a virtual deallocate() function. This function is exclusively used for plugins, and its addition to the interface will be discussed in Chapter 7.

MODERN C++ DESIGN NOTE: THE OVERRIDE KEYWORD

The override keyword was introduced in C++11. Functionally, it prevents a common error that is often surprising to new C++ programmers. Consider the following code snippet:

```cpp
class Base
{
public:
  virtual void foo(int);
};

class Derived : public Base
{
public:
  void foo(double);
};

Base* p = new Derived;
p->foo(2.1);
```

Which function is called? Most novice C++ programmers assume that Derived::foo() is called because they expect that Derived's foo() is overriding Base's implementation. However, because the signature of the foo() function differs between the base and derived classes, Base's foo() actually hides Derived's implementation since overloading cannot occur across scope boundaries. Therefore, the call, p->foo(), will call Base's foo() regardless of the argument's type. Interestingly enough, for the same reason

```cpp
Derived d;
d->foo(2);
```

can never call anything but Derived's foo().

In C++03 and C++11, the preceding code behaves in exactly the same confusing, but technically correct, way. However, starting in C++11, a derived class may optionally mark overriding functions with the override keyword:

```cpp
class Derived : public Base
{
public:
  void foo(double) override;
};
```

91

Now, the compiler will flag the declaration as an error because the programmer explicitly declared that the derived function should override. Thus, the addition of the override keyword prevents a perplexing bug from occurring by allowing the programmer to disambiguate his intentions.

From a design perspective, the override keyword explicitly marks the function as being an override. While this may not seem important, it is quite useful when working on a large code base. When implementing a derived class whose base class is in another distinct part of the code, it is convenient to know which functions override base class functions and which do not without having to look at the base class's declaration.

The Undo Strategy

Having defined the abstract interface for our commands, we next move on to designing the undo strategy. Technically, because the undo() command in our interface is a pure virtual, we could simply waive our hands and claim that the implementation of undo is each concrete command's problem. However, this would be both inelegant and inefficient. Instead, we seek some functional commonality for all commands (or at least groupings of commands) that might enable us to implement undo at a higher level than at each leaf node in the command hierarchy.

As was previously discussed, undo can be implemented either via command inversion or state reconstruction (or some combination of the two). Command inversion was already shown to be problematic because the inverse problem is ill-posed (specifically, it has multiple solutions) for some commands. Let's therefore examine state reconstruction as a generalized undo strategy for pdCalc.

We begin our analysis by considering a use case, the addition operation. Addition removes two elements from the stack, adds them together, and returns the result. A simple undo could be implemented by dropping the result from the stack and restoring the original operands, provided these operands were stored by the execute() command. Now, consider subtraction, or multiplication, or division. These commands can also be undone by dropping their result and restoring their operands. Could it be so simple to implement undo for all commands that we would simply need to store the top two values from the stack during execute() and implement undo by dropping the command's result and restoring the stored operands? No. Consider sine, cosine, and tangent. They each take one operand from the stack and return a single result. Consider swap. It takes two operands from the stack and returns two results (the operands in the opposite order). A perfectly uniform strategy for undo cannot be implemented over all commands. That said, we shouldn't just give up hope and return to implementing undo individually for every command.

Just because all commands in our calculator must descend from the Command class, no rule requires this inheritance to be the direct inheritance depicted in Figure 4-1. Consider, instead, the command hierarchy depicted in Figure 4-2. While some commands still directly inherit from the Command base class, we have created two new subclasses, UnaryCommand and BinaryCommand, from which more specialized commands can be inherited. In fact, as will be seen shortly, these two new base classes are themselves abstract.

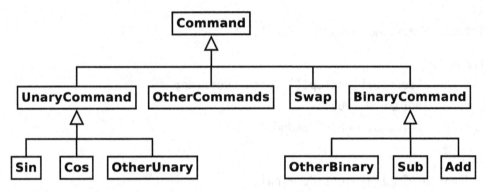

Figure 4-2. *A multilevel hierarchy for the calculator's command pattern*

Our preceding use case analysis identified two significant subcategories of operations that implement undo uniformly for their respective members: binary commands (commands that take two operands and return one result) and unary commands (commands that take one operand and return one result). Thus, we can simplify our implementation significantly by generically handling undo for these two classes of commands. While commands not fitting into either the unary or binary command family will still be required to implement undo() individually, these two subcategories account for about 75% of the core commands of the calculator. Creating these two abstractions will save a significant amount of work.

Let's examine the UnaryCommand class. By definition, all unary commands require one argument and return one value. For example, $f(x) = \sin(x)$ takes one number x from the stack and returns the result, $f(x)$, onto the stack. As previously stated, the reason for considering all unary functions together as a family is because regardless of the function, all unary commands implement both forward execution and undo identically, differing only in the functional form of *f*. Additionally, they also all must minimally meet the same precondition. Namely, there must be at least one element on the stack.

In code, the aforementioned common traits of unary commands are enforced by overriding executeImpl(), undoImpl(), and checkPreconditionsImpl() in the UnaryCommand base class and creating a new unaryOperation() pure virtual that delegates the precise implementation of each command to a further derived class. The result is a UnaryCommand class with the following declaration:

```
class UnaryCommand : public Command
 {
 public:
   virtual ~UnaryCommand() = default;

 protected:
   void checkPreconditionsImpl() const override;
   UnaryCommand() = default;
   UnaryCommand(const UnaryCommand&);

 private:
   void executeImpl() override final;
   void undoImpl() override final;
   virtual double unaryOperation(double top) const = 0;

   double top_;
};
```

Note that both the executeImpl() and undoImpl() functions are marked final, but the checkPreconditionsImpl() function is not. The entire reason for the UnaryCommand class to exist is to optimize the undo operation for all its descendants. Therefore, in order to be classified as a unary command, a derived class must accept UnaryCommand's handling of undo and execute. We enforce this constraint by disabling the ability of derived classes to override undoImpl() and executeImpl() by using the final keyword. We'll see a more detailed explanation of the final keyword in a sidebar later in this chapter. The checkPreconditionsImpl() function is different. While all unary commands share the common precondition that at least one element must be present on the stack, individual functions may require further preconditions.

For example, consider the unary function arcsine, which requires its operand to be in the range [−1, 1]. The Arcsine class must be allowed to implement its own version of the checkPreconditionsImpl() function, which should call UnaryCommand's checkPreconditionsImpl() before performing its own precondition check.

For completeness, let's examine the implementation of the three overridden functions from Command. Checking the precondition is trivial; we ensure at least one element is on the stack. If not, an exception is thrown:

```
void UnaryCommand::checkPreconditionsImpl() const
{
  if( Stack::Instance().size() < 1 )
    throw Exception{"Stack must have at least one element"};
}
```

The executeImpl() command is also quite straightforward:

```
void UnaryCommand::executeImpl()
 {
   top_ = Stack::Instance().pop(true);
   Stack::Instance().push( unaryOperation(top_) );
 }
```

The top element is popped from the stack and stored in the UnaryCommand's state for the purpose of undo. Remember, because we have already checked the precondition, we can be assured that unaryOperation() will complete without an error. As previously stated, commands with special preconditions will still need to implement checkPreconditionsImpl(), but they can at least delegate the unary precondition check upward to UnaryCommand's checkPreconditionsImpl() function. In one fell swoop, we then dispatch the unary function operation to a further derived class and push its result back onto the stack.

The only peculiarity in UnaryCommand's executeImpl() function is the boolean argument to the stack's pop command. This boolean optionally suppresses the emission of a stack changed event. Because we know that the following push command to the stack will immediately alter the stack again, there is no need to issue two subsequent stack changed events. The suppression of this event permits the command implementer to lump the action of the command into one user apparent event. Although this boolean argument to Stack's pop() was not part of the original design, this functionality can be added to the Stack class now as a convenience. Remember, design is iterative.

The final member function to examine is undoImpl():

```
void UnaryCommand::undoImpl()
{
    Stack::Instance().pop(true);
    Stack::Instance().push(top_);
}
```

This function also has the expected obvious implementation. The result of the unary operation is dropped from the stack, and the previous top element, which was stored in the top_ member of the class during the execution of executeImpl(), is restored to the stack.

As an example of using the UnaryCommand class, we present a partial implementation of the sine command:

```
class Sine : public UnaryCommand
{
private:
  double unaryOperation(double t) const override { return std::sin(t); }
};
```

Clearly, the advantage of using the UnaryCommand as a base class instead of the highest-level Command class is that we have removed the need to implement undoImpl() and checkPreconditionsImpl(), and we replaced the implementation of executeImpl() with the slightly simpler unaryOperation(). Not only do we need less code overall, but because the implementations of undoImpl() and checkPreconditionsImpl() would be identical over all unary commands, we reduce code repetition as well, which is always a positive.

Binary commands are implemented in an analogous manner to unary commands. The only difference is that the function for executing the operation takes two commands as operands and correspondingly must store both of these values for undo. The complete definition for the BinaryCommand class can be found alongside the Command and UnaryCommand classes in the Command.m.cpp file found in the GitHub source code repository.

Concrete Commands

Defining the aforementioned Command, UnaryCommand, and BinaryCommand classes completed the abstract interface for using the command pattern in the calculator. Getting these interfaces correct encompasses the lion's share of the design for commands. However, at this point, our calculator is yet to have a single concrete command (other than the partial Sine class implementation). This section will finally rectify that problem, and the core functionality of our calculator will begin to take shape.

The core commands of the calculator are all defined in the CoreCommands.m.cpp file. What are core commands? I have defined the core commands to be the set of commands that encompass the functionality distilled from the requirements listed in Chapter 1. A unique core command exists for each distinct action the calculator must perform. Why did I term these the core commands? They are the core commands because they are compiled and linked alongside the calculator and are therefore available immediately when the calculator loads. They are, in fact, an intrinsic part of the calculator. This is in contrast to plugin commands, which may be optionally loaded by the calculator dynamically during runtime. Plugin commands are discussed in detail in Chapter 7.

Interestingly enough, although the Command, UnaryCommand, and BinaryCommand classes were defined and exported from the command module, the core commands are all contained in the CoreCommands partition of the command dispatcher module. The CoreCommands are not exported from the command dispatcher module, except for testing. This design is justified because unlike the abstract command classes, the core commands, by definition, are those commands directly built into pdCalc, and the usage of these classes is entirely within the command dispatcher module itself.

While one might suspect that we now need to perform an analysis to determine the core commands, it turns out that this analysis has already been done. Specifically, the core commands were defined by the actions described in the use cases from Chapter 2. The astute reader will even recall that the exception listings in the use cases define each command's precondition. Therefore, with reference to the use cases as necessary, one can trivially derive the core commands. For convenience, they are all listed in Table 4-1.

Table 4-1. *The core commands listed by their immediate abstract base class*

Command	UnaryCommand	BinaryCommand
EnterCommand	Sine	Add
SwapTopOfStack	Cosine	Subtract
DropTopOfStack	Tangent	Multiply
Duplicate	Arcsine	Divide
ClearStack	Arccosine	Power
	Arctangent	Root
	Negate	

In comparing the aforementioned list of core commands to the use cases from Chapter 2, one notes the conspicuous absence of undo and redo as commands even though they are both actions the user can request the calculator to perform. These two commands are special because they act on other commands in the system. For this reason, they are not implemented as commands in the command pattern sense. Instead, they are handled intrinsically by the yet-to-be-discussed CommandManager, which is the class responsible for requesting commands, executing commands, and requesting undo and redo actions. The undo and redo actions (as opposed to the undo and redo operations defined by each command) will be discussed in detail in Section 4.4.

The implementation of each core command, including the checking of preconditions, the forward operation, and the undo implementation, is relatively straightforward. Most of the command classes can be implemented in about 20 lines of code. The interested reader is referred to the repository source code if they wish to examine the details.

An Alternative to Deep Command Hierarchies

Creating a separate Command class for each operation is a very classical way of implementing the command pattern. Modern C++, however, gives us a very compelling alternative that enables us to flatten the hierarchy. Specifically, we can use lambda expressions (see sidebar) to encapsulate operations instead of creating additional derived classes and then use the standard function class (see sidebar) to store these operations in a class at the UnaryCommand or BinaryCommand level. To make the discussion concrete, let's consider an alternative partial design to the BinaryCommand class:

```cpp
class BinaryCommandAlternative final : public Command
{
  using BinaryCommandOp = double(double, double);
public:
  BinaryCommandAlternative(string_view help,
    function<BinaryCommandOp> f);

private:
  void checkPreconditionsImpl() const override;
  const char* helpMessageImpl() const override;
  void executeImpl() override;
  void undoImpl() override;

  double top_;
  double next_;
  string helpMsg_;
  function<BinaryCommandOp> command_;
};
```

Now, instead of an abstract BinaryCommand that implements executeImpl() by deferral to a binaryOperation() virtual function, we declare a concrete and final (see sidebar) class that accepts a callable target and implements executeImpl() by invoking this target. In fact, the only material difference between BinaryCommand and BinaryCommandAlternative is a subtle difference in the implementation of the executeImpl() command:

```cpp
void BinaryCommandAlternative::executeImpl()
{
  top_ = Stack::Instance().pop(true);
  next_ = Stack::Instance().pop(true);
  // invoke callable target instead of virtual dispatch:
  Stack::Instance().push( command_(next_, top_) );
}
```

Now, as an example, instead of declaring a `Multiply` class and instantiating a `Multiply` object:

```
auto mult = new Multiply;
```

we create a `BinaryCommandAlternative` capable of multiplication:

```
auto mult = new BinaryCommandAlternative{ "help msg",
  [](double d, double f){ return d * f; } };
```

For completeness, we mention that because no classes further derive from `BinaryCommandAlternative`, we must handle help messages directly in the constructor rather than in a derived class. Additionally, as implemented, `BinaryCommandAlternative` only handles the binary precondition. However, additional preconditions could be handled in an analogous fashion to the handling of the binary operation. That is, the constructor could accept and store a lambda to execute the precondition test after the test for two stack arguments in `checkPreconditionsImpl()`.

Obviously, unary commands could be handled similarly to binary commands through the creation of a `UnaryCommandAlternative` class. With enough templates, I'm quite certain you could even unify binary and unary commands into one class. Be forewarned, though. Too much cleverness, while impressive at the water cooler, does not usually lead to maintainable code. Keeping separate classes for binary commands and unary commands in this flattened command hierarchy probably strikes an appropriate balance between terseness and understandability.

The implementation difference between `BinaryCommand`'s `executeImpl()` and `BinaryCommandAlternative`'s `executeImpl()` is fairly small. However, we should not understate the magnitude of this change. The end result is a significant design difference in the implementation of the command pattern. Is one better than the other in the general case? I do not think such a statement can be made unequivocally; each design has trade-offs. The `BinaryCommand` strategy is the classic implementation of the command pattern, and most experienced developers will recognize it as such. The source code is very easy to read, maintain, and test. For every command, exactly one class is created that performs exactly one operation. The `BinaryCommandAlternative`, on the other hand, is very concise. Rather than having *n* classes for *n* operations, only one class exists, and each operation is defined by a lambda in the constructor. If paucity of code is your objective, this alternative style is hard to beat. However, because lambdas are, by definition, anonymous objects, some clarity is lost by not naming each binary operation in the system.

Which strategy is better for pdCalc, the deep command hierarchy or the shallow command hierarchy? Personally, I prefer the deep command hierarchy because of the clarity that naming each object brings. However, for such simple operations, like addition and subtraction, I think one could make a good argument that the reduced line count improves clarity more than what is lost through anonymity. Because of my personal preference, I implemented most of the commands using the deep hierarchy and the `BinaryCommand` class. Nonetheless, I did implement multiplication via the `BinaryCommandAlternative` to illustrate the implementation in practice. In a production system, I would highly recommend choosing one strategy or the other. Implementing both patterns in the same system is certainly more confusing than adopting one, even if the one chosen is deemed suboptimal.

MODERN C++ DESIGN NOTE: LAMBDAS, STANDARD FUNCTION, AND THE FINAL KEYWORD

Lambdas, standard `function`, and the `final` keyword are actually three independent modern C++ concepts. We'll therefore address them separately.

Lambdas:

Lambdas (more formally, lambda expressions) can be thought of as anonymous function objects. The easiest way to reason about lambdas is to consider their function object equivalent. The syntax for defining a lambda is given by the following:

[*capture-list*](*argument-list*){*function-body*}

The preceding lambda syntax identically equates to a function object that stores the *capture-list* as member variables via a constructor and provides an `operator() const` member function with arguments provided by *argument-list* and a function body provided by *function-body*. The return type of the `operator()` is generally deduced from the function body, but it can be manually specified using the alternative function return type syntax (i.e., `->` `ret` between the argument list and the function body), if desired. The type of the parameters to *argument-list* can either be specified or automatically deduced using `auto`. When the *argument-list* is automatically deduced, the function object equivalent to this generic lambda has a templated `operator()`.

Given the equivalence between a lambda expression and a function object, lambdas do not actually provide new functionality to C++. Anything that can be done in C++11 with a lambda can be done in C++03 with a different syntax. What lambdas do provide, however, is a compelling, concise syntax for the declaration of inline, anonymous functions. Two very common use cases for lambdas are as predicates for STL algorithms and targets for asynchronous tasks. Some have even argued that the lambda syntax is so compelling that there is no longer a need to write `for` loops in high-level code since they can be replaced with a lambda and an algorithm. Personally, I find this point of view too extreme.

In the alternative design to binary commands, we saw yet another use for lambdas. They can be stored in objects and then called on demand to provide different options for implementing algorithms. In some respects, this paradigm encodes a microapplication of the strategy pattern. To avoid confusion with the command pattern, I specifically did not introduce the strategy pattern in the main text. The interested reader is referred to Gamma et al. [11] for details.

Standard `function`:

The `function` class is part of the C++ standard library. This class provides a generic wrapper around any callable target, converting this callable target into a function object. Essentially, any C++ construct that can be called like a function is a callable target. This includes functions, lambdas, and member functions.

Standard `function` provides two very useful features. First, it provides a generic facility for interfacing with any callable target. That is, in template programming, storing a callable target in a `function` object unifies the calling semantics on the target independent of the underlying type. Second, `function` enables the storage of otherwise difficult-to-store types, like lambda expressions. In the design of the `BinaryCommandAlternative`, we made use of the `function` class to store lambdas to implement small algorithms to overlay the strategy pattern onto the command pattern. Although not actually utilized in pdCalc, the generic nature of the `function` class actually enables the `BinaryCommandAlternative` constructor to accept callable targets other than lambdas.

The `final` keyword:

The `final` keyword, introduced in C++11, enables a class designer to declare either that a class cannot be inherited from or a virtual function may not be further overridden. For those programmers coming from either C# or Java, you'll know that C++ is late to the game in finally (pun intended) adding this facility.

Before C++11, nasty hacks needed to be used to prevent further derivation of a class. Beginning with C++11, the `final` keyword enables the compiler to enforce this constraint. Prior to C++11, many C++ designers argued that the `final` keyword was unnecessary. A designer wanting a class to be noninheritable could just make the destructor nonvirtual, thereby implying that deriving from this class was outside the designer's intent. Anyone who has seen code inheriting from STL containers will know how well developers tend to follow intent not enforced by the compiler. How often have you heard a fellow developer say, "Sure, that's a bad idea, in general, but, don't worry, it's fine in my special case." This oft uttered comment is almost inevitably followed by a week-long debugging session to track down obscure bugs.

Why might you want to prevent inheriting from a class or overriding a previously declared virtual function? Likely, because you have a situation where inheritance, while being well defined by the language, simply makes no sense, logically. A concrete example of this is pdCalc's `BinaryCommandAlternative` class. While you could attempt to derive from it and override the `executeImpl()` member function (i.e., without the `final` keyword in place), the intent of the class is to terminate the hierarchy and provide the binary operation via a callable target. Inheriting from `BinaryCommandAlternative` is outside the scope of its design. Preventing derivation is therefore likely to prevent subtle semantic errors. Earlier in this chapter, when introducing the `UnaryCommand` class, we saw a situation where deriving from a class while simultaneously prohibiting the overriding of a subset of its virtual functions enforced the designer's intended usage.

4.3 The Command Factory

Our calculator now has all of the commands required to meet its requirements. However, we have not yet defined the infrastructure necessary for storing commands and subsequently accessing them on demand. In this section, we'll explore several design strategies for storing and retrieving commands.

4.3.1 The CommandFactory Class

At first glance, instantiating a new command seems like a trivial problem to solve. For example, if a user requests the addition of two numbers, the following code will perform this function:

```
Command* cmd = new Add;
cmd->execute();
```

Great, problem solved, right? Not really. How is this code called? Where does this code appear? What happens if new core commands are added (i.e., requirements change)? What if new commands are added dynamically (as in plugins)? What seems like an easy problem to solve is actually more complex than initially expected. Let's explore possible design alternatives by answering the preceding questions.

First, we ask the question of how the code is called. Part of the calculator's requirements is to have both a command line interface (CLI) and a graphical user interface (GUI). Clearly, the request to initialize a command will derive somewhere in the user interface in response to a user's action. Let's consider how the user interface would handle subtraction. Suppose that the GUI has a subtraction button, and when this button is clicked, a function is called to initialize and execute the subtraction command (we'll ignore undo, momentarily). Now consider the CLI. When the subtraction token is recognized, a similar function is called. At first, one might expect that we could call the same function, provided it existed in the business logic layer instead of in the user interface layer. However, the mechanism for GUI callbacks makes this impossible because it would force an undesired dependency in the business logic layer on the GUI's widget library (e.g., in Qt, a button callback is a slot in a class, which requires the callback's class to be a Q_OBJECT). Alternatively, the GUI could deploy double indirection to dispatch each command (each button click would call a function which would call a function in the business logic layer). This scenario seems both inelegant and inefficient.

While the preceding strategy appears rather cumbersome, this initialization scheme has a structural deficit much deeper than inconvenience. In the model-view-controller architecture we have adopted for pdCalc, the views are not permitted direct access to the controller. Since the commands rightly belong to the controller, direct initialization of commands by the UI violates our foundational architecture.

How do we solve this new problem? Recall from Table 2-2 that the command dispatcher's only public interface is the event handling function commandEntered(const string&). This realization actually answers the first two questions we originally posed: How is the initialization and execution code called and where does it reside? This code must be triggered indirectly via an event from the UI to the command dispatcher with the specific command encoded via a string. The code itself must reside in the command dispatcher. Note that this interface has the additional benefit of removing duplication between the CLI and the GUI in creating new commands. Now, both user interfaces can simply create commands by raising the commandEntered event and specifying the command by string. We'll see how each user interface implements raising this event in Chapters 5 and 6, respectively.

From the aforementioned analysis, we are motivated to add a new class to the command dispatcher with the responsibility of owning and allocating commands. We'll call this class the CommandFactory. For the moment, we'll assume that another part of the command dispatcher (the CommandInterpreter class) receives the commandEntered() event and requests the appropriate command from the CommandFactory (via commandEntered()'s string argument), and yet another component of the command dispatcher (the CommandManager class) subsequently executes the command (and handles undo and redo). That is, we have decoupled the initialization and storage of commands from their dispatch and execution. The CommandManager and CommandInterpreter classes are the subjects of upcoming sections. For now, we'll focus on command storage, initialization, and retrieval.

Our task now is to implement a function capable of instantiating any class derived from the Command class given only a string argument indicating its specific type. As one might expect, dissociating object creation from type is a common occurrence in design. Any such construct that provides this abstraction is generally known as a factory. Here, we introduce a particular embodiment, the factory function design pattern.

Before progressing, I should point out the semantic difference between a factory function and the factory method pattern, as defined by the Gang of Four [11]. As previously mentioned, a factory, generically, is a mechanism for separating the selection of the specific derived class in a hierarchy from the point of logical instantiation. Whereas the factory method pattern implements a factory via a separate class hierarchy, a factory function is simply a single function interface that implements the factory concept without a class hierarchy.

Typically, a factory function is implemented by calling a function that takes a flag (an integer, an enumeration, a string, etc.) to delimit the specialization of a hierarchy and returns a base class pointer. Let's examine an artificial example. Suppose we have a hierarchy of Shapes with the derived classes Circle, Triangle, and Rectangle. Furthermore, suppose we have defined the following enumerated class:

```
enum class ShapeType {Circle, Triangle, Rectangle};
```

The following factory function could be used to create shapes:

```
unique_ptr<Shape> shapeFactory(ShapeType t)
{
  switch(t)
```

```
  {
  case ShapeType::Circle:
    return make_unique<Circle>();
  case ShapeType::Triangle:
    return make_unique<Triangle>();
  case ShapeType::Rectangle:
    return make_unique<Rectangle>();
  }
}
```

A `Circle` could be created by the following function call:

```
auto s = shapeFactory(ShapeType::Circle);
```

Why is the preceding construction anymore useful than typing

```
auto s = make_unique<Circle>();
```

Truthfully, given the similar compile time dependency, it's not. Instead, however, consider a factory function that accepts a `string` argument instead of an enumerated type (replacing the `switch` statement with a series of `if` statements). We can now construct a `Circle` with the following code:

```
string t = "circle";
auto s = shapeFactory(t);
```

The aforementioned is a much more useful construct than direct instantiation using a class name or enumerated type because discovery of the value of t can be deferred to runtime. For example, typical usages of the factory function are for instantiating specific derived classes whose types are discovered from configuration files, input files, or dynamic user interactions (i.e., via a UI).

Returning to pdCalc, we wish to design a class, the `CommandFactory`, that instantiates a specific `Command` given its `string` identifier as obtained from the event data generated from a user interaction. We therefore begin the interface for our `CommandFactory` class with a single factory function that returns a `Command` given a `string` argument:

```
class CommandFactory
{
public:
```

```
  unique_ptr<Command> allocateCommand(const string&) const;
};
```

The interface employs a smart pointer return type to make explicit that the caller owns the memory for the newly constructed command.

Let's now consider what an implementation for allocateCommand() might look like. This exercise will assist us in modifying the design for more flexibility.

```
unique_ptr<Command> CommandFactory::allocateCommand(const string& c)
const
{
  if(c == "+") return make_unique<Add>();
  else if(c == "-") return make_unique<Subtract>();
  // ...all known commands...
  else return nullptr;
}
```

The preceding interface is simple and effective, but it is limited by requiring a priori knowledge of every command in the system. In general, such a design would be highly undesirable and inconvenient for several reasons. First, adding a new core command to the system would require modifying the factory's initialization function. Second, deploying runtime plugin commands would require a completely different implementation. Third, this strategy creates unwanted coupling between the instantiation of specific commands and their storage. Instead, we would prefer a design where the CommandFactory relies only on the abstract interface defined by the Command base class.

The preceding problem is solved by application of a simple pattern known as the prototype pattern [11]. The prototype pattern is a creational pattern where a prototype object is stored, and new objects of this type are created simply by copying the prototype. Now, consider a design that treats our CommandFactory as merely a container of command prototypes. Furthermore, let the prototypes all be stored by Command pointer, say, in a hash table, using a string as the key (maybe the same string raised in the commandEntered() event). Then, new commands could be added (or removed) dynamically by adding (or removing) a new prototype command. To implement this strategy, we make the following additions to our `CommandFactory` class:

```
class CommandFactory
{
public:
  unique_ptr<Command> allocateCommand(const string&) const;
  void registerCommand(const string& name, unique_ptr<Command> c);

private:
  using Factory = unordered_map<string, unique_ptr<Command>>;
  Factory factory_;
};
```

The implementation for registering a command is quite simple:

```
void CommandFactory::registerCommand(const string& name,
unique_ptr<Command> c)
{
  if( factory_.contains(name) )
    // handle duplicate command error
  else
    factory_.emplace( name, std::move(c) );
}
```

Here, we check whether or not the command is already in the factory. If it is, then we handle the error. If not, then we move the command argument into the factory, where the command becomes the prototype for the command name. Note that the use of `unique_ptr` indicates that registering a command transfers ownership of this prototype to the command factory. In practice, the core commands are all registered via a function in the `CommandFactory.m.cpp` file, and a similar function exists inside each plugin to register the plugin commands (we'll see this interface when we examine the construction of plugins in Chapter 7). These function are called during initialization of the calculator and during plugin initialization, respectively. Optionally, the command factory can be augmented with a deregister command with the obvious implementation.

Using our new design, we can rewrite the allocateCommand() function as follows:

```
unique_ptr<Command> CommandFactory::allocateCommand(const string& name)
const
{
  if( factory_.contains(name) )
  {
    const auto& command = factory_.find(name)->second;
    return unique_ptr<Command>( command->clone() );
  }
  else return nullptr;
}
```

Now, if the command is found in the factory, a copy of the prototype is returned.
If the command is not found, a nullptr is returned (alternatively, an exception could
be thrown). The copy of the prototype is returned in a unique_ptr indicating that the
caller now owns this copy of the command. Note the use of the clone() function from
the Command class. The clone function was originally added to the Command class with
the promise of future justification. As is now evident, we require the clone() function
in order to copy Commands polymorphically for our implementation of the prototype
pattern. Of course, had we not had the foresight to implement a cloning function for all
commands at the time that the Command class was designed, it could easily be added now.
Remember, you won't get the design perfect on the first pass, so get used to the idea of
iterative design.

Essentially, registerCommand() and allocateCommand() embody the minimally
complete interface for the CommandFactory class. However, if you examine the included
source code for this class, you will see some differences. First, additional functions
were added to the interface. The additional functions are mostly convenience and
syntactic sugar. Second, I used an alias, CommandPtr, instead of directly using unique_
ptr<Command>. For the purposes of this chapter, just think of CommandPtr as being
defined by the following using statement:

```
using CommandPtr = std::unique_ptr<Command>;
```

The real alias, which can be found in Command.m.cpp, is slightly more complicated.
Additionally, I used a function MakeCommandPtr() rather than the unique_ptr's
constructor to create CommandPtrs. The reasons for these differences will be explained in
detail in Chapter 7.

Finally, the only other part of the interface from the repository code not already discussed that impacts the design is the choice to make the CommandFactory a singleton. The reason for this decision is simple. Regardless of how many different command interpreters exist in the system (interestingly enough, we'll eventually see a case for having multiple command interpreters), the prototypes for functions never change. Therefore, making the CommandFactory a singleton centralizes the storage, allocation, and retrieval of all commands for the calculator.

MODERN C++ DESIGN NOTE: UNIFORM INITIALIZATION

You might have noticed that I routinely use curly braces for initialization. For developers who have been programming in C++ for a long time, the use of curly braces to initialize a class (i.e., call its constructor) may appear odd. While we are accustomed to a list syntax for initializing arrays:

```
int a[] = { 1, 2, 3 };
```

using curly braces to initialize classes is a new feature in C++11. While parentheses may still be used for calling constructors, the new syntax using curly braces, called uniform initialization, is the preferred syntax for modern C++. While the two initialization mechanisms functionally perform the same task, the new syntax has three advantages:

1. Uniform initialization is nonnarrowing:

    ```
    class A { A(int a); };
    A a(7.8); // ok, truncates
    A a{7.8}; // error, narrows
    ```

2. Uniform initialization (combined with initializer lists) permits initializing user-defined types with lists:

    ```
    vector<double> v{ 1.1, 1.2, 1.3 };
    // valid since C++11; initializes vector with 3 doubles
    ```

3. Uniform initialization is never mistakenly parsed as a function:

    ```
    struct B { B(); void foo(); };
    B b(); // Are you declaring a function that returns a B?
    b.foo(); // error, requesting foo() in non-class type b
    B b2{}; // ok, default construction
    b2.foo(); // ok, call B::foo()
    ```

There is only one big caveat when using uniform initialization: a list constructor is always called before any other constructor. The canonical example comes from the STL vector class, which has an initializer list constructor and a separate constructor accepting an integer to define the vector's size. Because initializer list constructors are called before any other constructor if curly braces are used, we have the following different behaviors:

```
vector<int> v(3); // vector, size 3, all elements initialized to 0
vector<int> v{3}; // vector with 1 element initialized to 3
```

Fortunately, the preceding situation does not arise often. However, when it does, you must understand the difference between uniform initialization and function style initialization.

From a design perspective, the main advantage of uniform initialization is that user-defined types may be designed to accept lists of identically typed values for construction. Therefore, containers, such as vectors, may be statically initialized with a list of values rather than default initialized followed by successive assignment. This modern C++ feature enables initialization of derived types to use the same syntax for initialization as built in array types, a syntactical feature missing in C++03.

4.3.2 Registering Core Commands

We have now defined the core commands of the calculator and a class for loading and serving the commands on demand. However, we have not discussed a method for loading the core commands into the CommandFactory. In order to function properly, the loading of all the core commands must only be performed once, and it must be performed before the calculator is used. Essentially, this defines an initialization requirement for the command dispatcher module. A finalization function is not needed since deregistering the core commands when exiting the program is unnecessary.

The best place to call an initialization operation for the command dispatcher is in the main() function of the calculator. Therefore, we simply create a global RegisterCoreCommands() function, implement it in the CommandFactory.m.cpp file, ensure the function is exported from the module, and call it from main(). The reason to create a global function instead of registering the core commands in the CommandFactory's constructor is to avoid coupling the CommandFactory class with the derived classes of the command hierarchy. An alternative would have been to define the RegisterCoreCommands() in the CoreCommands.m.cpp file, but this would have required additional interface files, implementation files, and module exports. The registration function, of course, could have been called something like `InitCommandDispatcher()`, but I prefer a name that more specifically describes the functionality.

Implicitly, we have just extended the interface to the command dispatcher module (originally defined in Table 2-2), albeit fairly trivially. Should we have been able to anticipate this part of the interface in advance? Probably not. This interface update was necessitated by a design decision at a level significantly more detailed than the high-level decomposition of Chapter 2. I find slightly modifying a key interface during development to be an acceptable way of designing a program. A design strategy requiring immutability is simply too rigid to be practical. However, note that easy acceptance of a key interface modification during development is in contrast with the acceptance of a key interface modification after release, a decision that should only be made after significant consideration for how the change will affect clients already using your code.

4.4 The Command Manager

Having designed the command infrastructure and created a factory for the storage, initialization, and retrieval of commands in the system, we are now ready to design a class with responsibility for executing commands on demand and managing undo and redo. This class is called the `CommandManager`. Essentially, it manages the lifetime of commands by calling the `execute()` function on each command and subsequently retaining each command in a manner appropriate for implementing unlimited undo and redo. We'll start by defining the interface for the `CommandManager` and conclude the section by discussing the strategy for implementing unlimited undo and redo.

4.4.1 The Interface

The interface for the `CommandManager` is remarkably simple and straightforward. The `CommandManager` needs an interface for accepting commands to be executed, for undoing commands, and for redoing commands. Optionally, one could also include an interface for querying the available number of undo and redo operations, which might be important for the implementation of a GUI (e.g., for redo size equals zero, gray out the redo button). Once a command is passed to the `CommandManager`, the `CommandManager` owns the lifetime of the command. Therefore, the interface for the `CommandManager` should enforce owning semantics. Combining, we have the following complete interface for the `CommandManager`:

```
class CommandManager
{
public:
  size_t getUndoSize() const;
  size_t getRedoSize() const;
  void executeCommand(unique_ptr<Command> c);
  void undo();
  void redo();
};
```

In the actual code listed in `CommandManager.m.cpp`, the interface additionally defines an `enum class` for selecting the undo/redo implementation strategy during construction. These strategies are discussed in the following section. I've included this option for illustrative purposes only. A production code would simply implement one undo/redo strategy and not make the underlying data structure customizable at construction.

4.4.2 Implementing Undo and Redo

To implement unlimited undo and redo, we must have a dynamically growable data structure capable of storing and revisiting commands in the order they were executed. Although one could contrive many different data structures to satisfy this requirement, we'll examine two equally good strategies. Both strategies have been implemented for the calculator and can be seen in the `CommandManager.m.cpp` file.

this figure will be printed in b/w

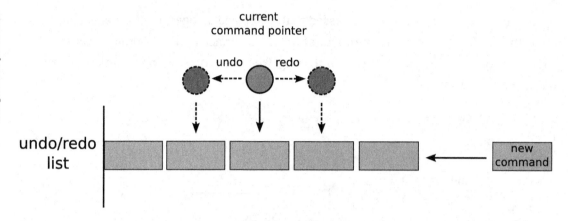

Figure 4-3. *The undo/redo list strategy*

Consider the data structure in Figure 4-3, which I have termed the list strategy. After a command is executed, it is added to a list (the implementation could be a `list`, `vector`, or other suitable ordered container), and a pointer (or index) is updated to point to the last command executed. Whenever undo is called, the command currently pointed to is undone, and the pointer moves to the left (the direction of earlier commands). When redo is called, the command pointer moves to the right (the direction of later commands), and the newly pointed to command is executed. Boundary conditions exist when the current command pointer reaches either the far left (no more commands exist to be undone) or far right (no more commands exist to be redone). These boundary conditions can be handled either by disabling the mechanism that enables the user to call the command (e.g., gray out the undo or redo button) or by simply ignoring an undo or redo command that would cause the pointer to overrun the boundary. Of course, every time a new command is executed, the entire list to the right of the current command pointer must be flushed before the new command is added to the undo/redo list. This flushing of the list is necessary to prevent the undo/redo list from becoming a tree with multiple redo branches.

As an alternative, consider the data structure in Figure 4-4, which I have termed the stack strategy. Instead of maintaining a list of commands in the order in which they were executed, we maintain two stacks: one for the undo commands and one for the redo commands. After a new command is executed, it is pushed onto the undo stack. Commands are undone by popping the top entry from the undo stack, undoing the command, and pushing the command onto the redo stack. Commands are redone by popping the top entry from the redo stack, executing the command, and pushing the command onto the undo stack. Boundary conditions exist and are trivially identified by the sizes of the stacks. Executing a new command requires flushing the redo stack.

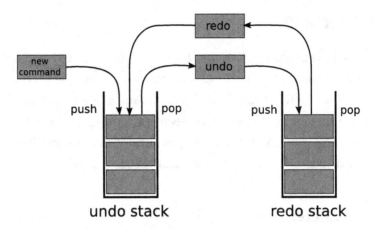

Figure 4-4. *The undo/redo stack strategy*

Practically, choosing between implementing undo and redo via either the stack or list strategy is largely a personal preference. The list strategy requires only one data container and less data movement. However, the stack strategy is slightly easier to implement because it requires no indexing or pointer shifting. That said, both strategies are fairly easy to implement and require very little code. Once you have implemented and tested either strategy, the CommandManager can easily be reused in future projects requiring undo and redo functionality, provided commands are implemented via the command pattern. For even more generality, the CommandManager could be templated on the abstract command class. For simplicity, I chose to implement the included CommandManager specifically for the abstract Command class previously discussed.

4.5 The Command Interpreter

The final component of the command dispatcher module is the CommandInterpreter class. As was previously stated, the CommandInterpreter class serves two primary roles. The first role is to serve as the primary interface to the command dispatcher module. The second role is to interpret each command, request the appropriate command from the CommandFactory, and pass each command to the CommandManager for execution. We address these two roles sequentially.

4.5.1 The Interface

For all the complications in the implementation of the command dispatcher module, the interface to the CommandInterpreter class is remarkably simple (as are most good interfaces). As was discussed in Chapter 2, the command dispatcher module's interface consists entirely of a single function used to execute a command; the command itself is specified by a string argument. This function is, naturally, the executeCommand() event handler previously discussed. Thus, the CommandInterpreter class's interface is given by the following:

```
class CommandInterpreter
{
  class CommandInterpreterImpl;
public:
  CommandInterpreter(UserInterface& ui);
  void executeCommand(const string& command);

private:
  unique_ptr<CommandInterpreterImpl> pimpl_;
};
```

Recall that the fundamental architecture of the calculator is based on the model-view-controller pattern and that the CommandInterpreter, as a component of the controller, is permitted to have direct access to both the model (stack) and view (user interface). Thus, the CommandInterpreter's constructor takes a reference to an abstract UserInterface class, the details of which are discussed in Chapter 5. A direct reference to the stack is unneeded since the stack was implemented as a singleton. The actual implementation of the CommandInterpreter is deferred to a private implementation class, CommandInterpreterImpl. We'll discuss this pattern of using a pointer to an implementation class, known as the pimpl idiom, in the next subsection.

An alternative design to the one previously mentioned would be to make the CommandInterpreter class an observer, directly. As discussed in Chapter 3, I prefer designs that use intermediary event observers. In Chapter 5, we'll discuss the design and implementation of a CommandIssuedObserver proxy class to broker events between user interfaces and the CommandInterpreter class. Although the CommandIssuedObserver is described alongside the user interface, it actually belongs to the command dispatcher module.

The Pimpl Idiom

In the first version of this book, I extensively used the pimpl pattern in pdCalc's implementation. However, when declaring classes in C++ module interfaces instead of in header files, I find that I use the pimpl pattern significantly less frequently. Despite my decreased usage of the pattern, because of its prominence in C++ code, the pimpl idiom is still worth discussing. Therefore, we'll describe the pimpl pattern itself, why it was historically important, and where the pimpl pattern still makes sense in the presence of modules.

If you look at enough C++ code, you will eventually find many classes with a curious single member variable often named `pimpl_` (or something similar) abstracting implementation details (a C++ specialization of the bridge pattern). For those unfamiliar with the term pimpl, it is shorthand notation for pointer to implementation. In practice, instead of declaring all of a class's implementation in that class's declaration, you instead forward declare a pointer to a "hidden" implementation class and fully declare and define this "hidden" class in a separate implementation file. Containing and using an incomplete type (the `pimpl` variable) is permissible provided the `pimpl` variable is only dereferenced in the source file containing its complete declaration. For example, consider class A in the following with a public interface consisting of functions `f()` and `g()`; a private implementation with functions `u()`, `v()`, and `w()`; and private data `v_` and `m_`:

```
class A
{
public:
  void f();
  void g();

private:
  void u();
  void v();
  void w();
  vector<double> v_;
  map<string, int> m_;
};
```

Instead of visually exposing the private interface of A to consumers of this class (in a header file or module interface unit), using the pimpl idiom, we write

```
class A
{
  class AImpl;
public:
  void f();
  void g();

private:
  unique_ptr<AImpl> pimpl_;
};
```

where u, v, w, v_, and m_ are now all be a part of class AImpl, which would be both declared and defined only in the implementation file associated with class A. To ensure AImpl cannot be accessed by any other classes, we declare this implementation class to be a private class wholly defined within A. Sutter and Alexandrescu [34] give a brief explanation of the advantages of the pimpl idiom. Assuming the use of a header/implementation file pair (as opposed to a module), one of the main advantages is that by moving the private interface of class A from A.h to A.cpp, we no longer need to recompile any code consuming class A when only A's private interface changes. For large-scale software projects, the time savings during compilation can be significant.

For code that has even a moderately complex private interface, I tend to use the pimpl idiom regardless of its implications on compile times. The exception to my general rule is for code that is computationally intensive (i.e., code where the indirection overhead of the pimpl is significant). Assuming a legacy header implementation, in addition to the compilation benefits of not having to recompile files including A.h when only class AImpl changes, I find that the pimpl idiom adds significant clarity to the code. This clarity derives from the ability to hide helper functions and classes in implementation files rather than listing them in interface files. In this manner, interface files truly reflect only the bare essentials of the interface and thus prevent class bloat, at least at the visible interface level. For any other programmer simply consuming your class, the implementation details are visually hidden and therefore do not distract from your hopefully well-documented, limited, public interface. The pimpl idiom truly is the epitome of encapsulation.

Do Modules Obviate the Pimpl Idiom?

C++20 modules bring several design and implementation benefits to interfaces. Do these benefits obviate the need for the pimpl idiom? To answer this question, we need to enumerate the reasons the pimpl pattern is used and determine if modules deprecate the need for this idiom.

The first reason the pimpl pattern is used is to speed up compilations. In the classical header file inclusion model, the pimpl pattern decouples the dependency between a class's private implementation and its public declaration. This decoupling implies that translation units dependent on a pimpl-ed class's header file do not need to be recompiled when changes are only made to the private implementation class since those changes would appear in a separately compiled source file rather than in the pimpl-ed class's header file. Modules partially solve this problem. To understand why, we'll need to delve briefly into the module compilation model.

Suppose we have a function foo defined in foo.cpp that consumes class A. In the header inclusion model, A would be declared in A.h and defined in A.cpp; A.h would be included in foo.cpp. The header inclusion model essentially pastes the contents of A.h into foo.cpp when foo.cpp is compiled. Therefore, any changes in A.h force the recompiling of foo.cpp, which includes the recompilation of the entire contents of A.h since it was textually included into foo.cpp. This situation is problematic when A.h is large, and this situation is doubly problematic since this recompilation of the contents of A.h occurs for every consumer of this class. Of course, any changes in A.cpp do not cause the recompilation of its consumers because the consumers of A depend only on A.h, not on A.cpp. This compilation dependency is exactly why the pimpl-ing benefits us by moving implementation details of A from A.h to A.cpp.

The compilation model for modules is different than the header inclusion model. Modules are not textually included into their consumers; instead, they are imported. Modules do not require separate header and implementation files, and imports do not directly require visibility of declarations. Instead, importing modules relies on the compiler creating compiled module interfaces (CMIs), which is, unfortunately, a compiler-dependent process. For example, gcc caches CMIs automatically when modules are compiled, while clang relies on the build system manually defining a CMI precompilation step. Regardless, the module import mechanism provides a distinct advantage over the header inclusion model because the CMI is compiled once when the module is built, eliminating the need to recompile the definitions in a header file each time the header is included. Of course, the preceding explanation of the module's compilation is slightly simplified, as modules can be split into module definition and module implementation files, and CMIs are both compiler version specific and even compilation option specific. Nonetheless, modules partially solve the first reason we use the pimpl idiom. If class A were defined in a module, ModuleA, instead of in A.h, any change to A's definition would still require recompilation of A's consumers. However, the recompilation of the former content of A.h would be precompiled once into a CMI rather than being textually included and recompiled with each consumer. Yes, each consumer would still need to be recompiled, but these compiles should be faster. Given ample tooling support, it is even possible that recompilation of consumers would be unnecessary if the build tool could detect the differences between public and private changes in a CMI.

The second reason the pimpl pattern is used is that the pimpl pattern hides implementation names and additional types from consuming compilation units. Why does this matter given that implementation details would appear in the private section of a class and be inaccessible to consumers? Oddly enough, even though private names are restricted from use, they participate in overload resolution. Consider the following example:

Listing 4-1. Visibility versus accessibility

```
// A.h
class A
{
public:
  void bar(double);

private:
  void bar(int);
};

// foo.cpp
#include "A.h"
void foo()
{
  A a;
  a.bar(7.0); // OK, calls A::bar(double)
  a.bar(7); // error, tries calling inaccessible A::bar(int)
}
```

If A::bar(int) had instead been hidden in a private implementation class, the erroneous line in the preceding function foo() would have compiled with an implicit conversion of the number 7 from an int to a double.

Do modules solve the preceding problem? Again, the answer is only partially. For the analogous example given in Listing 4-1 where class A would be refactored into an export from a module, the same error would result. However, let's consider the following even simpler example:

```cpp
// AMod.cpp
export module AMod;
export void bar(double);
void bar(int);
// implementations of bar
```

```cpp
// foo.cpp
import AMod;

void foo()
{
  bar(7);
  bar(7.0);
}
```

The preceding compiles, but only bar(double) is called. That is, while bar(int) is human visible, it is not compiler visible. Interestingly enough, bar(int) does remain reachable even though it is not visible. Let's return to our class example and modify the pimpl pattern for modules. We can now write

```cpp
// AMod.cpp
export module AMod;

struct AImpl
{
  void bar(int){}
};
```

```
export class A
{
public:
  void bar(double);
  void baz(int i){impl_.bar(i);}

private:
  AImpl impl_;
};

// foo.cpp
import AMod;

void foo()
{
  A a;
  a.bar(7);
  a.bar(7.0);
  a.baz(7);
}
```

The preceding example shows that we still must use the pimpl pattern to remove the name ambiguity for bar(). However, because modules can hide visibility without blocking reachability, we can construct our pimpl without a pointer indirection while still leaving AImpl hidden from consumers from an instantiation standpoint. This last fact brings us to our next dilemma.

Assuming the client does not have full source code access, the pimpl pattern enables us to hide implementation details from human eyes by moving these details from the human-readable interface, the header file, into the implementation file delivered to the client only as compiled binary code. Do modules permit hiding class implementation details from human eyes without resorting to the pimpl idiom? Unfortunately, no. Modules provide a language feature for enabling the compiler to hide visibility from consuming code, not from humans. While modules can be decomposed into separate module interface and module implementation units, the module interface unit must be human readable as the CMI cannot be used across compiler versions or settings reliably. That is, if a module's interface must be exportable, the source code for its implementation must be distributable. This previous statement extends to the case where we define the implementation details of class A in its own module, AMod.Impl, and import AMod.Impl into AMod (without reexporting AMod.Impl). The lack of binary portability of the CMI implies that any module interface units imported by AMod must also be shipped with the module interface unit of AMod, just like nested header files. Additionally, analogous to a header file class declaration, a module interface unit-exported class declaration must contain sufficient information to instantiate an object. Therefore, types must be fully visible (even if not accessible), meaning that to hide code from human eyes, we must resort to the implementation of the pimpl pattern that uses pointer indirection rather than the more efficient method previously mentioned that utilizes class composition. Modules do not solve the human visibility problem solved by pimpl-ing private class implementation details.

Finally, my opinion is that the pimpl pattern stylistically simplifies interface code by minimizing the overall number of lines of code appearing in the visual representation of a class's client interface. Many may not care about, or even acknowledge, this advantage of the pimpl idiom. This stylistic advantage applies to both header files and module interface units.

In summary, if you were using the pimpl pattern solely for its compilation efficiency benefits, modules, once matured, will likely obviate this usage of the pimpl idiom. If you were using the pimpl pattern to avoid collisions, modules may partially solve your problem. Finally, if you were using the pimpl idiom to remove implementation details from distributed interface source to avoid human visibility or just to clean up the interface, then modules do not help at all. The conclusion reached at the end of this section is that modules may partially obviate the pimpl idiom depending on your usage. While I still use the pimpl pattern, I do find I use it less frequently with modules than I do with header files.

4.5.2 Implementation Details

Typically in this book, we have not focused on the implementation details of classes. In this case, though, the implementation of the CommandInterpreterImpl class is particularly instructive. The main function of the CommandInterpreterImpl class is to implement the function executeCommand(). This function must receive command requests, interpret these requests, retrieve commands, request execution of commands, and gracefully handle unknown commands. Had we started our decomposition of the command dispatcher module from the top-down, trying to implement this function cleanly would have been exceedingly difficult. However, due to our bottom-up approach, the implementation of executeCommand() is largely an exercise in gluing together existing components. Consider the following implementation, where the manager_ object is an instance of the CommandManager class:

```
1   void CommandInterpreter::CommandInterpreterImpl::executeCommand(const
2   string command&)
3   {
4     if(double d; isNum(command, d) )
5       manager_.executeCommand(MakeCommandPtr<EnterNumber>(d));
6     else if(command == "undo")
7       manager_.undo();
8     else if(command == "redo")
9       manager_.redo();
10    else
11    {
12      if( auto c = CommandFactory::Instance().allocateCommand(command) )
13      {
14        try
15        {
16          manager_.executeCommand( std::move(c) );
17        }
18        catch(Exception& e)
19        {
20          ui_.postMessage( e.what() );
21        }
22      }
23      else
24      {
25        auto t = std::format("Command {} is not a known command", command);
26        ui_.postMessage(t);
27      }
28    }
29
30    return;
31  }
```

Lines 4–9 handle special commands. A special command is any command that is not entered in the command factory. In the preceding code, this includes entering a new number, undo, and redo. If a special command is not encountered, then it is assumed that the command can be found in the command factory; command factory requests are made on line 12. If `nullptr` is returned from the command factory, the error is handled in lines 25-26. Otherwise, the command is executed by the command manager. Note that the execution of commands is handled in a try/catch block. In this manner, we are able to trap errors caused by command precondition failures and report these errors in the user interface. The `CommandManager`'s implementation ensures that commands failing a precondition are not entered onto the undo stack.

The actual implementation of `executeCommand()` found in `CommandInterpreter.cpp` differs slightly from the preceding code. First, the actual implementation includes two additional special commands. The first of these additional special commands is help. The help command can be issued to print a brief explanatory message for all of the commands currently in the command factory. While the implementation generically prints the help information to the user interface, I only exposed the help command in the CLI (i.e., my GUI's implementation does not have a help button). The second special command deals with the handling of stored procedures. Stored procedures are explained in Chapter 8. Additionally, I placed the try/catch block in its own function. This was done simply to shorten the `executeCommand()` function and separate the logic of command interpretation from command execution.

Depending on your familiarity with the evolution of the language's syntax since C++17, two code statements in the implementation of `executeCommand()` may or may not have been new to you: an initializer in an if statement and the `std::format()` function. We'll examine these two new features in the following sidebar.

MODERN C++ DESIGN NOTE: IF STATEMENT INITIALIZERS AND `STD::FORMAT()`

Initialization in if statements was introduced in C++17, and the `std::format()` function was introduced in C++20. Let's examine both of these new features.

If statement initializers:

Prior to C++17, how often did you find yourself in the following (or similar) situation?

```
auto i = getAnInt();
if(i % 2 == 0 ) { /* do even things with i */ }
else { /* do odd things with i */}
```

How often did you wish you could scope i to the if statement similarly to how you might scope a variable to a for loop? In C++17, this dilemma was remedied with the extension of the if statement to include an optional clause for initialization. Now, instead, we can write

```
if(auto i = getAnInt(); i % 2 == 0 ) { /* do even things with i */ }
else { /* do odd things with i */}
```

Does this feature radically change what you can do with C++? No, but it is convenient, and it brings consistency to the scoping and initialization rules for if statements and for loops. An analogous feature added initialization to switch statements. What about while loops? No, no new syntax was added for while loops. Why not? No new syntax was needed. We've always been able to express this construct with for loops. That is, we have the following equivalence:

```
while(auto keepGoing = foo(); keepGoing) //not C++
{ /* do something that updates keepGoing */ }
```

is the same as

```
for(auto keepGoing = foo(); keepGoing;)
{ /* do something that updates keepGoing */ }
```

std::format():

Are you one of the people who never liked the overly verbose syntax of iostream string formatting and longed for a type-safe analog to sprintf() for C++? If you were, then std::format() will really excite you!

C++20 added a formatting library with several different formatting functions, two of which are used in pdCalc: format() and format_to(). The format() function has the following logical signature:

```
template<class... Args>
string format(string_view fmtStr, const Args&... args);
```

where fmtStr is a formatted string that accepts any number of typed arguments. The formatted string is an ordinary string that, by default, replaces any occurrences of {}s with the arguments, in order. {}s can either be empty (default formatting) or can contain user-specified formatting arguments. The return value of the function is the formatted string with all of the {}s replaced by the formatted arguments. As an example:

```
cout << format("{0} to {1} decimal places: {2:.{1}f}", "pi", 4, 3.1415927);
```

produces

```
pi to four decimal places: 3.1416
```

In the preceding example, I used numbered arguments to the format specifiers to enable reuse of the second argument, the precision value. Additionally, the example demonstrates how an argument can either be printed or used as a variable to a format specifier. Trust me when I say that the aforementioned only scratches the surface of the standard formatting.

Using `format()` allows you to format a single string. If you instead need a string builder, you can use `format_to()`. `format_to()` formats strings using the same syntax as `format()` except, instead of returning a formatted string, `format_to()` accepts an output iterator as its first argument and returns this same output iterator advanced by the formatted string. When the output iterator is a `back_inserter<string>`, then `format_to()` essentially replaces an `ostringstream`.

I must admit, I am not one of those people who were bothered by the overly verbose syntax of the `iostream` library. However, I have not used an `ostream` to format text since I started using the C++20 formatting library. I guess I actually was bothered by the previous syntax but didn't even know it!

4.6 Revisiting Earlier Decisions

At this point, we have finished two of the main modules of our calculator: the stack and the command dispatcher. Let's revisit our original design to discuss a significant subtle deviation that has arisen.

Recall from Chapter 2 that our original design handled errors by raising events in the stack and command dispatcher, and these events were to be handled by the user interface. The reason for this decision was for consistency. While the command dispatcher has a reference to the user interface, the stack does not. Therefore, we decided to simply let both modules notify the user interface of errors via events. The astute reader will notice, however, that the command dispatcher, as previously designed, never raises error events. Instead, it directly calls the user interface when errors occur. Have we not then broken the consistency that was intentionally designed into the system? No. Actually, we implicitly redesigned the error handling mechanism of the system during the design of the command dispatcher so that no error events are ever raised by either the stack or the command dispatcher. Let's examine why.

As we just stated, it is obvious from its implementation that the command dispatcher does not raise error events, but what happened to stack events? We didn't change the Stack class's source code, so how did error events get eliminated? In the original design, the stack indirectly notified the user interface when errors occurred by raising events. The two possible stack error conditions were popping an empty stack and swapping the top two elements of an insufficiently sized stack. While designing the commands, I realized that if a command triggered either of these error conditions, the user interface would be notified, but the command dispatcher would not be (it is not an observer of stack events). In either error scenario, a command would have completed, albeit unsuccessfully, and been placed erroneously on the undo stack. I then realized that either the command dispatcher would have to trap stack errors and prevent erroneous placement onto the undo stack, or commands should not be permitted to make stack errors. As the final design demonstrates, I chose the easier and cleaner implementation of using preconditions before executing commands to prevent stack errors from occurring, thus implicitly suppressing stack errors.

The big question is, why didn't I change the text describing the original design and the corresponding code to reflect the change in the error reporting? Simply stated, I wanted the reader to see that mistakes do occur. Design is an iterative process, and a book trying to teach design by example should embrace that fact rather than hide it. Designs should be somewhat fluid (but maybe with a high viscosity). It is much better to change a bad design decision early than to stick with it despite encountering evidence demonstrating flaws in the original design. The later a bad design is changed, the higher the cost will be to fix it, and the more pain the developers will incur while trying to implement a mistake. As for changing the code itself, I would have removed the superfluous code from the Stack class in a production system when I performed the refactor unless the Stack class was being designed for reuse in another program that handled errors via events. After all, as a generic design, the mechanism of reporting errors by raising events is not flawed. In hindsight, this mechanism was simply not right for pdCalc.

The Command Line Interface

This is a very exciting chapter. While command line interfaces (CLI) may not have the cachet of modern graphical user interfaces (GUI), especially those of phones, tablets, or the Web, the CLI is still a remarkably useful and effective user interface. This chapter details the design and implementation of the command line interface for pdCalc. By the end of this chapter, we will, for the first time, have a functioning, albeit feature incomplete, calculator, a significant milestone in our development.

5.1 The User Interface Abstraction

While we could design a fully functioning CLI in isolation, we know from our requirements that the feature complete calculator must have both a CLI and a GUI. Therefore, our overall design will be better served by first considering the commonality between these two interfaces and factoring this functionality into a common abstraction. Let's consider two design alternatives to constructing a user interface abstraction: a top-down approach and a bottom-up approach.

Designing an abstract interface before considering the concrete types is akin to top-down design. In terms of a user interface, you first consider the barest essentials to which any UI must conform and create an abstract interface based on this minimalist concept. Refinement to the interface becomes necessary when the abstract concept misses something required to implement a concrete type. Designing an abstract interface after considering the concrete types is akin to bottom-up design. Again, in terms of a user interface, you first consider the needs of all the concrete types (CLI and GUI, in this case), look for the commonality between all types, and then distill the common features

129

© Adam Singer 2022
A. B. Singer, *Practical C++ Design*, https://doi.org/10.1007/978-1-4842-7407-1_5

into an abstraction. Refinement to the interface becomes necessary when you add a new concrete type that requires additional features not considered when the abstraction was originally distilled.

Which strategy is better, in general, for creating an abstract interface, top-down or bottom-up? As is typical, the answer depends on the particular situation, personal comfort, and style. In this particular scenario, we are better served starting from the abstraction and working downward toward the concrete types (the top-down approach).

Why? In this instance, the top-down approach is essentially free. The user interface is one of pdCalc's high-level modules, and we already defined the abstract interface for the UI module in Chapter 2 when we performed our initial decomposition. Let's now turn the abstract module interface into a practical object-oriented design.

5.1.1 The Abstract Interface

The point of having an abstract interface for the UI is to enable the rest of the program to interact with the user interface without regard to whether the current interface is graphical, command line, or something else entirely. Ideally, we will be able to factor the abstract interface to the minimum number of functions required to use each concrete interface. Any functions sharing an implementation can be defined in the base class, while any functions requiring unique implementations based on the concrete type can be declared as virtual in the abstract base class and defined in the derived classes. The concept is fairly straightforward, but, as usual, the devil is in the details.

Figure 5-1. *A minimal interface hierarchy*

Consider the hierarchy depicted in Figure 5-1. Our goal is to design a minimal but complete interface, consistent with the Liskov Substitution Principle, for pdCalc's UserInterface class that will work for both the CLI and the GUI. As was previously discussed, we already defined a high-level interface for this UI in Chapter 2. Let's start from this predefined interface and refactor as necessary.

Referring to Table 2-2, we see that the complete interface for the `UserInterface` class consists of two event handling functions, `postMessage()` and `stackChanged()`, and one `UserInterface` raised event, `commandEntered()`. Interestingly, the `UserInterface` class is a publisher, an observer, an abstract user interface class, and the primary component of a module interface.

The two event handling functions, `postMessage()` and `stackChanged()`, are straightforward at the interface level. As we have done with previous observers, we will simply add these two functions to the public interface of the `UserInterface` class and create proxy observer classes to broker the communication by the publisher and the actual observer. These proxies are discussed in detail in the "User Interface Observers" section. Concrete user interfaces must handle the implementations for event handling uniquely based on how the individual UI interacts with the user. Hence, `postMessage()` and `stackChanged()` must both be pure virtual. Because there is no need for the `UserInterface` class to interject during event handling, I chose, for simplicity, to forgo the NVI pattern. However, as was discussed in Chapter 4, one could instead use the NVI pattern with trivial forwarding nonvirtual interface functions.

The `UserInterface` class's role as a publisher is slightly more complicated than its role as an observer. As we saw in Chapter 3 when designing the `Stack` class, the `Stack` implemented the publisher interface rather than substituted as a publisher. We therefore concluded that inheritance from the `Publisher` class should be private. For the `UserInterface` class, the relationship to the `Publisher` class is similar except the `UserInterface` class itself is not the publisher. The `UserInterface` class is an abstract interface for user interfaces in the system and is inheriting from the `Publisher` class only to enforce the notion that user interfaces must implement the publisher interface themselves. Both the CLI and the GUI classes will need to access public functions from `Publisher` (e.g., to raise events). Thus, the protected mode of inheritance is appropriate in this instance.

Further, recall from Chapter 3 that in order for the `Stack` class to implement the publisher interface, once we used private inheritance, we needed to hoist the `Publisher` class's `attach()` and `detach()` functions into the `Stack`'s public interface. The same is true here using protected inheritance. The question, however, is, should the hoisting occur in the `UserInterface` class or in its derived classes? To answer this question, we need to ask how particular user interfaces will be used by pdCalc. Clearly, either a CLI or a GUI *is-a* `UserInterface`. Therefore, concrete user interfaces will publicly inherit from `UserInterface` and be expected to obey the LSP. Attaching or detaching events to or from a particular user interface must therefore be able to be accomplished without knowing the underlying UI type. Thus, the attach() and detach() functions must be visible as part of UserInterface's public interface. Interestingly, in a rather unique implementation of the observer pattern, part of the publisher interface is implemented at the UserInterface level, while another part of the publisher interface is implemented at the derived class level.

Combining all of the preceding points, we can finally define the UserInterface class:

```
export module pdCalc.userInterface;

export class UserInterface : protected Publisher
{
public:
  UserInterface();
  virtual ~UserInterface();

  virtual void postMessage(string_view m) = 0;
  virtual void stackChanged() = 0;

  using Publisher::attach;
  using Publisher::detach;
  static string CommandEntered();
};
```

The CommandEntered() function returns a string that is the name of the command entered event. It is needed for attaching or detaching this event and can be given any name unique to events in the UserInterface class.

For completeness, we show the final user interface hierarchy in Figure 5-2. The class diagram illustrates the relationship between the CLI, the GUI, the abstract UserInterface class, and the publisher interface. Remember that the inheritance between the UserInterface class and the Publisher class is protected, so a UserInterface (or subsequent derived class) cannot be used as a Publisher. As was previously stated, however, the intent for the inheritances between the concrete CLI and GUI classes and the abstract UserInterface class are public, allowing an instantiation of either concrete type to be substituted as a UserInterface.

Figure 5-2. *The user interface hierarchy*

5.1.2 User Interface Events

Defining the UserInterface class does not complete the interface for the UI. Because the UserInterface class is an event publisher, we must also define the event data class that corresponds to the commandEntered() event. Additionally, defining the UserInterface class finally completes a publisher/observer pair, so we are finally ready to design and implement event proxy classes to broker events between the user interface and both the command dispatcher and the stack.

In Chapter 4, we saw that all commands are delivered to the command dispatcher via events. Specifically, the UI raises an event containing a specific command encoded as a string argument, the CommandInterpreter receives this event, and the string argument is passed to the CommandFactory, where a concrete command is retrieved for processing. As far as the command dispatcher is concerned, handling commandEntered() events is the same, irrespective of whether the encoded command string derives from the CLI or the GUI. Likewise, when the Stack class raises a stackChanged() event, the Stack is indifferent to the particular UserInterface that handles this event. We are therefore motivated to treat the issuing of commandEntered() events and the handling of stackChanged() events uniformly at the UserInterface class level in the user interface hierarchy.

We begin by examining the common infrastructure for raising commandEntered() events. The commandEntered() event is registered for all user interfaces in the constructor of the UserInterface class. Therefore, any derived user interface class can simply raise this event by calling the raise() function defined by the Publisher interface, which, by protected inheritance, is part of any concrete UI's implementation. The signature of the raise() function requires the name of the event and the event's data. Because the event's name is predefined in the UserInterface's constructor, the only additional functionality required to raise a command entered event is a uniform object for handling event data. Let's now look at its design.

Command Data

In Chapter 3, we designed our event system to use push semantics for passing event data. Recall that push semantics simply means that the publisher creates an object containing the necessary information to handle an event and pushes that object to the observers when an event is raised. We also examined two techniques for handling event data. In the polymorphic technique, an event data object must publicly inherit from an abstract EventData class. Observers receive the event data through the abstract interface when the event is raised, and they retrieve the data by downcasting the event data to the appropriate derived class. In the type erasure technique, the event data does not need to derive from a common base class, provided a concrete observer understands how to any_cast the data to the appropriate type. The implementation of pdCalc implements events using the type erasure method. Since both techniques were described in Chapter 3, only the type erasure technique actually used in pdCalc will be discussed in the following.

For command entered events, the event data is trivially a string containing either a number to be entered on the stack or the name of a command to be issued. While we could create a distinct CommandEnteredData class that would accept this string in its constructor, the type erasure method actually admits a much simpler solution: the event data can simply be the string itself. When the event is caught by an observer, event data d is recovered by any_cast<string>(d) instead of any_cast<CommandEnteredData>(d).

Neither design for commandEntered() event data can be considered superior to the other – they just make opposing trade-offs. Using a CommandEnteredData class gives extra type specificity through abstraction at the expense of additional code and an additional function call to retrieve the abstracted string. Using a plain string as the event's data is simple, lightweight, and efficient, but lacks the clarity enforced by the class abstraction. For a complex code base, introducing a new class to abstract the event data would probably be preferred. However, since we already described the class abstraction event data strategy in Chapter 3, for illustrative purposes, the commandEntered() event's data was implemented using a plain string.

While the mechanics for determining how and when to raise a `commandEntered()` event is somewhat different between the CLI and the GUI, both raise events by ultimately calling `Publisher`'s `raise()` function with a `string` that encodes the particular command being issued. That is, for some command string, `cmd`, the following code raises a `commandEntered()` event in the CLI, the GUI, or any other user interface that might inherit from `UserInterface`:

```
raise(UserInterface::CommandEntered(), cmd);
```

Now that we can raise UI events, let's see how they're handled.

User Interface Observers

The goal for this subsection is to construct the mechanics to enable classes to listen to events. Because the abstract user interface is both a source and sink for events, the UI serves as an ideal candidate to demonstrate how publishers and observers interact with each other.

In Chapter 3, we saw that observers are classes that register for and listen to events raised by publishers. Thus far, we have encountered both the `CommandInterpreter` and `UserInterface` classes that both need to observe events. While it is possible to make the `CommandInterpreter` or `UserInterface` an observer directly, I prefer constructing a dedicated observer intermediary between the publisher and the class that needs to observe an event. I have often nebulously referred to this intermediary as a proxy. We are now ready to give a more concrete meaning to this term.

The proxy pattern [11] is a design pattern that uses a class, the proxy, to serve as the interface for something else. The something else, let's call it the target, is not strictly defined. It could be a network connection, a file, an object in memory, or, as in our case, simply another class. Often, the proxy pattern is used when the underlying target is impossible, inconvenient, or expensive to replicate. The proxy pattern uses a class buffer to allow the system to perceive the target as an object independent of its underlying composition. In our context, we are using the proxy pattern simply to buffer communication between publishers and observers.

Why are we bothering with the proxy pattern here? This strategy has several distinct advantages. First, it increases clarity in the target class's public interface by replacing a generically named `notify()` function with a descriptively named event handling function. Second, an otherwise unnecessary inheritance from the `Observer` class is removed. Eliminating this dependency reduces coupling, increases cohesion, and facilitates reuse of the target in a setting where it is not an observer. Third, using a proxy class eliminates the ambiguity that arises for a target class that needs to listen to multiple events. Without using proxy classes, an observer would be required to disambiguate events in its single notify() function. Using an individual proxy for each event enables each event to call a unique handler function in the target object. The main disadvantage of implementing the observer pattern using a proxy is the slight cost of one extra indirection for handling each event. However, in situations where using the observer pattern is appropriate, the cost of an extra indirection is negligible.

Using the proxy pattern for implementing the observer pattern leads to the following two classes for handling commandEntered() and stackChanged() events: CommandIssuedObserver and StackUpdatedObserver, respectively. The CommandIssuedObserver mediates between commandEntered() events raised by the UI and observation in the command dispatcher. The StackUpdatedObserver mediates between stackChanged() events raised by the stack and observation in the UI. The implementation for both of these classes is relatively straightforward and very similar. By way of example, let's examine the implementation for CommandIssuedObserver.

The declaration for CommandIssuedObserver is given by the following:

```
class CommandIssuedObserver : public Observer
{
public:
  explicit CommandIssuedObserver(CommandInterpreter& ci);

private:
  void notifyImpl(const any&) override;
  CommandInterpreter& ci_;
};
```

Because it mediates events between the UI as a publisher and the CommandInterpreter as the target of the observer, the CommandIssuedObserver's constructor takes a reference to a CommandInterpreter instance, which it retains to callback to the command dispatcher when the UI raises a commandEntered() event. Recall that the CommandIssuedObserver will be stored by the UI in the Publisher's event symbol table when the observer is attached to the event. The implementation of notifyImpl() is simply an any cast of the function's parameter to a string followed by a call to CommandInterpreter's commandEntered() function.

Of course, before an event is triggered, the `CommandIssuedObserver` must be registered with the UI. For completeness, the following code illustrates how to accomplish this task:

```
ui.attach( UserInterface::CommandEntered(),
  make_unique<CommandIssuedObserver>(ci) );
```

where `ui` is a `UserInterface` reference and `ci` is a `CommandInterpreter` instance. Note that since the `attach()` function was intentionally hoisted into the abstract `UserInterface` scope, attaching through a reference allows us to reuse the same call for both the CLI and the GUI. That is, registering events is accomplished through the abstract UI interface, which greatly simplifies user interface setup in pdCalc's `main()` routine. The declaration and registration of `StackUpdatedObserver` are analogous.

The complete implementation of the observer proxy classes can be found in `AppObservers.m.cpp`. While the usage of the observer proxies is intertwined with the event observing classes, the proxies are not part of the interface for the target classes.

Hence, they are included in their own file. The attachment of the proxies to events is performed in `main.cpp`. This code structure preserves the loose binding between publishers and observers. Specifically, publishers know which events they can raise, but not who will observe them, while observers know which events they will watch, but not who raises them. Code external to both publishers and their observers binds the two together.

5.2 The Concrete CLI Class

The remainder of this chapter is devoted to detailing the CLI concrete class, a member of the user interface module. Let's start by reexamining the CLI's requirements.

5.2.1 Requirements

The requirements for pdCalc indicate that the calculator must have a command line interface, but what, precisely, is a CLI? My definition for a command line interface is any user interface to a program that responds to user commands interactively through text. Even if your definition for a command line interface is somewhat different, I believe we can certainly agree that a broad requirement simply indicating a program should have a CLI is woefully insufficient.

In a production development situation, when you encounter a requirement too vague to design a component, you should immediately seek clarification from your client. Notice I said *when* and not *if*. Regardless of how much effort you place up front trying to refine requirements, you always have incomplete, inconsistent, or changing requirements. This usually arises for a few reasons. Sometimes, it is due to a conscious effort not to spend the upfront time refining requirements. Sometimes, it arises from an inexperienced team member not understanding how to gather requirements properly. Often, however, it simply arises because the end user doesn't know what they truly want or need until the product starts to take shape. I find this true even for small development projects for which I am my own customer! While you as the implementer always retain the expedient option of refining a requirement without engaging your customer, my experience indicates that this path invariably leads to rewriting the code repeatedly: once for what you thought the user wanted, once for what the user thought they wanted, and once for what the user actually wanted.

Obviously, for our case study, we only have a hypothetical end user, so we'll simply do the refinement ourselves. We specify the following:

1. The CLI should accept a text command for any command defined for the calculator (those that exists in the command factory plus undo, redo, help, and exit).

2. The help command should display a list of all available commands and a short explanatory message.

3. The CLI should accept space-separated commands in the order in which they should be processed. Recall that this order corresponds to Reverse Polish Notation. All commands on a line are processed after return is pressed.

4. After commands are processed, the interface should display at most the top four elements of the stack plus the stack's current size.

Surprisingly, the minimal requirements previously listed are sufficient to build a simple CLI. While these requirements are somewhat arbitrary, something specific needed to be chosen in order to describe a design and implementation. If you don't like the resulting CLI, I highly encourage you to specify your own requirements and modify the design and implementation accordingly.

5.2.2 The CLI Design

The design of the CLI is remarkably simple. Because our overall architectural design placed the entire "business logic" of the calculator in the backend, the frontend is merely a thin layer that does nothing more than accept and tokenize input from the user, pass that input to the controller sequentially, and display the results. Let's begin by describing the interface.

The Interface

From the analysis we performed earlier in the chapter, we know that the concrete CLI class will inherit from the abstract UserInterface class. This inheritance is public because the CLI *is-a* UserInterface and must substitute as one. Hence, the CLI must implement the UserInterface's two abstract pure virtual functions: postMessage() and stackChanged(). These two methods are only called polymorphically through a UserInterface reference; therefore, both methods become part of the private interface of the CLI. Other than construction and destruction, the only functionality that the CLI needs to expose publicly is a command that starts its execution. This function drives the entire CLI and only returns (normally) when the user requests to quit the program. Combining the aforementioned, the entire interface for the CLI can be given by the following:

```
export module pdCalc.userInterface;

export class Cli : public UserInterface
{
public:
  Cli(istream& in, ostream& out);
  ~Cli();

  void execute(bool suppressStartupMessage = false, bool echo = false);

private:
  void postMessage(string_view m) override;
  void stackChanged() override;
};
```

While the interface is mostly self-explanatory, the arguments to both the constructor and the execute() function are worth explaining. To meet the requirements previously described, the execute() function could be written with no arguments. The two arguments included in the interface are simply optional features that can be turned on. The first argument dictates whether or not a banner is displayed when the CLI starts. The second argument controls command echoing. If echo is set to true, then each command is repeated before displaying the result. Both of these features could be hard-coded in the CLI, but I chose to add them as arguments to the execute() method for added flexibility.

The arguments to the constructor are slightly less obvious than the arguments to the execute() command. Almost by definition, a CLI takes input from cin and outputs results to cout or maybe cerr. However, hard-coding these standard I/O streams arbitrarily limits the usage of this class to that of a traditional CLI. Usually, I advocate limiting functionality to exactly what you need instead of anticipating more general usage. However, using C++ stream I/O is one of my few exceptions to my rule of thumb.

Let's discuss why using references to base class C++ I/O streams is generally a good design practice. First, the desire to use different I/O modes is quite common. Specifically, redirection to or from files is a frequently requested modification to a CLI. In fact, we'll see this request in Chapter 8! Second, implementing the generic vs. specific interface adds virtually no complexity. For example, instead of directly writing to cout, one simply keeps a reference to an output stream and writes to that instead. In the base case, this reference simply points to cout. Finally, using arbitrary stream input and output greatly simplifies testing. While the program may instantiate the Cli class using cin and cout, tests can instantiate the Cli class with either a file stream or a string stream. In this manner, interactive stream inputs and outputs can be simulated using strings or files. This strategy simplifies testing of the Cli class since inputs can be easily passed in and outputs easily captured as strings rather than through standard input and output.

Finally, note that the Cli class is declared as a part of the userInterface module in the UserInterface.m.cpp file, while it is defined in the partition userInterface:Cli in the file Cli.m.cpp. This somewhat strange construction is required due to an otherwise circular reference that would be created between UserInterface.m.cpp and Cli.m.cpp. Another alternative would have been to simply define the Cli class in the userInterface module instead of a partition, likely renaming Cli.m.cpp to UserInterface.cpp. This implementation detail has no bearing on the design of pdCalc – it is only a curiosity of file organization.

The Implementation

The implementation of the Cli class is worth examining to observe the simplicity enabled by the modularity of pdCalc's design. The entire implementation of the Cli class is effectively contained in the execute() and postMessage() member functions. The execute() function drives the CLI. It presents a startup message to the end user, waits for commands to be entered, tokenizes these commands, and raises events to signal to the command dispatcher that a new command has been entered. The stackChanged() function is an observer proxy callback target that writes the top of the stack to the command line after the stackChanged() event is raised. Essentially, the CLI reduces to two I/O routines where execute() handles input and stackChanged() handles output. Let's look at the implementations for these two functions starting with the execute() function:

```
void Cli::execute(bool suppressStartupMessage, bool echo)
{
  if(!suppressStartupMessage) startupMessage();

  for(string line; std::getline(in_, line, '\n'); )
  {
    istringstream iss{line};
    // Tokenizer must be one of LazyTokenizer or GreedyTokenizer.
    // See discussion below.
    Tokenizer tokenizer{iss};
    for(auto i : tokenizer)
    {
      if(echo) out_ << i << endl;
      if(i == "exit" || i == "quit")
        return;
      else
        raise(UserInterface::CommandEntered(), i);
    }
  }

  return;
}
```

141

The main algorithm for the CLI is fairly simple. First, the CLI waits for the user to input a line. Second, this input line is tokenized by the `Tokenizer` class. The CLI then loops over each token in the input line and raises an event with the token string as the event's data. The CLI terminates when it encounters either a `quit` or an `exit` token.

The only piece of the `execute()` function not previously explained is the `Tokenizer` class. Simply, the `Tokenizer` class is responsible for taking a string of text and splitting this string into individual space-separated tokens. Neither the CLI nor the `Tokenizer` determines the validity of tokens. Tokens are simply raised as events for the command dispatcher module to process. Note that as an alternative to writing your own, many libraries (e.g., boost) provide simple tokenizers.

The tokenization algorithm is relatively straightforward; we'll see two separate implementations momentarily. First, however, why choose a class design for the `Tokenizer` instead of, say, a design employing a function returning a `vector` of `strings`? Realistically, both designs functionally work, and both designs are equally easy to test and maintain. However, I prefer the class design because it provides a distinct type for the `Tokenizer`. Let's examine the advantages of creating a distinct type for tokenization.

Suppose we wanted to tokenize input in function `foo()` but process tokens in a separate function, `bar()`. Consider the following two possible pairs of functions to achieve this goal:

```
// use a Tokenizer class
Tokenizer foo(string_view);
void bar(const Tokenizer&);

// use a vector of strings
vector<string> foo(string_view);
void bar(const vector<string>&);
```

First, using a `Tokenizer` class, the signatures for both `foo()` and `bar()` immediately inform the programmer the intent of the functions. We know these functions involve tokenization. Using a `vector` of `strings` leaves ambiguity without further documentation (I intentionally did not provide names for the arguments). More importantly, however, typing the tokenizer enables the compiler to ensure that `bar()` can only be called with a `Tokenizer` class as an argument, thus preventing a programmer from accidentally calling `bar()` with an unrelated collection of `strings`. Another benefit of the class design is that a `Tokenizer` class encapsulates the data structure that represents a collection of tokens. This encapsulation shields the interface to `bar()` from a decision to change the underlying data structure from, for example, a `vector` of `strings` to a `list` of `strings` (or, a generator, as we'll see shortly). Finally, a `Tokenizer` class can encapsulate additional state information about tokenization (e.g., the original, pretokenized input), if desired. A collection of `strings` is obviously limited to carrying only the tokens themselves.

We now turn to the implementation of the `Tokenizer` class. I chose to present two separate implementations: a greedy tokenization and a lazy tokenization. The first approach, greedy tokenization, was the approach I took in the first edition of this book. The second approach, lazy tokenization, was only made trivial with the introduction of coroutines in C++20.

In order to demonstrate the interchangeability of the two algorithms, I implemented both behind an identical conceptual interface. However, because the two classes are not intended to be used polymorphically, the interface is not enforced via inheritance. Let's examine this hypothetical interface:

```
class TokenizerInterface
{
public:
  explicit TokenizerInterface(istream&);
  ~TokenizerInterface();

  size_t nTokens() const;

  // not a "real" interface class - just using auto conceptually
  auto begin();
  auto end();
};
```

A tokenizer can be constructed from an input stream, it can state how many tokens it has parsed, and it can return an iterator to the beginning and ending of the token stream. Of course, more functionality can be added, but these member functions comprise the minimal set required for parsing tokens in pdCalc. Let's now look at the individual implementations.

What makes a tokenization algorithm greedy, and what makes one lazy? Both implementations initialize tokenization in the constructor. However, the greedy algorithm parses all of the tokens in the stream immediately and stores them in a container for future use. The iterator interface in `TokenizerInterface` simply resolves to a forwarding request to the underlying container, for example, a `vector<string>`, in the GreedyTokenizer. No tokenization occurs when a user iterates over the tokens; tokenization already greedily occurred during construction. The following is a simple implementation of the greedy tokenization algorithm (which also pops all entries to lowercase):

```cpp
void GreedyTokenizer::tokenize(istream& is)
{
  for(istream_iterator<string> i{is}; i != istream_iterator<string>{};
  ++i)
  {
    string t;
    ranges::transform(*i, back_inserter<string>(t), ::tolower);
    tokens_.push_back( std::move(t) );
  }


  return;
}
```

In contrast, let's look at the lazy tokenization algorithm. Lazy tokenization only parses each token as the next one is requested. This lazy algorithm is made trivially possible by C++20 coroutines, which are discussed in the sidebar. First, however, let's examine the LazyTokenizer's implementation:

Listing 5-1. Lazy tokenizer

```cpp
cppcoro::generator<string> LazyTokenizer::tokenize(std::istream& is)
{
  for(istream_iterator<string> i{is}; i != istream_iterator<string>{};
  ++i)
  {
    string t;
    ranges::transform(*i, back_inserter<string>(t), ::tolower);
    ++nTokens_;
    co_yield t;
  }

  co_return;
}
```

Two differences exist between the greedy and lazy implementations. First, trivially, the lazy routine needs to count and store the number of tokens (nTokens_) that are parsed. This step is unnecessary for the greedy algorithm because it retains all the tokens in a vector, which knows its own size. The second difference is that the lazy algorithm uses the co_yield operator and returns a generator (part of the cppcoro library [7]), which is discussed in detail in the sidebar. Essentially, the co_yield operator signals to the compiler that this function is a coroutine, which can be preempted and subsequently restarted at the point it yielded, in this case, resuming the for loop to parse the next token. co_yield permits returning a value, in this case, our lazily evaluated token.

It should be noted that while the two tokenizers have the same interface, their behavior is slightly different. First, the greedy tokenizer parses the stream once, but the tokens can be iterated over as many times as desired. The nTokens() function always returns the total number of tokens in the stream because the stream is completely parsed before nTokens() can be called. In contrast, the lazy tokenizer can only be iterated over once because the iteration causes the tokenization. The nTokens() function therefore returns the number of tokens parsed up to that point, which may be smaller than the total number of tokens in the input stream. Of course, if multiple iterations over the LazyTokenizer are desired, tokens could always be stored in a container as the stream was lazily parsed. The two tokenizers would then behave the same once the parse was completed.

Implementations of both the greedy tokenizer and the lazy tokenizer are provided in the Tokenizer.m.cpp source file. By default, pdCalc is configured to only use the lazy tokenizer. However, the two tokenizers are completely interchangeable. If you wish to try the greedy tokenizer, just change the tokenizer instantiated in CLI's execute() function. Obviously, switching between the two tokenizers could be made compile time configurable using static polymorphism.

MODERN C++ DESIGN NOTE: COROUTINES AND GENERATORS

Coroutines are an old idea finally made standard in C++20. In my opinion, coroutines are a mix in terms of usability. Writing a coroutine itself is fairly straightforward, provided you don't need to write the support code for managing the lifetime of the coroutine. In concrete terms, relative to Listing 5-1, implementing tokenize() is easy, but implementing generator<> is hard.

Unfortunately, a common library for coroutine utilization was not adopted as part of the C++20 standard (maybe C++23?). Fortunately, however, the high-quality cppcoro coroutines library exists [7], and you can rest assured knowing that its author has already implemented the hard parts of using coroutines for you. In my initial implementation of Listing 5-1, I wrote my own generator class. My implementation was not generic and was quite sloppy, but it did work as expected. However, understanding the implementation was not instructive to understanding pdCalc's design. Ultimately, I decided that describing the detailed implementation of coroutines was beyond the scope of this book. Instead, I decided to use cppcoro's generator class directly. The MIT licensed `generator.hpp` is included with pdCalc and is located in `3rdparty/cppcoro`. Those readers interested in understanding the details of coroutines are referred to the excellent blog posts [6] by Lewis Baker, the creator of cppcoro. Our discussion will instead focus on the higher-level design goals of what coroutines are conceptually and how we are able to use them to better pdCalc's design.

Coroutines are a generalization of subroutines that allow suspension of control by programatically ceding execution from within. Coroutines maintain their state and can be resumed later from the point at which they relinquished control. Effectively, coroutines provide a language mechanism to support cooperative multitasking (vs. the preemptive multitasking of threads).

One of the types that coroutines enable is generators. Generators are objects that generate a sequence as they are iterated upon. They are particularly useful when the sequence is infinite. The canonical implementation of a generator seems to be the generation of the Fibonacci numbers. The Fibonacci numbers, F_n, are defined by the following recursion:

$$F_0 = 0, \qquad F_1 = 1, \quad F_n = F_{n-1} + F_{n-2}, n > 1$$

Without using coroutines, the sequence can be trivially generated to the nth number with the following function:

```cpp
auto fibLoop(unsigned int n)
{
  vector<long long> v(n+1);
  v[0] = 0;

  if(n > 0) v[1] = 1;

  for(auto i = 2u; i < v.size(); ++i)
    v[i] = v[i-1] + v[i-2];

  return v;
}
```

Unfortunately, we must perform a greedy evaluation of all numbers up to the *n*th number. fibLoop() does not allow a lazy, sequential evaluation of the Fibonacci numbers by calling the function repeatedly.

Let's try to create a function that can generate the next number in the Fibonacci sequence each time it's called. The following code is our first attempt:

```
long long fibStatic()
{
  static long long cur = 0;
  static long long prev = 1;

  auto t = cur;
  cur += prev;
  prev = t;

  return prev;
}
```

The code works as long as we only want to generate the Fibonacci sequence once per program execution in a single-threaded environment. To fix the problem that the code can only be called once, we could add a reset flag as a parameter. However, now we're just adding hacks, and we still haven't fixed our inability to run in a multithreaded environment. Let's try again.

Our next attempt leads to a rather complicated solution involving a Fibonacci class and an iterator:

```
class Fibonacci
{
  class fibonacci_iterator
  {
  public:
    using iterator_category = std::input_iterator_tag;
    using difference_type = std::ptrdiff_t;
    using value_type = long long;
    using reference = long long&;
    using pointer = long long*;

    fibonacci_iterator(){}
    fibonacci_iterator(Fibonacci* f): f_{f}{}
```

```cpp
    long long operator*() const { return f_->cur_; }
    fibonacci_iterator& operator++(){f_->next(); return *this;}
    void operator++(int){ operator++(); }

    auto operator<=>(const fibonacci_iterator&) const = default;

  private:
    Fibonacci* f_ = nullptr;
  };
public:

  using iterator = fibonacci_iterator;

  iterator begin() { return fibonacci_iterator{this}; }
  iterator end() { return fibonacci_iterator{}; }

private:
  void next()
  {
    long long t = cur_;
    cur_ += prev_;
    prev_ = t;
  }

  long long cur_ = 0l;
  long long prev_ = 1l;
};
```

Ouch! The preceding code is sloppy, incomplete, and really quite horrendous to perform what seemed like an easy task. Making use of the ranges library (see next sidebar), it does, however, enable us to generate and use Fibonacci numbers in a beautifully succinct fashion:

```cpp
Fibonacci fib;
```

```cpp
// grab the first 10 Fibonacci numbers and use them one at a time
ranges::for_each(fib | views::take(10), [](auto fn){useFib(fn);});
```

If you are unfamiliar with the preceding syntax, especially the functional style of piping a range to a view, don't fret. The ranges library is another new feature of C++20, which I'll very briefly introduce in the next sidebar.

Simple things should be easy, and here is where coroutines and generators shine. What if we could provide the simplicity of `fibLoop()`, the one-by-one semantics of `fibStatic()`, and the expressiveness and safety of class `Fibonacci`. This would be possible if there were a language mechanism that would essentially allow us to write a function that could be interrupted and resumed, yielding a value each time the function were suspended. Of course, this feature is precisely what coroutines provide. We can now simply write

```
cppcoro::generator<long long> fibonacci()
{
  long long prev = 1;
  long long cur = 0;
  while(true)
  {
    co_yield cur;
    long long t = cur;
    cur += prev;
    prev = t;
  }
}
```

The preceding coroutine is an infinite but interruptible loop. The `co_yield` expression causes the coroutine to suspend and yield the current Fibonacci number. cppcoro's `generator` class hides the complicated mechanics of suspending and resuming `fibonacci()` behind a simple-to-use iterator interface. When the generator iterator is dereferenced, the value of the current Fibonacci number is returned. When the forward iterator is advanced, `fibonacci()` is resumed, continuing the infinite loop until `co_yield` is encountered again. In this manner, we can use and access an infinite loop in a finite fashion, which provides a very clean implementation for computing Fibonacci numbers to a finite but not predetermined depth. As before, the coroutine can be used trivially:

```
auto fib = fibonacci();
```

```
// grab the first 10 Fibonacci numbers and use them one at a time
ranges::for_each(fib | views::take(10), [](auto fn){useFib(fn);});
```

At this point, hopefully Listing 5-1 makes sense. Our lazy tokenizer is simply a generator of string tokens that are produced by looping over a stream, extracting each whitespace-separated string, and suspending execution until the next token is requested. It's a beautiful design made easy by new C++20 language features.

Before departing this sidebar, I want to share one quick tip that I learned the hard way: Carefully watch the lifetime of any values passed to a coroutine by reference. In fact, I would go so far as to say avoid passing values by reference to coroutines. Consider my failed first attempt at writing a string constructor for `LazyTokenizer`:

```
LazyTokenizer::LazyTokenizer(const std::string& s)
: nTokens_{0}
{
  istringstream t{s};
  generator_ = tokenize(t);
}
```

The preceding seemingly correct code will compile, but the tokenizer will cause a segmentation fault when it is used. The reason is that while the `tokenize()` function appears to be a regular function call that simply returns, it is not. `tokenize()` is a resumable coroutine that is accessed via its returned generator, which, in this case, is stored in `generator_`. Here, `generator_`, a member variable, has a lifetime longer than the local variable `t`. When `tokenize()` is first called, everything works fine. The generator is initialized and in a ready state. However, since `tokenize()` captures its stream argument by reference, when the coroutine is advanced via iteration over `generator_`, `t` has gone out of scope and has been destroyed. Inside `tokenize()`, we are left advancing an `istream_iterator<string>` that is iterating over a destroyed `istringstream`. Obviously, this code will fail. Once you've reasoned this failure out, it makes perfect sense. However, to me, it was nonobvious the first time I encountered this error because my experience has trained me to interpret `tokenize()` as a single pass through function that only exists until control is returned to the caller. Of course, coroutine call semantics are different as coroutines exist until destroyed. The return of control to the caller does not destroy the local context inside the coroutine, which could contain references to function arguments. Instead, that state is stored for later resumption. Any referred to objects that have since gone out of scope become invalid. Programmer beware.

As a final part of the CLI's implementation, we examine a simplified version of the `stackChanged()` function:

```
void Cli::stackChanged()
{
  unsigned int nElements{4};
  auto v = Stack::Instance().getElements(nElements);
```

```
string s{"\n"};
auto bi = std::back_inserter(s);

for( auto j = v.size(); auto i : views::reverse(v) )
  std::format_to(bi, "{}:\t{:.12g}\n", j--, i);

postMessage(s);
}
```

The implementation in `Cli.m.cpp` differs only in the fanciness of the printing. Note that whenever the stack changes, the CLI simply picks the top four (as specified in our requirements) entries of the stack (`getElements()` returns the minimum of `nElements` and the size of the stack), formats them in a `string`, and passes this string to the `postMessage()` function. For the CLI, `postMessage()` simply writes the string to the output stream.

Before we move on, let's pause and reflect on how clean and brief the implementation for the CLI is. This simplicity is a direct result of pdCalc's overall design. Whereas many user interfaces intermix the "business logic" with the display code, we meticulously designed these two layers to be independent. Interpretation and processing of commands, the "business logic," resides entirely in the command dispatcher. Therefore, the CLI is only responsible for accepting commands, tokenizing commands, and reporting results. Furthermore, based on the design of our event system, the CLI has no direct coupling to the command dispatcher, a decision consistent with our MVC architecture. The command dispatcher does have a direct link to the user interface, but because of our abstraction, the command dispatcher binds to an abstract `UserInterface` rather than a specific user interface implementation. In this way, the `Cli` perfectly substitutes as a `UserInterface` (application of the LSP) and can trivially be swapped in or out as any one of many unique views to the calculator. While this flexibility may seem like overkill for the design of a calculator, the modularity of all of the components is beneficial from both a testing and separation of concerns standpoint even if the calculator were not slated to have another user interface.

MODERN C++ DESIGN NOTE: THE RANGES LIBRARY

The ranges library is one of the big four features of C++20, and a simple sidebar in no way does this library justice. However, we'll take a very quick detour to get a cursory introduction.

The ranges library introduces, among a few other features, three major new constructs: the ranges concept, the range algorithms, and views. Ignoring the detailed C++ mechanics of how ranges are implemented with C++ concepts, logically, a range is an iterable collection demarcated by a beginning and an ending. While you may choose to implement your own ranges, beginning in C++20, the STL containers are ranges, so ranges are immediately accessible to everyone.

Great, vectors are ranges, so now what? The first immediate benefit you will see from ranges is the improved syntax of their accompanying algorithms. Suppose you need to sort a vector of strings, v (we'll assume by the default sorting criteria). Prior to ranges, using the standard library, you would have written the following code:

```
std::sort( begin(v), end(v) );
```

The preceding syntax isn't terrible, but given we wanted to sort the entire vector, why couldn't we just call sort(v)? Well, now you can. Because a vector is a range, we can call the range-based equivalent algorithm:

```
std::ranges::sort(v);
```

That's much cleaner. Most, if not all, of the standard algorithms now come with range-based equivalents.

If range-based algorithmic syntax is all we would have gotten with the ranges library, I would have been underwhelmed. However, we get much more because ranges come with views. Loosely, a view is a lazily evaluated range adapter. Let's consider an example. Suppose you have a vector, v, of 20 integers and want to store the square of the last five even numbers you encounter in vector, t (yes, an admittedly contrived example). The following single executable line of code will accomplish this feat:

```
// note, code assumes
// namespace ranges = std::ranges;
// namespace views = std::ranges::views;
```

```
ranges::copy( v | views::filter([](int i){return i % 2 == 0;})
                | views::reverse
                | views::take(5)
                | views::transform([](int i){return i * i;})
                , back_inserter(t) );
```

Three important things are occurring in the single line of code shown previously. First, and most obvious, all of the views are chained together. Second, the chaining of the views enables us to perform all of these operations in one loop over v. Third, because views are lazily evaluated, only the necessary actions are taken. For example, we're not reversing all of v, only the even numbers. Additionally, we're not squaring all of the even numbers, only the last five (or fewer if there are less than five even numbers in v).

While the preceding code is both compact and efficient, I'm willing to concede it may not be the most readable. Sure, the views reverse and take clearly state what they're doing, but understanding what filter and transform do require also understanding their embedded lambda expressions. Fortunately, we can store views in variables and apply them as follows:

```
auto takeEven = views::filter([](int i){ return i % 2 == 0; });
auto square = views::transform([](int i){return i * i;});

ranges::copy(v | takeEven | views::reverse | views::take(5) | square,
        back_inserter(t));
```

That's clearer. The ability to trivially create new named views from existing views both increases readability and enables reusability.

I'll conclude this sidebar the same way I began it, by stating that this small sidebar in no way does ranges justice. If, however, this sidebar piqued your interest, I encourage you to read Eric Niebler's article introducing ranges [26] and the Range-v3 User Manual [25]. Eric Niebler's Range-v3 library formed the basis on which the C++ standard ranges library was built.

5.3 Tying It Together: A Working Program

Before we conclude our chapter on the CLI, it is worthwhile to write a simple main program that ties all of the components together to demonstrate a working calculator. pdCalc's actual implementation in main.cpp is significantly more complicated because it handles multiple user interfaces and plugins. Eventually, we will build up to understanding the full implementation in main.cpp, but for now, the following code

153

will enable us to execute a working calculator with a command line interface (of course, including the appropriate header files and module imports):

```cpp
int main()
{
  Cli cli{std::cin, std::cout};

  CommandInterpreter ci{cli};

  RegisterCoreCommands(cli);

  cli.attach(UserInterface::CommandEntered(),
    make_unique<CommandIssuedObserver>(ci) );

  Stack::Instance().attach(Stack::StackChanged(),
    make_unique<StackUpdatedObserver>(cli) );

  cli.execute();

  return 0;
}
```

Due to the modularity of the design, the entire calculator can be set up, assembled, and executed in just six executable statements! The logic within the main() function is easy to follow. From a maintenance perspective, any new programmer to the project would easily be able to trace the calculator's logic and see that the functionality for each module is clearly divided into distinct abstractions. As will be seen in future chapters, the abstraction is even more powerful as more modules are added.

To get you started quickly, a project is included in the repository source code that builds an executable, pdCalc-simple-cli, using the preceding main() function as the application's driver. The executable is a stand-alone CLI that includes all of the features discussed up to this point in the book.

In the next chapter, we'll consider the design of the graphical user interface for our calculator. As soon as the GUI is complete, many users will quickly dismiss the CLI as simply an exercise or a relic from a previous era. Before doing so, I'd like to encourage the reader not to be so quick to judge the humble CLI. CLIs are very efficient interfaces, and they are typically much easier to script for tasks requiring large deployments or automation. As for pdCalc, personally, I prefer the CLI to the GUI due to its ease of use. Of course, maybe that is just an indication that I, too, am a relic from a previous era.

The Graphical User Interface

In this chapter, we will explore the design of the graphical user interface (GUI) for pdCalc. Anytime one designs a GUI, a widget platform needs to be selected. As previously noted, I chose to use Qt for the creation of the GUI. That said, this is not a how-to chapter on using Qt to design an interface. Rather, I assume that the reader has a working knowledge of Qt, and the chapter itself focuses on design aspects of the GUI. In fact, as much as possible, I will defer the reader to the source code to see detailed aspects of the widget implementations. Any discussion of the Qt implementation is either merely incidental or worthy of particular emphasis. If you have no interest in GUI design, this chapter can be skipped entirely with virtually no loss in continuity.

6.1 Requirements

In Chapter 5, we began our analysis of the command line interface (CLI) by deriving an interface abstraction that would be used by both the CLI and the GUI. Obviously, we will reuse this interface here, and we therefore already know the abstract interface to which our overall user interface must conform. We thus begin this chapter by defining the requirements for the GUI specialization.

As with the CLI, we quickly discover that the requirements from Chapter 1 are woefully inadequate for specifying a graphical user interface. The given requirements are only functional. That is, we know what buttons and operations the calculator should support, but we know nothing about the expected appearance.

© Adam Singer 2022
A. B. Singer, *Practical C++ Design*, https://doi.org/10.1007/978-1-4842-7407-1_6

In a commercial project, one would (hopefully) engage the client, a graphic artist, and a user experience expert to assist in designing the GUI. For our case study, it suffices to fully specify our own requirements:

1. The GUI should have a window that displays both input and output. The output is the top six entries of the current stack.

2. The GUI should have clickable buttons for entering numbers and all supported commands.

3. The GUI should have a status display area for displaying error messages.

The preceding requirements still do not explain what the calculator should actually look like. For that, we need a picture. Figure 6-1 shows the working calculator as it appears on my Windows desktop (Windows 10 using Qt 5.15.2). To show the finished GUI as a prototype for designing the GUI is most certainly "cheating." Hopefully, this shortcut does not detract from the realism of the case study too much. Obviously, one would not have a finished product at this stage in the development. In a production setting, one might have mock-ups drawn either by hand or with a program such as Microsoft PowerPoint, Adobe Illustrator, or Inkscape. Alternatively, maybe the GUI is being modeled from a physical object, and the designer either has photographs or direct access to that object. For example, one might be designing a GUI to replace a physical control system, and the requirements specify that the interface must display identical dials and gauges (to reduce operator retraining costs).

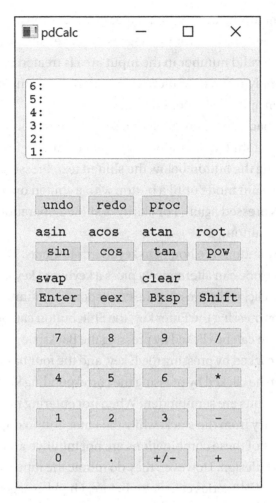

Figure 6-1. *The GUI on Windows with no plugins*

The GUI for pdCalc was inspired by my HP48S calculator. For those familiar with any of the Hewlett-Packard calculators in this series, the interface will feel somewhat familiar. For those not familiar with this series of calculators (likely, the majority of readers), the following description explains the basic behavior of the GUI.

The top third of the GUI is a dedicated input/output (I/O) window. The I/O window displays labels for the top six stack levels on the left, with the top of the stack being at the bottom of the window. Values on the stack appear on the right side of the window on the line corresponding to the number's location on the stack. As the user enters a number, the stack reduces to showing only the top five stack elements, while the number being entered is displayed left justified on the bottom line. A number is terminated and entered onto the stack by pressing the enter button.

Assuming sufficient input, an operation takes place as soon as the button is pressed. If insufficient input is present, an error message is displayed above the I/O window. With respect to commands, a valid number in the input area is treated as the top number on the stack. That is, applying an operation while entering a number is equivalent to pressing enter and then applying the operation.

To economize on space, some buttons have a shifted operation above and to the left of the button itself. These shifted operations can be activated by first pressing the shift button and then pressing the button below the shifted text. Pressing the shift button places the calculator in shift mode until a button with a shifted operation is pressed or until the shift button is pressed again. For clarity, a shifted operation is often the inverse of the operation on the button.

To ease input, many buttons are bound to keyboard shortcuts. That is, in addition to pressing the GUI button, one can alternatively press a keyboard key instead. For example, number buttons can be clicked by pressing the corresponding number key, the Enter button can be clicked by pressing the Enter key, the Shift button can be clicked by pressing the S key, the Bksp button can be clicked by pressing the Backspace key, the exponentiation operation (eex) can be clicked by pressing the E key, and the four basic arithmetic operations (+, -, *, /) can be clicked by pressing the corresponding keyboard keys.

Finally, a few operations are semihidden. When not entering numbers, the backspace button drops the top entry from the stack, while the enter button duplicates the top entry on the stack. Some of these combinations are not intuitive and therefore might not represent very good GUI design. However, they do mimic the input used on the HP48S. If you have never used an HP48 series calculator before, I highly suggest building and familiarizing yourself with the GUI from the GitHub repository before continuing.

If you're wondering what a `proc` key does, it executes stored procedures. It is one of the "new" requirements we'll encounter in Chapter 8.

One's first critique about the GUI might be that it is not very pretty. I would agree. The purpose of the GUI in this chapter is not to demonstrate advanced Qt features. Rather, the purpose is to illustrate how to design a code base to be modular, robust, reliable, and extensible. Adding code to make the GUI more attractive rather than functional would distract from this message. Of course, the design permits a prettier GUI, so feel free to make your own pretty GUI on top of the provided infrastructure.

We now have sufficient detail to design and implement the calculator's GUI. However, before we begin, a short discussion on alternatives for building GUIs is warranted.

6.2 Building GUIs

Essentially, two distinct paths exist for building a GUI: construct the GUI in an Integrated Development Environment (IDE) or construct the GUI in code. Here, I loosely use the term code to indicate building the GUI by text, whether it be by using a traditional programming language like C++ or a declarative markup syntax like XML. Of course, between the two extremes is the hybrid approach, which utilizes elements from both IDEs and code.

6.2.1 Building GUIs in IDEs

If all you need is a simple GUI, then, certainly, designing and building your GUI in an IDE is the easier route. Most IDEs have a graphical interface for laying out visual elements onto a canvas, which, for example, might represent a dialog box or a widget. Once a new canvas is set up, the user visually builds the GUI by dragging and dropping existing widgets onto the canvas. Existing widgets consist of the built-in graphical elements of the GUI toolkit (e.g., a push button) as well as custom widgets that have been enabled for drag-and-drop in the IDE framework. Once the layout is complete, actions can be tied together either graphically or with a little bit of code. Ultimately, the IDE creates code corresponding to the graphically laid out GUI, and this IDE-created code is compiled with the rest of your source code.

Building a GUI using an IDE has both advantages and disadvantages. Some of the advantages are as follows. First, because the process is visual, you can easily see the GUI's appearance as you perform the layout. This is in direct contrast with writing code for the GUI, where you only see the look of the GUI after compiling and executing the code. The difference is very much akin to the difference between using a WYSIWYG text editor like Microsoft Word and a markup language like LaTeX for writing a paper. Second, the IDE works by automatically generating code behind the scenes, so the graphical approach can significantly reduce the amount of coding required to write a GUI. Third, IDEs typically list the properties of a GUI element in a property sheet, making it trivial to stylize a GUI without constantly consulting the API documentation. This is especially useful for rarely used features.

Some of the disadvantages to using an IDE to build a GUI are as follows. First, you are limited to the subset of the API that the IDE chooses to expose. Sometimes, the full API is exposed, and sometimes, it is not. If you need functionality that the IDE's author chose not to grant you, you'll be forced into writing your own code. That is, the IDE may limit fine-tuned control of GUI elements. Second, for repetitive GUI elements, you may have to perform the same operation many times (e.g., clicking to make text red in all push buttons), while in code, it's easy to encapsulate any repeated task in a class or function call. Third, using the IDE to design a GUI limits the GUI to decisions that can be made at compile time. If you need to dynamically change the structure of a GUI, you'll need to write code for that. Fourth, designing a GUI in an IDE ties your code to a specific vendor product. In a corporate environment, this may not be a significant concern because the development environment may be uniform throughout the company. However, for an open source, distributed project, not every developer who might want to contribute to your code base will want to be restricted to the same IDE you chose.

6.2.2 Building GUIs in Code

Building a GUI in code is exactly what the name implies. Rather than graphically placing widgets on a canvas, you instead write code to interact with the GUI toolkit. Several different options exist for how the code can be written, and often, more than one option is available to you for any given GUI toolkit. First, you can almost always write source code in the language of the toolkit. For example, in Qt, you can build your GUI entirely by writing C++ in a very imperative style (i.e., you direct the GUI's behavior explicitly). Second, some GUI toolkits permit a declarative style (i.e., you write markup code describing the style of GUI elements, but the toolkit defines the elements' behaviors). Finally, some toolkits use a script-based interface for constructing a GUI (often JavaScript or a JavaScript derivative syntax) perhaps in conjunction with a declarative markup. In the context of this chapter, building a GUI in code refers exclusively to coding in C++ against Qt's desktop widget set.

As you might expect, building a GUI in code has nearly the opposite trade-offs as building a GUI with an IDE. The advantages are as follows. First, the full API to the widgets is completely exposed. Therefore, the programmer has as much fine-tuned control as desired. If the widget library designer wanted a user to be able to do something, you can do it in code. Second, repetitive GUI elements are easily managed through the use of abstraction. For example, in designing a calculator, instead of having to customize every button manually, we can create a button class and simply instantiate it. Third, adding widgets dynamically at runtime is easy. For pdCalc, this advantage will be important in fulfilling the requirement to support dynamic plugins. Fourth, designing a GUI in code grants complete IDE independence, provided that the build system is independent of the IDE.

While building a GUI in code has many advantages, disadvantages exist as well. First, the layout is not visual. In order to see the GUI take shape, you must compile and execute the code. If it looks wrong, you have to tweak the code, try again, and repeat this process until you get it right. This can be exceedingly tedious and time consuming. Second, you must author all of the code yourself. Whereas an IDE will autogenerate a significant portion of the GUI code, particularly the parts related to the layout, when you are writing code, you must do all the work manually. Finally, when writing a GUI in code, you will not have access to all of a widget's properties succinctly on a property sheet. Typically, you'll need to consult the documentation more frequently. That said, good IDE code completion can help significantly with this task. Someone may cry foul to my last remark claiming, "It's unfair to indicate that using an IDE can mitigate a disadvantage of not using an IDE." Remember, unless you're writing your source code in a pure text editor (unlikely), the code editor is still likely a sophisticated IDE. My comparison is between building a GUI using an IDE's graphical GUI layout tool and writing the code manually using a modern code editor, likely itself an IDE.

6.2.3 Which GUI Building Method Is Better?

The answer to the overly general question in the section header is, of course, neither. Which technique is better for building a GUI is entirely context dependent. When you encounter this question in your own coding pursuits, consult the preceding trade-offs, and make the choice most sensible for your situation. Often, the best solution is a hybrid strategy where some parts of the GUI will be laid out graphically while other parts of the GUI will be built entirely from code.

A more specific question in our context is, "Which GUI building method is better for pdCalc?" For this application, the trade-offs heavily favor a code-based approach. First, the visual layout for the calculator is fairly trivial (a status window, a display widget, and a grid of buttons) and easily accomplished in code. This fact immediately removes the most significant advantage of the IDE approach, handling complex layout visually. Second, the creation and layout of the buttons are repetitive but easily encapsulated, one of the advantages of a code-based approach. Finally, because the calculator must support runtime plugins, the code approach works better for dynamically adding widget elements (runtime discovered buttons).

In the remainder of this chapter, we'll explore the design of pdCalc's GUI in code. In particular, the main emphasis will be on the design of components and their interfaces. Because our focus is not on widget construction, many implementation details will be glossed over. Never fear, however. If you are interested in the details, all of the code is available for your perusal in the GitHub repository.

6.3 Modularization

From the outset of this book, we have discussed decomposition strategies for the calculator. Using the MVC architectural pattern, we split our design into a model, a view, and a controller. In Chapter 4, we saw that one of the main modules, the command dispatcher, was split into subcomponents. Whereas the CLI module was simple enough to be implemented with a single class, the GUI module is sufficiently complex that decomposition is useful. Recall from Chapter 2 that when we refer to the GUI module, we are referring only to a module as a logical construct since Qt, at the time of writing, does not yet support C++20 modules.

In Chapter 5, we determined that any user interface for our system must inherit from the UserInterface abstract class. Essentially, the UserInterface class defines the abstract interface of the view in the MVC pattern. While the GUI module must inherit from UserInterface and hence present the same abstract interface to the controller, we are free to decompose the internals of the GUI however we see fit. We'll again use our guiding principles of loose coupling and strong cohesion to modularize the GUI.

When I decompose a module, I first think in terms of strong cohesion. That is, I attempt to break the module into small components that each do one thing (and do it well). Let's try that with the GUI. First, any Qt GUI must have a main window, defined by inheriting QMainWindow. The main window is also the entry point to the MVC view, so our main window must also inherit from UserInterface. The MainWindow is our first class. Next, visually inspecting Figure 6-1, the calculator is obviously divided into a component used for input (a collection of buttons) and a component used for display. We therefore add two more classes: the InputWidget and the Display. We've already discussed that an advantage of using the code approach to building a GUI is to abstract the repeated creation of buttons, so we'll make a CommandButton class as well. Finally, I added a component responsible for managing the look-and-feel of the calculator (e.g., fonts, margins, spacing, etc.) that I aptly named the LookAndFeel class. A component for stored procedure entry also exists, but we will delay the discussion of that component until Chapter 8. Let's now look at the design of each class, starting with the CommandButton. We'll discuss any necessary refinements to this initial decomposition if and when they arise.

6.3.1 The CommandButton Abstraction

We begin our discussion by describing how buttons are abstracted. This is a sensible place to begin since buttons underlie the input mechanism for both numbers and commands to the calculator.

Qt provides a push button widget class that displays a clickable button that emits a signal when the button is clicked. This QPushButton class provides the basis for the functionality that we require for number and command input. One prospective design we could employ would be to use QPushButtons as is. This design would require explicitly writing code to connect each QPushButton manually to its own customized slot. However, this approach is repetitive, tedious, and highly error prone. Moreover, some buttons need additional functionality not provided by the QPushButton API (e.g., shifted input). Therefore, we instead seek a button abstraction for our program that builds upon the QPushButton, supplements this Qt class with additional functionality, but also simultaneously restricts the QPushButton's interface to meet exactly our requirements. We'll call this class the CommandButton.

In pattern parlance, we are proposing something that acts as both an adapter and a facade. We saw the adapter pattern in Chapter 3. The facade pattern is a close cousin. Whereas the adapter pattern is responsible for converting one interface into another (possibly with some adaptation), the facade pattern is responsible for providing a unified interface to a set of interfaces in a subsystem (often as a simplification). Our CommandButton is tasked with doing both. We are both simplifying the QPushButton interface to a restricted subset that pdCalc needs but simultaneously adapting QPushButton's functionality to match the requirements of our problem. So, is CommandButton a facade or an adapter? The difference is irrelevant; it shares characteristics of each. Remember, it is important to understand the objectives of different patterns and adapt them according to your needs. Try not to get lost in rote implementations from the Gang of Four [11] for the sake of pattern purity.

The CommandButton Design

Introductory remarks aside, we still must determine what exactly our CommandButton needs to do and how it will interact with the rest of the GUI. In many ways, a CommandButton looks and acts similarly to a QPushButton. For example, a CommandButton must present a visual button that can be clicked, and after the button is clicked, it should emit some kind of signal to let other GUI components know a click action has occurred. Unlike a standard QPushButton, however, our CommandButton must support both a standard and shifted state (e.g., a button that supports both sin and arcsin). This support should be both visual (both states should be shown by our CommandButton widget) and functional (click signals must describe both a standard click and a shifted click). We therefore have two design questions to answer. First, how do we design and implement the widget to appear correctly on the screen? Second, how will the calculator, in general, handle shifted operations?

Let's first address the CommandButton appearance problem. Sure, we could implement our button from scratch, paint the screen manually, and use mouse events to trap button clicks, but that's overkill for CommandButton. Instead, we seek a solution that reuses Qt's QPushButton class. We essentially have two options for reuse: inheritance and encapsulation.

First, let's consider reusing the QPushButton class in the CommandButton class's design via inheritance. This approach is reasonable since one could logically adopt the viewpoint that a CommandButton *is-a* QPushButton. This approach, however, suffers from an immediate deficiency. An *is-a* relationship implies public inheritance, which means that the entire public interface of QPushButton would become part of the public interface for CommandButton. However, we already determined that for simplicity within pdCalc, we want CommandButton to have a restricted interface (the facade pattern). OK, let's try private inheritance and modify our viewpoint to an *implements-a* relationship between CommandButton and QPushButton. Now we encounter a second deficiency. Without public inheritance from QPushButton, CommandButton loses its indirect inheritance of the QWidget class, a prerequisite in Qt for a class to be a user interface object. Therefore, any implementation inheriting QPushButton privately would also require public inheritance from QWidget. However, because QPushButton also inherits from QWidget, the multiple inheritance of both of these classes by CommandButton would lead to ambiguities and is thus disallowed. We must seek an alternative design.

Now, consider encapsulating a QPushButton within a CommandButton (i.e., CommandButton *has-a* QPushButton). We probably should have started with this option since general practice indicates we should prefer encapsulation to inheritance whenever possible. However, many developers tend to start with inheritance, and I wanted to discuss the drawbacks of that approach without resorting merely to C++ best practices canon. Aside from breaking the strong inheritance relationship, choosing an encapsulation approach overcomes the two drawbacks of using inheritance previously discussed. First, since the QPushButton will be encapsulated within a CommandButton, we are free to expose only those parts of the QPushButton interface (or none at all) that make sense for our application. Second, by using encapsulation, we'll avoid the multiple inheritance mess of inheriting from both the QWidget and QPushButton classes, simultaneously. Note that I do not object, in principle, to designs that use multiple inheritance. Multiple inheritance is simply ambiguous in this instance.

Encapsulating relationships can either take the form of composition or aggregation. Which is right for the CommandButton class? Consider two classes, A and B, where A is encapsulating B. In a composite relationship, B is an integral part of A. In code, the relationship is expressed as follows:

```
class A
{
  // ...
private:
  B b_;
};
```

In contrast, aggregation implies that A is merely using a B object internally. In code, aggregation is expressed as follows:

```
class A
{
  // ...
private:
  B* b_; // or some suitable smart pointer or reference
};
```

For our application, I think aggregation makes more sense. That is, our CommandButton uses a QPushButton rather than is composed from a QPushButton. The difference is subtle, and an equally logical argument could be made for declaring the relationship to be composition. That said, both designs work mechanically within Qt, so your compiler really won't care how you choose to express the relationship.

Now that we have decided to aggregate the QPushButton within the CommandButton, we can proceed with the overall design of the CommandButton class. Our CommandButton must support both a primary and a secondary command. Visually, I chose to display the primary command on the button and the secondary command in blue above and to the left of the button (we'll discuss how the shifted state operates momentarily). Therefore, the CommandButton merely instantiates a QPushButton and a QLabel and places them both in a QVBoxLayout. The QPushButton displays the text for the primary command, and the QLabel displays the text for the shifted command. The layout is depicted in Figure 6-2. To complete the design, as previously stated, in order to interact graphically with the rest of the GUI, the CommandButton must publicly inherit from the QWidget class. The design results in a reusable CommandButton widget class for a generic push button declaring both a primary and secondary command. Because the push button action is achieved by using a QPushButton, the overall implementation of the CommandButton class is remarkably simple.

One final small detail for reusing the QPushButton remains. Obviously, because the QPushButton is encapsulated privately in the CommandButton, clients cannot externally connect to the QPushButton's clicked() signal, rendering it impossible for client code to know when a CommandButton is clicked. This design is actually intentional. The CommandButton will internally trap the QPushButton's clicked() signal and subsequently reemit its own signal. The design of this public CommandButton signal is intricately linked to the handling of the shifted state.

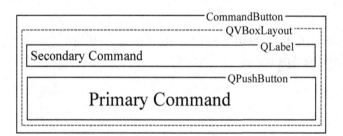

Figure 6-2. *The layout of the* CommandButton

We now return to modeling the shifted state within the calculator. We have two practical options. The first option is to have CommandButtons understand when the calculator is in the shifted state and only signal the correct shifted or unshifted command. Alternatively, the second option is to have CommandButtons signal with both the shifted and unshifted commands and let the receiver of the signal sort out the calculator's current state. Let's examine both options.

The first option, having CommandButtons know if the calculator is in a shifted or unshifted state, is fairly easy to implement. In one implementation, the shift button notifies every button (via Qt signals and slots) when it is pressed, and the buttons toggle between the shifted and unshifted state. If desired, one could even swap the text in the shift position with the text on the button every time the shifted state is toggled. Alternatively, the shift button can be connected to one slot that sets a global shift state flag that buttons can query when they signal that a click has occurred. In either implementation scenario, when the button is clicked, only the command for the current state is signaled, and the receiver of this command eventually forwards the single command out of the GUI via a commandEntered() event.

In the second option, the CommandButtons are not required to know anything about the calculator's state. Instead, when a button is clicked, it signals the click with both the shifted and unshifted states. Essentially, a button just informs its listeners when it is clicked and provides both possible commands. The receiver is then responsible for determining which of the possible commands to raise in the commandEntered() event. The receiver presumably must be responsible for tracking the shifted state (or be able to poll another class or variable holding that state).

For the CommandButton, both designs for handling the calculator's state work fairly well. However, personally, I prefer the design that does not require CommandButtons to know anything about the shifted state. In my opinion, this design promotes better cohesion and looser coupling. The design is more cohesive because a CommandButton should be responsible for displaying a clickable widget and notifying the system when the button is clicked. Requiring CommandButtons to understand calculator states encroaches on the independence of their abstraction. Instead of just being generic clickable buttons with two commands, the buttons become integrally tied to the concept of the calculator's global state. Additionally, by forcing CommandButtons to understand the calculator's state, the coupling in the system is increased by forcing CommandButtons to be unnecessarily interconnected to either the shift button or to the class they must poll. The only advantage gained by notifying every CommandButton when the shift button is pressed is the ability to swap the labels for the primary and secondary commands. Of course, label swapping could be implemented independently of the CommandButton's signal arguments.

The CommandButton Interface

Getting the design right is the hard part. With the design in hand, the interface practically writes itself. Let's examine a simplified version of the CommandButton class's definition:

```
class CommandButton : public QWidget
{
  Q_OBJECT // needed by all Qt objects with signals and slots
public:
  CommandButton(const string& dispPrimaryCmd, const string& primaryCmd,
    const string& dispShftCmd, const string& shftCmd,
    QWidget* parent = nullptr);

  CommandButton(const string& dispPrimaryCmd, const string& primaryCmd,
    QWidget* parent = nullptr);

private slots:
  void onClicked();

signals:
  void clicked(string primCmd, string shftCmd);
};
```

The CommandButton class has two constructors: the four-argument overload and the two-argument overload. The four-argument overload permits specification of both a primary command and a secondary command, while the two-argument overload permits the specification of only a primary command. Each command requires two strings for full specification. The first string equates to the text the label will present in the GUI, either on the button or in the shifted command location. The second string equates to the text command to be raised by the commandEntered() event. One could simplify the interface by requiring these two strings to be identical. However, I chose to add the flexibility of displaying a different text than that required by the command dispatcher. Note that we require overloads instead of default arguments due to the trailing parent pointer.

The only other public part of the interface is the clicked() signal that is emitted with both the primary and shifted commands for the button. The rationale behind a two argument vs. one argument signal was previously discussed. Despite being private, I also listed the onClicked() slot in CommandButton's interface to highlight the private slot that must be created to catch the internal QPushButton's clicked() signal. The onClicked() function's sole purpose is to trap the QPushButton's clicked() signal and instead emit the CommandButton's clicked() signal with the two function arguments.

If you look at the actual declaration of the CommandButton class in CommandButton.h, you will see a few additional functions as part of CommandButton's public interface. These are simply forwarding functions that either change the appearance (e.g., text color) or add visual elements (e.g., a tool tip) to the underlying QPushButton. While these functions are part of CommandButton's interface, they are functionally optional and are independent of CommandButton's underlying design.

6.3.2 Getting Input

The GUI is required to take two distinct types of inputs from the user: numbers and commands. Both input types are entered by the user via CommandButtons (or keyboard shortcuts mapped to these buttons) arranged in a grid. This collection of CommandButtons, their layout, and their associated signals to the rest of the GUI compose the InputWidget class.

Command entry is conceptually straightforward. A CommandButton is clicked, and a signal is emitted reflecting the command for that particular button. Ultimately, another part of the GUI will receive this signal and raise a commandEntered() event to be handled by the command dispatcher.

Entering numbers is a bit more complicated than entering commands. In the CLI, we had the luxury of simply allowing the user to type numbers and press enter when the input was complete. In the GUI, however, we have no such built-in mechanism (assuming we want a GUI more sophisticated than a CLI in a Qt window). While the calculator does have a Command for entering numbers, remember that it assumes complete numbers, not individual digits. Therefore, the GUI must have a mechanism for constructing numbers.

Building a number consists of entering digits as well as special symbols such as the decimal point, the plus/minus operator, or the exponentiation operator. Additionally, as the user types, they might make errors, so we'll want to enable basic editing (e.g., backspace) as well. The assembly of numbers is a two-step process. The InputWidget is only responsible for emitting the button clicks required for composing and editing numbers. Another part of the GUI will receive these signals and assemble complete number input.

The Design of the InputWidget

Conceptually, the design of the InputWidget class is straightforward. The widget must display the buttons needed for generating and editing input, bind these buttons to keys (if desired), and signal when these buttons are clicked. As previously mentioned, the InputWidget contains buttons for both digit entry and command entry. Therefore, it is responsible for the digits 0–9, the plus/minus button, the decimal button, the exponentiation button, the enter button, the backspace button, the shift button, and a button for each command. Recall that as an economization, the CommandButton class permits two distinct commands per visual button.

For consistency throughout the GUI, we'll use the CommandButton exclusively as the representation for all of the input buttons, even for buttons that neither issue commands nor have secondary operations (e.g., the 0 button). How convenient that our design for the CommandButton is so flexible! However, that decision still leaves us with two outstanding design issues, which are how do we lay out the buttons visually and what do we do when a button is clicked.

Two options exist for placing buttons in the InputWidget. First, the InputWidget itself owns a layout, it places all the buttons in this internal layout, and then the InputWidget itself can be placed somewhere on the main window. The alternative is for the InputWidget to accept an externally owned layout during construction and place its CommandButtons on that layout. In general, having the InputWidget own its own layout is the superior design. It has improved cohesion and decreased coupling over the alternative approach. The only exception where having the InputWidget accept an external layout would be preferred would be if the design called for other classes to share the same layout for the placement of additional widgets. In that special case, using a shared layout owned externally to both classes would be cleaner.

Let's now turn our attention to what happens when a button is clicked within the InputWidget. Because the InputWidget encapsulates the CommandButtons, the clicked() signal for each CommandButton is not directly accessible to consumers of the InputWidget class. Therefore, the InputWidget must catch all of its CommandButtons' clicks and reemit them. For calculator commands like sine or tangent, reemitting the click is a trivial forwarding command. In fact, Qt enables a shorthand notation for connecting a CommandButton's clicked() signal directly to an InputWidget commandEntered() signal, forgoing the need to pass through a private slot in the InputWidget. Digits, number editing buttons (e.g., plus/minus, backspace), and calculator state buttons (e.g., shift) are better handled by catching the particular `clicked()` signal from the `CommandButton` in a private slot in the `InputWidget` and subsequently emitting an `InputWidget` signal for each of these actions.

As just described, as each input button is pressed, the `InputWidget` must emit its own signal. At one extreme, the `InputWidget` could have individual signals for each internal `CommandButton`. At the other extreme, the `InputWidget` could emit only one signal regardless of the button pressed and differentiate the action via an argument. As expected, for our design, we'll seek some middle ground that shares elements from each extreme.

Essentially, the `InputWidget` accepts three distinct types of input: a modifier (e.g., enter, backspace, plus/minus, shift), a scientific notation character (e.g., 0–9, decimal, exponentiation), or a command (e.g., sine, cosine, etc.). Each modifier requires a unique response; therefore, each modifier binds to its own separate signal. Scientific notation characters, on the other hand, can be handled uniformly simply by displaying the input character on the screen (the role of the `Display` class). Thus, scientific notation characters are all handled by emitting a single signal that encodes the specific character as an argument. Finally, commands are handled by emitting a single signal that simply forwards the primary and secondary commands, verbatim, as function arguments to the signal.

In constructing the signal handling, it is import to maintain the `InputWidget` as a class for signaling raw user input to the rest of the GUI. Having the `InputWidget` interpret button presses leads to problems. For example, suppose we designed the `InputWidget` to aggregate characters and only emit complete, valid numbers. Since this strategy implies that no signal would be emitted per character entry, characters could neither be displayed nor edited until the number was completed. This situation is obviously unacceptable, as a user would definitely expect to see each character on the screen as they entered it.

Let's now turn our attention to translating our design into a minimal interface for the `InputWidget`.

The Interface of the InputWidget

We begin the discussion of the `InputWidget`'s interface by presenting the class declaration. As expected, our clear design leads to a straightforward interface.

```cpp
class InputWidget : public QWidget
{
  Q_OBJECT
public:
  explicit InputWidget(QWidget* parent = nullptr);

signals:
  void characterEntered(char c);

  void enterPressed();
  void backspacePressed();
  void plusMinusPressed();
  void shiftPressed();

  void commandEntered(string, string);
};
```

Essentially, the entire class interface is defined by the signals corresponding to user input events. Specifically, we have one signal indicating entry of any scientific notation character, one signal to forward command button clicks, and individual signals indicating clicking of the backspace, enter, plus/minus, or shift buttons, respectively.

If you look in the GitHub repository source code in the InputWidget.cpp file, you will find a few additional public functions and signals. These extra functions are necessary to implement two features introduced in subsequent chapters. First, an addCommandButton() function and a setupFinalButtons() function are needed to accommodate the dynamic addition of plugin buttons, a feature introduced in Chapter 7. Second, a procedurePressed() signal is needed to indicate a user request to use a stored procedure. Stored procedures are introduced in Chapter 8.

6.3.3 The Display

Conceptually, the calculator has two displays: one for input and one for output. This abstraction can be implemented visually either as two separate displays or as one merged input/output display. Both designs are perfectly valid; each is illustrated in Figure 6-3.

Figure 6-3. *Input and output display options*

Choosing one style of I/O vs. the other ultimately reduces to the customer's preference. Having no particular affinity for either style, I chose a merged display because it looks more like the display of my HP48S calculator. With a display style chosen, let's now focus on the design implications this choice implies.

With a separate on-screen widget for input and output, as seen in Figure 6-3a, the choice to have separate input and output display classes would be obvious. The input display would have slots to receive the InputWidget's signals, and the output display would have slots to receive completed numbers (from the input display) and stack updates. The cohesion would be strong, and the separation of components would be appropriate.

Our design, however, calls for a commingled input/output display, as seen in Figure 6-3b. The commingled design significantly alters the sensibility of using independent input and output display classes. While lumping input and output display concerns into one class does decrease the cohesion of the display, trying to maintain two independent classes both pointing to the same on-screen widget would lead to an awkward implementation. For example, choosing which class should own the underlying Qt widget is arbitrary likely resulting in a shared widget design (using a shared_ptr, perhaps?). However, in this scenario, should the input or the output display class initialize the on-screen widget? Would it make sense for the input display to signal the output display if the input display shared a pointer to the single display widget? The answer is simply that a two class design is not tenable for a merged I/O display widget even though we might prefer to separate input and output display concerns.

The aforementioned discussion identifies a few interesting points. First, the visual presentation of the design on screen can legitimately alter the design and implementation of the underlying components. While this may seem obvious once presented with a concrete GUI example, the indirect implication is that GUI class design may need to change significantly if the on-screen widgets are changed only slightly. Second, situations exist where the result is cleaner when the design directly contradicts the elements of good design postulated in Chapter 2. Obviously, the guidelines in Chapter 2 are meant to aid the design process, not to serve as inviolable rules. That said, my general advice is to aim to preserve clarity over adherence to guidelines but only violate best practices judiciously.

Now that we've decided to pursue a single I/O display with a single underlying `Display` class, let's look at its design.

The Design of the Display Class

I confess. My original design and implementation for the `Display` class was inept. Instead of using proper analysis techniques and upfront design, I grew the design organically (i.e., alongside the implementation). However, as soon as my design forced the `Display` class to emit `commandEntered()` signals for the GUI to function properly, I knew the design had a "bad smell" to it. The class responsible for painting numbers on the screen should probably not be interpreting commands. That said, the implementation worked properly, so I left the code as it was and completed the calculator. However, when I finally started writing about the design, I had so much difficulty trying to formulate a rationale for my design that I finally had to admit to myself that the design was fatally flawed and desperately needed a rewrite.

Obviously, after redesigning the display, I could have simply chosen to describe only the improved product. However, I think it is instructive to study my first misguided attempt, to discuss the telltale signs that the design had some serious problems, and finally to see the design that eventually emerged after a night of refactoring. Possibly, the most interesting lesson here is that bad designs can certainly lead to working code, so never assume that working code is an indicator of a good design. Additionally, bad designs, if localized, can be refactored, and sometimes, refactoring should be undertaken solely to increase clarity. Refactoring, of course, assumes your project schedule contains enough contingency time to pause periodically just to pay down technical debt. We now begin by briefly studying my mistake before returning to a better design.

A Poor Design

From the preceding analysis, we determined that the calculator should have one unified `Display` class handling both input and output. The fundamental mistake in my design for the display derived from incorrectly interpreting that one `Display` class implied no additional classes for orthogonal concerns. Hence, I proceeded to lump all functionality not handled by the InputWidget class into a single Display class. Let's start along that path. However, rather than completing the design and implementation as I had previously done, we'll stop and redesign the class as soon as we see the first fatal flaw emerges (which is what I should have done originally).

With a single Display class design, the Display is responsible for showing input from the user and output from the calculation engine. Showing the output is trivial. The Display class observes the stackChanged() event (indirectly, since it is not part of the GUI's external interface) and updates the screen display widget (a QLabel, in this case) with the new stack values. Conceptually, showing the input is trivial as well. The Display directly receives the signals emitted by the InputWidget class (e.g., characterEntered()) and updates the screen display widget with the current input. The simplicity of this interaction belies the fundamental problem with this design, which is that the input is not entered atomically for display. Instead, it is assembled over multiple signals by entering several characters independently and finalizing the input by pressing the enter button. This sequential construction of the input implies that the calculator must maintain an active input state, and input state has no business existing in a display widget.

At this point, you may inquire what, aside from ideological aversion, is wrong with the Display class maintaining an input state. Can't we just view the state as simply a display input buffer? Let's follow through with this design to see why it is flawed. Consider, for example, the backspace button, whose operation is overloaded based on the input state. If the current input buffer is nonempty, the backspace button erases one character from this buffer. However, if the current input buffer is empty, pressing the backspace button causes the issuance of the command to drop the top number from the stack. Since, under this design, the Display owns the input state and is the sink for the backspacePressed() signal, the Display must be the source of the drop number from stack command. Once the Display starts issuing commands, we've completely given up on cohesion, and it's time to find the pasta sauce because spaghetti code ensues. From here, instead of just abandoning the design, I doubled down, and my original design actually got worse. However, instead of proceeding further along this misguided path, let's simply move on to examining a better approach.

An Improved Display Design

Early in the discussion of the poor display design, I pointed out that the fatal mistake
came from assuming that a unified display necessitated a single class design. However,
as we've seen, this assumption was invalid. The emergence of state in the calculator
implies the need for at least two classes: one for the visual display and one for the state.

Does this remind you of a pattern we've already seen? The GUI needs to maintain
an internal state (a model). We're currently in the midst of designing a display (a view).
We have already designed a class, the InputWidget, for accepting input and issuing
commands (a controller). Obviously, the GUI itself is nothing more than an embodiment
of a familiar pattern, the model-view-controller (MVC). Note that relative to the MVC
archetype seen in Figure 2-2, the GUI can replace direct communication between the
controller and the model with indirect communication. This minor change, which
promotes decreased coupling, is facilitated by Qt's signals and slots mechanism.

We now focus our attention on the design of the newly introduced model class.
Upon completion of the model, we'll return to the Display class to finish its now simpler
design and interface.

6.3.4 The Model

The model class, which I aptly called the GuiModel, is responsible for the state of the
GUI. In order to achieve this goal properly, the model must be the sink for all signals that
cause the state of the system to change, and it must be the source of all signals indicating
that the state of the system has changed. Naturally, the model is also the repository for
the state of the system, and it should provide facilities for other components of the GUI
to query the model's state. Let's look at GuiModel's interface:

```
class GuiModel : public QObject
{
  Q_OBJECT
public:
  enum class ShiftState { Unshifted, Shifted };
  struct State { /* discussed below */ };

  GuiModel(QObject* parent = nullptr);
  ~GuiModel();
```

```
    void stackChanged(const vector<double>& v);

    const State& getState() const;
public slots:
    // called to toggle the calculator's shift state
    void onShift();

    // paired to InputWidget's signals
    void onCharacterEntered(char c);
    void onEnter();
    void onBackspace();
    void onPlusMinus();
    void onCommandEntered(string primaryCmd, string secondaryCmd);

signals:
    void modelChanged();
    void commandEntered(string s);
    void errorDetected(string s);
};
```

The six slots in the GuiModel class all correspond to signals emitted by the InputWidget class. The GuiModel interprets these requests, changes the internal state as appropriate, and emits one or more of its own signals. Of particular note is the commandEntered() signal. Whereas the GuiModel's onCommandEntered() slot accepts two arguments, the raw primary and secondary commands corresponding to the CommandButton that was pressed, the GuiModel is responsible for interpreting the shifted state of the GUI and only reemitting a commandEntered() signal with the active command.

The remainder of the GuiModel interface involves the GUI's state. We begin by discussing the rationale behind the nested State struct. Rather than declaring each piece of the model's state as a separate member within GuiModel, I find it much cleaner to lump all of the state parameters into one struct. This design facilitates the querying of the model's state by permitting the entire system state to be returned by const reference with one function call as opposed to requiring piecemeal access to individual state members. I chose to nest the State struct because it is an intrinsic part of GuiModel that serves no stand-alone purpose. Therefore, the State struct naturally belongs in GuiModel's scope, but its declaration must be publicly declared in order for other components of the GUI to be able to query the state.

The constituents of the State struct define the entire state of the GUI. In particular, this State struct comprises a data structure holding a copy of the maximum number of visible numbers on the stack, the current input buffer, an enumeration defining the shift state of the system, and a Qt enumeration defining the validity of the input buffer. The declaration is given as follows:

```
struct State
{
  vector<double> curStack;
  string curInput;
  ShiftState shiftState;
  QValidator::State curInputValidity;
};
```

An interesting question to ask is, why does the GuiModel's State buffer the visible numbers from the top of the stack? Given that the Stack class is a singleton, the Display could access the Stack directly. However, the Display only observes changes in the GuiModel (via the modelChanged() slot). Because state changes unrelated to stack changes occur frequently in the GUI (e.g., character entry), the Display would be forced to wastefully query the Stack on every modelChanged() event since the Display is not a direct observer of the stackChanged() event. On the other hand, the GuiModel is an observer of the stackChanged() event (indirectly via function call from the MainWindow). Therefore, the efficient solution is to have the GuiModel update a stack buffer only when the calculator's stack actually changes and give the Display class access to this buffer, which is guaranteed by construction to be current, for updating the screen.

6.3.5 The Display Redux

We are now ready to return our attention to the Display class. Having placed all of the state and state interactions in the GuiModel class, the Display class can be reduced simply to an object that watches for model changes and displays the current state of the calculator on the screen. Other than the constructor, the interface for the Display class consists of only two functions: the slot to be called when the model changes and a member function to be called to show messages in the status area. The latter function call is used to display errors detected within the GUI (e.g., invalid input) as well as errors detected in the command dispatcher (as transmitted via UserInterface's postMessage()). The entire interface for the Display class is given by the following:

```
class Display : public QWidget
{
    Q_OBJECT
public:
  explicit Display(const GuiModel& g, QWidget* parent = nullptr,
    int nLinesStack = 6, int minCharWide = 25);

  void showMessage(const string& m);

public slots:
  void onModelChanged();
};
```

The optional arguments to the Display class's constructor simply dictate visual appearance of the stack on the screen. Specifically, a client of the Display class has flexibility over the number of stack lines to display and the minimum width (in units of fixed width font characters) of the on-screen display.

6.3.6 Tying It Together: The Main Window

The main window is a fairly small class that serves a big purpose. To be precise, it serves three purposes in our application. First, as in most Qt-based GUIs, we need to provide a class that publicly inherits from QMainWindow that acts, naturally, as the main GUI window for the application. In particular, this is the class that is instantiated and shown in the function that launches the GUI. Following my typical creative naming style, I called this class the MainWindow. Second, the MainWindow serves as the interface class for the view module of the calculator. That is, the MainWindow also must publicly inherit from our abstract UserInterface class. Finally, the MainWindow class owns all of the previously discussed GUI components and glues these components together as necessary. For all practical purposes, gluing components together simply entails connecting signals to their corresponding slots. These straightforward implementation details can be found in the MainWindow.cpp source code file. We'll spend the remainder of this section discussing the MainWindow's design and interface.

We've written a Qt application; it's obvious that we'll have a descendant of QMainWindow somewhere. That, in and of itself, is not terribly interesting. What is interesting, however, is the decision to use multiple inheritance to make the same class also serve as the UserInterface to the rest of pdCalc. That said, is that truly an interesting decision, or does it just seem provocative because some developers have a strong aversion to multiple inheritance?

Indeed, I could have separated the QMainWindow and the UserInterface into two separate classes. In a GUI where the main window were decorated with menus, toolbars, and multiple underlying widgets, I, perhaps, would have separated the two. However, in our GUI, the QMainWindow base serves no purpose other than to provide an entry point for our Qt application. The MainWindow literally does nothing else in its QMainWindow role. To therefore create a separate MainWindow class with the sole purpose of containing a concrete specialization of a UserInterface class serves no purpose other than to avoid multiple inheritance. While some may disagree, I think a lack of multiple inheritance, in this instance, would actually complicate the design.

The situation described previously is actually an archetypal example of where multiple inheritance is an excellent choice. In particular, multiple inheritance excels in derived classes whose multiple base classes exhibit orthogonal functionality. In our case, one base class serves as the GUI entry point to Qt, while the other base class serves as the UserInterface specialization for pdCalc's GUI view. Notice that neither base class shares functionality, state, methods, or ancestors. Multiple inheritance is especially sensible in situations where at least one of the base classes is purely abstract (a class with no state and only pure virtual functions). The scenario of using multiple inheritance of purely abstract bases is so useful that it is permitted in programming languages that do not otherwise allow multiple inheritance (e.g., interfaces in both C# and Java).

The interface for the MainWindow consists simply of a constructor, the overrides for the two pure virtual functions in the UserInterface class, and a few functions for dynamically adding commands (we'll encounter these functions in Chapter 7 when we design plugins). For completeness, the interface for MainWindow is listed as follows:

```
class MainWindow : public QMainWindow, public UserInterface
{
  class MainWindowImpl;
public:
  MainWindow(int argc, char* argv[], QWidget* parent = nullptr);
```

```
void postMessage(string_view m) override;
void stackChanged() override;

// plugin functions...
};
```

6.3.7 Look-and-Feel

Before we conclude this chapter with some sample code to execute the GUI, we must return briefly to the final component of the GUI, the LookAndFeel class. The LookAndFeel class simply manages the dynamically customizable appearance of the GUI, such as font sizes and text colors. The interface is simple. For each point of customization, a function exists to return the requested setting. For example, to get the font for the display, we provide a function:

```
class LookAndFeel
{
public:
  // one function per customizable setting, e.g.,
  const QFont& getDisplayFont() const;
  // ...
}
```

Because we only need one LookAndFeel object in the calculator, the class is implemented as a singleton.

A great question to ask is, "Why do we need this class at all?" The answer is that it gives us the opportunity to dynamically modify the appearance of the calculator based on the current environment, and it centralizes in memory access to the look-and-feel of pdCalc. For example, suppose we had wanted to make our GUI DPI aware and choose font sizes accordingly (I didn't in the source code, but you might want to). With a static configuration file (or the conceptual equivalent, registry settings), we would have to customize the settings for each platform during the installation process. Either we would have to build customization within the installer for each platform, or we would have to write code to execute during the installation to create the appropriate static configuration file dynamically. If we have to write code, why not just put it in the source where it belongs? As an implementation decision, the LookAndFeel class could be designed simply to read a configuration file and buffer the appearance attributes in memory (a look-and-feel proxy object). That's the real power of the LookAndFeel class. It centralizes the location of appearance attributes so that only one class needs to be changed to effect global appearance changes. Maybe even more importantly, a LookAndFeel class insulates individual GUI components from the implementation details defining how the GUI discovers (and possibly adapts to) the settings on a particular platform.

The full implementation for the LookAndFeel class can be found in the LookAndFeel.cpp file. The current implementation is very simple. The LookAndFeel class provides a mechanism for standardizing the GUI's look-and-feel, but no implementation exists to allow user customization of the application. Chapter 8 briefly suggests some possible extensions one could make to the LookAndFeel class to make pdCalc user customizable.

6.4 A Working Program

We conclude this chapter with a working main() function for launching the GUI. Due to additional requirements we'll encounter in Chapter 7, the actual main() function for pdCalc is more complicated than the one listed below. However, the simplified version is worth listing to illustrate how to tie pdCalc's components together with the GUI to create a functioning, stand-alone executable.

```
int main(int argc, char* argv[])
{
  QApplication app{argc, argv};
  MainWindow gui{argc, argv};

  CommandInterpreter ci{gui};

  RegisterCoreCommands(gui);

  gui.attach(UserInterface::CommandEntered(),
    make_unique<CommandIssuedObserver>(ci) );

  Stack::Instance().attach(Stack::StackChanged(),
    make_unique<StackUpdatedObserver>( gui ) );

  gui.execute();

  return app.exec();
}
```

Note the similarities between the main() function for executing the GUI mentioned previously and the main() function for executing the CLI listed at the conclusion of Chapter 5. The likenesses are not accidental and are the result of pdCalc's modular design.

As with the CLI, to get you started quickly, a project is included in the repository source code that builds an executable, pdCalc-simple-gui, using the preceding main() function as the application's driver. The executable is a stand-alone GUI that includes all of the features discussed up to this point in the book.

6.5 A Microsoft Windows Build Note

pdCalc is designed to be both a GUI and a CLI. In Linux, no compile time distinction exists between a console application (CLI) and a windowed application (GUI). A unified application can be compiled with the same build flags for both styles. In Microsoft Windows, however, creating an application that behaves as both a CLI and a GUI is not quite as trivial because the operating system requires an application to declare during compilation the usage of either the console or the windows subsystem.

Why does the declaration of the subsystem matter on Windows? If an application is declared to be a windowed application, if it is launched from a command prompt, the application will simply return with no output (i.e., the application will appear as if it never executed). However, when the application's icon is double-clicked, the application launches without a background console. On the other hand, if an application is declared to be a console application, the GUI will appear when launched from a command prompt, but the GUI will launch with a background console if opened by double-clicking the application's icon.

Conventionally, Microsoft Windows applications are designed for one subsystem or the other. In the few instances where applications are developed with both a GUI and a CLI, developers have created techniques to avoid the preceding problem. One such technique creates two applications: a .com and a .exe that the operating system can appropriately call depending on the option selected via command line arguments.

In order to keep pdCalc's code simple and cross platform, I ignored this problem and simply built the GUI using the console subsystem (pdCalc-simple-gui, however, having no CLI, is built in windowed mode). Indeed, this means that if the application is launched by double-clicking pdCalc's icon, an extra console window will appear in the background. If you intend to use the application exclusively as a GUI, the problem can be remedied by building the program using the windows subsystem. If you make this change, remember that pdCalc's CLI will essentially be disabled. Building a windowed application can be accomplished by adding the WIN32 option to the add_executable() command of the CMakeLists.txt file responsible for building pdCalc's executable file (see the CMakeLists.txt file for pdCalc-simple-gui). If you need access to both the CLI and the GUI and the extraneous console drives you crazy, you have two realistic options. First, search the Internet for one of the techniques discussed previously and give it a try. Personally, I've never gone that route. Second, build two separate executables (maybe called pdCalc and pdCalc-cli) instead of one executable capable of switching modes based on command line arguments. The application's flexible architecture trivially supports either decision.

Plugins

You've probably read the chapter title, so you already know that this chapter is about plugins, specifically their design and implementation. Additionally, plugins will afford us the opportunity to explore design techniques to isolate platform specific features. Before we dive into the details, however, let's begin by defining what a plugin is.

7.1 What Is a Plugin?

A plugin is a software component that enables new functionality to be added to a program after the program's initial compile. In this chapter, we'll concentrate exclusively on runtime plugins, that is, plugins built as shared libraries (e.g., a POSIX .so or Windows .dll file) that are discoverable and loadable at runtime.

Plugins are useful in applications for a myriad of different reasons. Here are just a few examples. First, plugins are useful for allowing end users to add features to an existing program without the need to recompile. Often, these are new features that were completely unanticipated by the original application developers. Second, architecturally, plugins enable separation of a program into multiple optional pieces that can be individually shipped with a program. For example, consider a program (e.g., a web browser) that ships with some base functionality but allows users to add specialty features (e.g., an ad blocker). Third, plugins can be used for designing an application that can be customized to a specific client. For example, consider an electronic health record system that needs different functionality depending on whether the software is deployed at a hospital or a physician's individual practice. The necessary customizations could be captured by different modules that plug into a core system. Certainly, one can think of many additional applications for plugins.

In the context of pdCalc, plugins are shared libraries that provide new calculator commands and, optionally, new GUI buttons. How difficult could that task be? In Chapter 4, we created numerous commands and saw that adding new ones was fairly trivial. We simply inherited from the Command class (or one of its derived classes, such

© Adam Singer 2022
A. B. Singer, *Practical C++ Design*, https://doi.org/10.1007/978-1-4842-7407-1_7

as `UnaryCommand` or `BinaryCommand`), instantiated the command, and registered it with the `CommandFactory`. For example, take the sine command, which is declared in `CoreCommands.m.cpp` as follows:

```
class Sine : public UnaryCommand
{
  // implement Command virtual members
};
```

and registered in `CommandFactory.m.cpp` by the line

```
cf.registerCommand( "sin", MakeCommandPtr<Sine>() );
```

where `cf` is a `CommandFactory` reference. It turns out that this recipe can be followed almost exactly by a plugin command except for one crucial step. Since the plugin command's class name is unknown to pdCalc at compile time, we cannot use the plugin class's name for allocation.

This seemingly simple dilemma of not knowing the class names of plugin commands leads to the first problem we need to solve for plugins. Specifically, we'll need to establish an abstract interface by which plugin commands become discoverable to and registered within pdCalc. Once we've agreed upon a plugin interface, we'll quickly encounter the second fundamental plugin problem, which is how do you dynamically load a plugin to even make the names in the shared library available to pdCalc. To make our lives more complicated, the solution to this second problem is platform dependent, so we'll seek a design strategy that minimizes the platform dependency pain. The final problem we'll encounter is updating our existing code to add new commands and buttons dynamically. Maybe surprisingly, this last problem is the easiest to solve. Before we get started tackling our three problems, however, we need to consider a few rules for C++ plugins.

7.1.1 Rules For C++ Plugins

Plugins are not conceptually part of the C++ language. Rather, plugins are a manifestation of how the operating system dynamically loads and links shared libraries (hence the platform-specific nature of plugins). For any nontrivially sized project, the application is typically divided into an executable and several shared libraries (traditionally, .so files in Unix, .dylib files in Mac OS X, and .dll files in MS Windows).

Ordinarily, as C++ programmers, we remain blissfully unaware of the subtleties this structure entails because the executable and libraries are built in a homogeneous build environment (i.e., same compiler and standard libraries). For a practical plugin interface, however, we have no such guarantee. Instead, we must program defensively and assume the worst-case scenario, which is that plugins are built in a different but compatible environment to the main application. Here, we'll make the relatively weak assumption that the two environments, at minimum, share the same object model. Specifically, we require that the two environments use the same layout for handling the virtual function pointer (vptr). If you are unfamiliar with the concept of a virtual function pointer, all the gory details can be found in [18]. While in principle, C++ compiler writers may choose different vptr layouts, in practice, compilers typically use compatible layouts, especially different versions of the same compiler. Without this shared object model assumption, we would be forced to develop a C language–only plugin structure. Note that we must also assume that sizeof(T) is the same size for all types T in the main application and plugins. This eliminates, for example, having a 32-bit application and a 64-bit plugin because these two platforms have different pointer sizes.

How does programming in a heterogeneous environment affect the available programming techniques we can use? In the worst-case scenario, the main application might be built with both a different compiler and a different standard library. This fact has several serious implications. First, we cannot assume that allocation and deallocation of memory between plugins and the application are compatible. This means any memory new-ed in a plugin must be delete-ed in the same plugin. Second, we cannot assume that code from the standard library is compatible between any plugin and the main application. Therefore, our plugin interface cannot contain any standard containers. While standard library incompatibility might seem odd (it's the *standard* library, right?), remember that the standard specifies the interface, not the implementation (subject to some restrictions, such as vectors occupying contiguous memory). For example, different standard library implementations frequently have different string implementations. Some prefer the small string optimization, while others prefer using copy-on-write. Third, while we have assumed a compatible layout for the vptr in our objects, we cannot assume identical alignment. Therefore, plugin classes should not inherit from main application classes that have member variables defined in the base classes if these member variables are used in the main application. This follows since the main application's compiler may use a different memory offset to a member variable than what was defined by the plugin's compiler if each compiler uses different alignment. Fourth, due to name mangling variances across different compilers, exported interfaces must specify extern "C" linkage. The linkage requirement is bidirectional. Plugins should not call application functions without extern "C" linkage nor should the application call plugin functions without extern "C" linkage. Note that because noninline, nonvirtual member functions require linkage across compilation units (as opposed to virtual functions, which are called via the vptr through an offset in the virtual function table), the application should only call into plugin code through virtual functions, and plugin code should not call base class noninline, nonvirtual functions compiled in the main application. Fifth, exceptions are rarely portable across the binary interface between the main program and plugins, so we cannot throw exceptions in a plugin and try to catch them in the main application. Finally, C++20 modules are portable across plugin boundaries, but their compiled module interfaces (CMIs) are not. Any main application code encapsulated by a C++20 module that is required by a plugin must supply its module interface file to that plugin. This is essentially no different than supplying a header file to a plugin except, depending on the build system, the module interface file may need to be separately compiled or precompiled vs. simply included.

That was a mouthful. Let's recap by enumerating the rules for C++ plugins:

1. Memory allocated in a plugin must be deallocated in the same plugin.

2. Standard library components cannot be used in plugin interfaces.

3. Assume incompatible alignment. Avoid plugins inheriting from main application classes with member variables if the variables are used in the main application.

4. Functions exported from a plugin (to be called by the main application) must specify extern "C" linkage. Functions exported from the main application (to be called by plugins) must specify extern "C" linkage.

5. The main application should communicate with plugin-derived classes exclusively via virtual functions. Plugin-derived classes should not call noninline, nonvirtual main application base class functions.

6. Do not let exceptions thrown in plugins propagate to the main application.

7. Module CMIs are not distributable artifacts; distribute module interface files.

With these rules in mind, let's return to the three fundamental problems we must solve in order to design plugins.

7.2 Problem 1: The Plugin Interface

The plugin interface is responsible for several items. First, it must enable the discovery of both new commands and new GUI buttons. We'll see that this functionality is most effectively accomplished through a class interface. Second, the plugin must support a C linkage interface for allocating and deallocating the aforementioned plugin class. Third, pdCalc should provide a `PluginCommand` class derived from `Command` to assist in correctly writing plugin commands. Technically, a `PluginCommand` class is optional, but providing such an interface helps users conform to plugin rules three and six. Fourth, it is worthwhile for the plugin interface to provide a function for querying the API version that a plugin supports. Finally, pdCalc must provide C linkage for any of the functions it must make available for plugins to call. Specifically, plugin commands must be able to access the stack. We'll address these issues in sequence starting with the interface for discovering commands.

7.2.1 The Interface for Discovering Commands

The first problem we face is how to allocate commands from plugins where we know neither what commands the plugin provides nor the names of the classes we'll need to instantiate. We'll solve this problem by creating an abstract interface to which all plugins must conform that exports both commands and their names. First, let's address what functionality we'll need.

Recall from Chapter 4 that in order to load a new command into the calculator, we must register it with the `CommandFactory`. By design, the `CommandFactory` was specifically constructed to admit dynamic allocation of commands, precisely the functionality we need for plugin commands. For now, we'll assume that the plugin management system has access to the register command (we'll address this deficiency in Section 7.4).

The `CommandFactory`'s registration function requires a `string` name for the command and a `unique_ptr` that serves as a prototype for the command. Since pdCalc knows nothing a priori about the command names in a plugin, the plugin interface must first make the names discoverable. Second, since C++ lacks reflection as a language feature, the plugin interface must provide a way to create a prototype command to be associated with each of the discovered names. Again, by design, the abstract `Command` interface supports the prototype pattern via the `clone()` virtual member function. Let's see how these two prior design decisions effectively enable plugins.

Based on our C++ plugin rules mentioned previously, the only means we have to effect command discovery is to encapsulate it as a pure virtual interface to which all plugins must adhere. Ideally, our virtual function would return an associative container of `unique_ptr<CommandPtr>` values keyed by `strings`. However, our C++ plugin rules also stipulate that we cannot use standard containers, thus excluding `string`, `map`, `unordered_map`, and `unique_ptr`. Rather than (poorly) reimplementing custom versions of any of these containers, we'll just use a typically avoided, low-level facilities available to us, arrays of pointers.

The preceding design is enforced by creating a `Plugin` class to which all plugins must conform. The purpose of this abstract class is to standardize plugin command discovery. The class declaration is given by the following:

```
// module code will be omitted from additional plugin listings
export class pdCalc.plugins;

export class Plugin
{
public:
  Plugin();
  virtual ~Plugin();

  struct PluginDescriptor
  {
    int nCommands;
    char** commandNames;
    Command** commands;
  };

  virtual const PluginDescriptor& getPluginDescriptor() const = 0;
};
```

We now have an abstract plugin interface that, when specialized, requires a derived class to return a descriptor that provides the number of commands available, the names of these commands, and prototypes of the commands themselves. Obviously, the ordering of the command names must match the ordering of the command prototypes. An alternative design would be to define a CommandDescriptor as follows:

```
struct CommandDescriptor
{
  char* commandName;
  Command* command;
};
```

and have the PluginDescriptor hold an array of CommandDescriptors instead of separate arrays for names and commands. This choice is the classic struct of arrays or array of structs conundrum. Either choice is valid in this context, and somewhat arbitrarily, I chose the former for pdCalc's implementation.

Unfortunately, with raw pointers and raw arrays, the ambiguity of who owns the memory for the command names and command prototypes arises. Our inability to use standard containers forces us into an unfortunate design: contract via comment. Since our rules dictate that memory allocated in a plugin must be freed by the same plugin, the best strategy is to decree that plugins are responsible for deallocation of the PluginDescriptor and its constituents. As stated before, the memory contract is "enforced" by comment.

Great, our problem is solved. We create a plugin; let's call it MyPlugin, which inherits from Plugin. We'll see how to allocate and deallocate the plugin in Section 7.3. Inside of MyPlugin, we create new commands by inheriting from Command as usual. Since the plugin knows its own command names, unlike the main program, the plugin can allocate its command prototypes with the new operator. Then, in order to register all the plugin's commands, we simply allocate a plugin descriptor with both command names and command prototypes, return the descriptor by overriding the getPluginDescriptor() function, and let pdCalc register the commands. Since Commands must each implement a clone() function, pdCalc can copy the plugin command prototypes via this virtual function to register them with the CommandFactory. Trivially, string names for registration can be created from the commandNames array.

For an already allocated `Plugin* p`, the following code within pdCalc could implement registration:

```
const auto& d = p->getPluginDesciptor();
for(int i = 0; i < d.nCommands; ++i)
  CommandFactory::Instance().registerCommand( d.commandNames[i],
    MakeCommandPtr(d.commands[i]->clone()) );
```

At this point, you might recognize a dilemma we face with our plugins. Commands are allocated in a plugin, copied in the main program upon registration with the `CommandRegistry` via an allocation by the plugin's `clone()` function, and then ultimately deleted by the main program when `CommandRegistry`'s destructor executes. Even worse, every time a command is executed, the `CommandRegistry` clones its prototype, triggering a new statement in the plugin via `Command`'s `clone()` function. The lifetime of this executed command is managed by the `CommandManager` through its undo and redo stacks. Specifically, when a command is cleared from one of these stacks, `delete` is called in the main program when the `unique_ptr` holding the command is destroyed. At least, that's how it works without some tweaking. As was alluded to in Chapter 4, `CommandPtr` is more than a simple alias for `unique_ptr<Command>`. Let's now finally describe the mechanics behind the `CommandPtr` alias and the `MakeCommandPtr()` function that allow correct plugin command memory management.

Fundamentally, we first need a function to call `delete` in the appropriate compilation unit. The easiest solution to this problem is to add a `deallocate()` virtual function to the `Command` class. The responsibility of this function is to invoke `delete` in the correct compilation unit when `Command`s are destroyed. For all core commands, the correct behavior is simply to `delete` the class in the main program. Hence, we do not make the `deallocate()` function pure virtual, and we give it the following default implementation:

```
void Command::deallocate()
{
  delete this;
}
```

For plugin commands, the override for the `deallocate()` has the same definition, only the definition appears in the plugin's compiled code (say, in a base class used by commands in a particular plugin). Therefore, when `deallocate()` is invoked on a Command pointer in the main application, the virtual function dispatch ensures that delete is called from the correct compilation unit. Now, we just need a mechanism to ensure that we call deallocate() instead of directly calling delete when Commands are reclaimed. Fortunately, it's as if the standards committee anticipated our needs perfectly when they designed unique_ptr. Let's return to the CommandPtr alias to see how unique_ptr can be used to solve our problem.

Remarkably few lines of code are necessary to define a CommandPtr alias and to implement a MakeCommandPtr() function capable of invoking deallocate() instead of delete. The code makes use of unique_ptr's deleter object (see sidebar), which enables a custom routine to be called to reclaim the resource held by the unique_ptr when the unique_ptr's destructor is invoked. Let's look at the code:

```
inline void CommandDeleter(Command* p)
{
    if(p) p->deallocate();
    return;
}

using CommandPtr = unique_ptr<Command, decltype(&CommandDeleter)>;

inline auto MakeCommandPtr(Command* p)
{
    return CommandPtr{p, &CommandDeleter};
}
```

A brief explanation of the preceding dense code is warranted. A CommandPtr is simply an alias for a unique_ptr that contains a Command pointer that is reclaimed by calling the CommandDeleter() function at destruction. The CommandDeleter() function invoked by the unique_ptr is a simple inline function that calls the virtual deallocate() function previously defined. To ease the syntactic burden of creating CommandPtrs, we introduce an inlined MakeCommandPtr() helper function that constructs a CommandPtr from a Command pointer. That's it. Now, just as before, unique_ptrs automatically manage the memory for Commands. However, instead of directly calling delete on the underlying Command, the unique_ptr's destructor invokes the CommandDeleter function, which calls deallocate(), which issues a delete on the underlying Command in the correct compilation unit.

If you look at the source code for MakeCommandPtr(), in addition to the version of the function seen previously that takes a Command pointer argument, you will see a very different overload that uses a variadic template and perfect forwarding. This overloaded function must exist due to a different semantic usage of MakeCommandPtr() in the construction of stored procedures. We'll revisit the reasoning behind the two forms of the function in Chapter 8. If the suspense is overwhelming, feel free to skip ahead to Section 8.1.2.

MODERN C++ DESIGN NOTE: UNIQUE_PTR DESTRUCTION SEMANTICS

The unique_ptr<T,D> class template is a smart pointer that models unique ownership of a resource. The most common usage specifies only the first template parameter, T, which declares the type of pointer to be owned. The second parameter, D, specifies a custom delete callable object that is invoked during the destruction of a unique_ptr. Let's look at a conceptual model for the destructor for unique_ptr:

```
template<typename T, typename D = default_delete<T>>
class unique_ptr
{
  T* p_;
  D d_;

public:
  ~unique_ptr()
  {
    d_(p_);
  }
};
```

Rather than directly calling delete, unique_ptr's destructor passes the owned pointer to the deleter using function call semantics. Conceptually, default_delete is implemented as follows:

```
template<typename T>
struct default_delete
{
  void operator()(T* p)
```

```
  {
    delete p;
  }
};
```

That is, the `default_delete` simply `deletes` the underlying pointer contained by the `unique_ptr`. However, by specifying a custom deleter callable object during construction (the D template argument), `unique_ptr` can be used to free resources requiring customized deallocation semantics. As a trivial example, `unique_ptr`'s delete semantics allow us to create a simple RAII (resource acquisition is initialization) container class, `MyObj`, allocated by `malloc()`:

```
MyObj* m = static_cast<MyObj*>( malloc(sizeof(MyObj) ) );
auto p = unique_ptr<MyObj, decltype(&free)>{m, &free};
```

Of course, our design for pdCalc shows another instance of the usefulness of the custom delete semantics of `unique_ptr`. It should be noted that `shared_ptr` also accepts a custom deleter in an analogous fashion.

7.2.2 The Interface for Adding New GUI Buttons

Conceptually, dynamically adding buttons is not much different than dynamically adding commands. The main application does not know what buttons need to be imported from the plugin, so the `Plugin` interface must provide a virtual function providing a button descriptor. Unlike commands, however, the plugin does not actually need to allocate the button itself. Recall from Chapter 6 that the GUI `CommandButton` widget only requires text for construction. In particular, it needs the push button's display text (optionally, the shifted state text) and the command text issued with the `clicked()` signal. Therefore, even for plugin commands, the corresponding GUI button itself resides entirely in the main application; the plugin must only provide text. This leads to the following trivial interface in the `Plugin` class:

```
class Plugin
{
public:
  struct PluginButtonDescriptor
```

```
{
  int nButtons;
  char** dispPrimaryCmd; // primary command label
  char** primaryCmd; // primary command
  char** dispShftCmd; // shifted command label
  char** shftCmd; // shifted command
};

virtual const PluginButtonDescriptor* getPluginButtonDescriptor() const = 0;
};
```

Again, due to the rules we must follow for plugins, the interface must be comprised of low-level arrays of characters rather than a higher-level, STL construct. Again, we could have alternatively provided an interface that used an array of structs rather than a struct of arrays.

One interesting facet of the getPluginButtonDescriptor() function relative to the getPluginDescriptor() is the decision to return a pointer rather than a reference. The rationale behind this choice is that a plugin writer might wish to write a plugin that exports commands that do not have corresponding GUI buttons (i.e., CLI-only commands). The converse, of course, is nonsensical. That is, I cannot envision why someone would write a plugin that exported buttons for nonexistent commands. This practicality is captured in the return type for the two descriptor functions. Since both functions are pure virtual, Plugin specializations must implement them. Because getPluginDescriptor() returns a reference, it must export a nonnull descriptor. However, by returning a pointer to the descriptor, getPluginButtonDescriptor() is permitted to return a nullptr indicating that the plugin exports no buttons. One might argue that the getPluginButtonDescriptor() function should not be pure virtual and instead provide a default implementation that returns a nullptr. This decision is technically viable. However, by insisting a plugin author manually implement getPluginButtonDescriptor(), the interface forces the decision to be made explicitly.

7.2.3 Plugin Allocation and Deallocation

Our original problem was that the main program did not know the class name of plugin commands and therefore could not allocate them via a call to new. We solved this problem by creating an abstract Plugin interface responsible for exporting command prototypes, command names, and sufficient information for the GUI to create buttons. Of course, to implement this interface, plugins must derive from the Plugin class, thereby creating a specialization, the name of which the main application cannot know in advance. Seemingly, we have made no progress and have returned to our original problem.

Our new problem, similar as it may be to the original problem, is actually much easier to solve. The problem is solved by creating a single extern "C" allocation/ deallocation function pair in each plugin with prespecified names that allocate/ deallocate the Plugin specialization class via the base class pointer. To satisfy these requirements, we add the following two functions to the plugin interface:

```
extern "C" void* AllocPlugin();
extern "C" void DeallocPlugin(void*);
```

Obviously, the AllocPlugin() function allocates the Plugin specialization and returns it to the main application, while the DeallocPlugin() function deallocates the plugin once the main application is finished using it. Curiously, the AllocPlugin() and DeallocPlugin() functions use void pointers instead of Plugin pointers. This interface is necessary to preserve C linkage since an extern "C" interface must conform to C types. An unfortunate consequence of maintaining C linkage is the necessity of casting. The main application must cast the void* to a Plugin* before using it, and the shared library must cast the void* back to a Plugin* before calling delete. Note, however, that we do not need the concrete Plugin's class name. Thus, the AllocPlugin()/ DeallocPlugin() function pair solves our problem.

7.2.4 The Plugin Command Interface

Technically, a special plugin command interface is not necessary. However, providing such an interface facilitates writing plugin commands that obey the C++ plugin rules. Specifically, by creating a PluginCommand interface, we assure plugin developers of two key features. First, we provide an interface that guarantees that plugin commands do not inherit from a command class that has any state (to avoid alignment problems). This property is obvious by construction. Second, we adapt the checkPreconditionsImpl() function to create an exception-free interface across the plugin boundary. With this guidance in mind, we present the PluginCommand interface:

```
class PluginCommand : public Command
{
public:
  virtual ~PluginCommand();

private:
  virtual const char* checkPluginPreconditions() const noexcept = 0;
  virtual PluginCommand* clonePluginImpl() const noexcept = 0;

  void checkPreconditionsImpl() const override final;
  PluginCommand* cloneImpl() const override final;
};
```

While only mentioned briefly in Chapter 4, all of the pure virtual functions in the Command class are marked noexcept except for checkPreconditionsImpl() and cloneImpl() (see the sidebar on keyword noexcept). Therefore, to ensure that plugin commands do not originate exceptions, we simply implement the checkPreconditionsImpl() and cloneImpl() functions at the PluginCommand level of the hierarchy and create new, exception-free pure virtual functions for its derived classes to implement. checkPreconditionsImpl() and cloneImpl() are both marked final in the PluginCommand class to prevent specializations from inadvertently overriding either of these functions. The implementation for checkPreconditionsImpl() can trivially be written as follows:

```
void PluginCommand::checkPreconditionsImpl() const
{
  if( const char* p = checkPluginPreconditions() )
    throw Exception(p);

  return;
}
```

Note that the key idea behind the preceding implementation is that the PluginCommand class's implementation resides in the main application's compilation unit, while any specializations of this class reside in the plugin's compilation unit. Therefore, via virtual dispatch, a call to checkPreconditionsImpl() executes in the main application's compilation unit, and this function in turn calls the exception-free checkPluginPreconditions() function that resides in the plugin's compilation unit.

If an error occurs, the checkPreconditionsImpl() function receives the error via a pointer return value and subsequently originates an exception from the main application's compilation unit rather than from the plugin's compilation unit. If no precondition fails, checkPluginPreconditions() returns a nullptr, and no exception is thrown.

A similar trivial implementation for cloneImpl() can be found in Command.cpp. Plugin commands that inherit from PluginCommand instead of Command, UnaryCommand, or BinaryCommand are much more likely to avoid violating any of the C++ plugin rules and are therefore much less likely to generate difficult-to-diagnose plugin-specific runtime errors.

MODERN C++ DESIGN NOTE: NOEXCEPT

The C++98 standard admits using exception specifications. For example, the following specification indicates that the function foo() does not throw any exceptions (the throw specification is empty):

```
void foo() throw();
```

Unfortunately, many problems existed with C++98 exception specifications. While they were a noble attempt at specifying the exceptions a function could throw, they often did not behave as expected. For example, the compiler never guaranteed exception specifications at compile time but instead enforced this constraint through runtime checks. Even worse, declaring a no throw exception specification could impact code performance. For these reasons and more, many coding standards were written declaring one should simply avoid exception specifications (see, e.g., Standard 75 in [34]).

While specifying which specifications a function can throw has proven not to be terribly useful, specifying that a function cannot throw any exceptions can be an important interface consideration. Fortunately, the C++11 standard remedied the exception specification mess by introducing the noexcept keyword. For an in-depth discussion of the uses of the noexcept specifier, see Item 14 in [24]. For our discussion, we'll concentrate on the keyword's usefulness in design.

Performance optimization aside, the choice to use noexcept in a function's specification is largely a matter of preference. For most functions, no exception specification is the norm. Even if a function's code does not itself emit exceptions, it is difficult to ensure statically that nested function calls within a function do not emit any exceptions. Therefore, noexcept is enforced at runtime rather than guaranteed at compile time. Thus, my personal recommendation is to reserve the usage of the noexcept specifier for particular instances where making a strong statement about the intent of a function is necessary. pdCalc's Command hierarchy illustrates several situations where not throwing an exception is important for correct operation. This requirement is codified in the interface to inform developers that throwing exceptions will lead to runtime faults.

7.2.5 API Versioning

Invariably, over the lifetime of a long-lived application, the specification for plugins may change. This implies that a plugin written at one point in time may no longer function with an updated API version. For an application shipped as a single unit, the components composing the whole (i.e., the multiple shared libraries) are synchronized by the development schedule. For a complete application, versioning is used to express to the external world that the overall application has changed. However, because plugins are designed to be stand-alone from the main application's development, synchronizing plugin releases with application releases may be impossible. Furthermore, the plugin API may or may not change with each application release. Therefore, to ensure compatibility, we must version the plugin API separately from the main application. While you may not anticipate changing the plugin API in the future, if you don't add the ability to query plugins for their supported API version up front as part of the API itself, you'll have to introduce a breaking change to add this feature later. Depending on your requirements, such a breaking change may not be feasible, and you'll never be able to add API versioning. Therefore, even if it's not used initially, adding a function to query a plugin's supported API version in the plugin interface should be considered an implicit requirement. As is hopefully apparent, the API version is distinct from the application's version.

The actual API version numbering scheme can be as simple or as complicated as is deemed appropriate. On the simple side, it can be a single integer. On the more complicated side, it can be a structure containing several integers for major version, minor version, etc. For pdCalc, I chose a simple structure utilizing only a major version and a minor version number. The interface code is given by the following:

```
class Plugin
{
public:
  struct ApiVersion
  {
    int major;
    int minor;
  };

  virtual ApiVersion apiVersion() const = 0;
};
```

The main application simply calls the `apiVersion()` function before calling plugin functions to ensure the plugin is compatible. If incompatibility is detected, an error message can be displayed, and the incompatible plugin can be ignored or rejected. Alternatively, the main application can support multiple plugin versions, and the `ApiVersion` information informs the main application what functions the plugin supports.

7.2.6 Making the Stack Available

Part of the plugin interface consists of making plugins and their commands discoverable to pdCalc. The other part of pdCalc's plugin interface consists of making necessary parts of pdCalc's functionality available to plugins. Specifically, the implementation of new commands requires access to pdCalc's stack.

As we saw when we developed the core commands, commands require only very basic access to the stack. Specifically, they need the ability to push elements onto the stack, to pop elements off of the stack, and potentially to inspect elements from the stack (to implement preconditions). Our strategy for making this functionality available to the core commands was to implement the `Stack` class as a singleton with a public interface that included push, pop, and inspection member functions. However, this design fails to extend to plugin commands because it violates two of the C++ plugin rules. Namely, our current interface does not conform to C linkage (the stack provides a C++ class interface) and the current inspection function returns stack elements via an STL `vector`.

The solution to this problem is quite trivial. We simply add a new interface to the stack (preferably in a specially designated header file) consisting of a collection of global (outside the pdCalc namespace) extern "C" functions that translate between C linkage and C++ class linkage (the adapter pattern again). Recall that since the Stack class was implemented as a singleton, neither the plugins nor the global helper functions need to own a Stack reference or pointer. The helper functions directly access the Stack through its Instance() function. I chose to implement the following five functions in a separate StackPluginInterface.m.cpp module interface file:

```
export module pdCalc.stackinterface;
```

```
extern "C" void StackPush(double d, bool suppressChangeEvent);
extern "C" double StackPop(bool suppressChangeEvent);
extern "C" size_t StackSize();
extern "C" double StackFirstElement();
extern "C" double StackSecondElement();
```

For simplicity, since my example plugin did not need deeper access to the stack than the top two elements, I created only two inspection functions, StackFirstElement() and StackSecondElement(), for getting the top two elements of the stack. If desired, a function returning the elements of the stack to any depth could have been implemented. To maintain extern "C" linkage, the implementer of such a function would need to remember to use a raw array of doubles rather than an STL vector.

The complete, straightforward implementations for the preceding five functions appear in the StackPluginInterface.cpp file. As an example, the implementation of the StackSize() function is given by the following:

```
size_t StackSize()
{
  return pdCalc::Stack::Instance().size();
}
```

7.3 Problem 2: Loading Plugins

As previously stated, plugins are platform specific, and, inherently, the loading of plugins requires platform-specific code. In this section, we will consider two topics. First, we'll address the platform-specific code necessary for loading libraries and their respective symbols. Here, we'll look at two platform interfaces: POSIX (Linux, UNIX, Mac OS X) and win32 (MS Windows). Second, we'll explore a design strategy to mitigate the source code clutter often arising from the use of platform-specific code.

7.3.1 Platform-Specific Plugin Loading

In order to work with plugins, we only need three platform-specific functions: a function to open a shared library, a function to close a shared library, and a function to extract symbols from an opened shared library. Table 7-1 lists these functions and their associated header file by platform. Let's look at how these functions are used.

Table 7-1. *Plugin functions for different platforms*

	POSIX	win32
header	dlfcn.h	windows.h
load library	dlopen()	LoadLibrary()
close library	dlclose()	FreeLibrary()
get library symbol	dlsym()	GetProcAddress()

7.3.2 Loading, Using, and Closing a Shared Library

The first step in using a plugin is asking the runtime system to open the library and make its exportable symbols available to the current working program. The open command on each platform requires the name of the shared library to be opened (POSIX also requires a flag specifying the desired symbol binding, either lazy or immediate), and it returns an opaque handle to the library, which is used to refer to the library in subsequent function calls. On a POSIX system, the handle type is a void*, while on a win32 system, the handle type is an HINSTANCE (which, after some unraveling, is a typedef for a void*). As an example, the following code opens a plugin library, libPlugin.so, on a POSIX system:

```
void* handle = dlopen("libPlugin.so", RTLD_LAZY);
```

where the RTLD_LAZY option simply tells the runtime system to perform lazy binding, which resolves symbols as the code that references them is executed. The alternative option is RTLD_NOW, which resolves all undefined symbols in the library before dlopen() returns. The null pointer is returned if the open fails. A simple error handling scheme skips loading any functionality from a null plugin, warning the user that opening the plugin failed.

Aside from the different function names, the main platform-specific difference for opening a plugin is the canonical naming convention employed by the different platforms. For example, on Linux, shared libraries begin with lib and have a .so file extension. On Windows, shared libraries (usually called dynamically linked libraries, or, simply, DLLs) have no particular prefix and a .dll file extension. On Mac OS X, shared libraries conventionally are prefaced with lib and have the .dylib extension. Essentially, this naming convention matters only in two places. First, the build system should create plugins with an appropriate name for the respective platform. Second, the call to open a plugin should specify the name using the correct format. Since plugin names are specified at runtime, we need to ensure that plugin names are correctly specified by the user supplying the plugin.

Once a plugin has been opened, we'll need to export symbols from the shared library in order to call the functions contained within the plugin. This export is accomplished by calling either dlopen() or LoadLibrary() (depending on the platform), either of which uses a plugin function's string name to bind the plugin function to a function pointer. The bound plugin function is then called in the main application indirectly via this obtained function pointer.

In order to bind to a symbol in the shared library, we need to have a plugin handle (the return value from opening a plugin), to know the name of the function in the plugin we want to call, and to know the signature of the function we want to call. For pdCalc, the first plugin function we need to call is AllocPlugin() to allocate the embedded Plugin class (see Section 7.2.3). Because this function is declared as part of the plugin interface, we know both its name and its signature. As an example, on Windows, for an already-

loaded plugin pointed to by HINSTANCE handle, we bind to the plugin's AllocPlugin()
function to a function pointer with the following code:

```
// function pointer of AllocPlugin's type:
extern "C" { typedef void* (*PluginAllocator)(void); }
// bind the symbol from the plugin
auto alloc = GetProcAddress(handle, "AllocPlugin");
// cast the symbol from void* (return of GetProcAddress)
// to the function pointer type of AllocPlugin
PluginAllocator allocator{ reinterpret_cast<PluginAllocator>(alloc) };
```

Subsequently, the plugin's Plugin specialization is allocated by the following:

```
// only dereference if the function was bound properly
if(allocator)
{
  // dereference the allocator, call the function,
  // cast the void* return to a Plugin*
  auto p = static_cast<Plugin*>((*allocator)());
}
```

The concrete Plugin is now available for use (e.g., loading plugin commands, querying
the supported plugin API) through the abstract Plugin interface.

An analogous sequence of code is required to bind and execute the plugin's
DeallocPlugin() function upon plugin deallocation. The interested reader is referred
to the platform-specific code in the GitHub repository for the details. Remember that
before deallocating a plugin, since commands allocated by the plugin are resident
in memory in the main application (but must be reclaimed in the plugin), a plugin
must not be closed until all of its commands are freed. Examples of plugin commands
resident in the main application's memory space are command prototypes in the
CommandFactory and commands on the undo/redo stack in the CommandManager.

Since a plugin is an acquired resource, we should release it when we are finished
using it. This action is performed on a POSIX platform by calling dlclose() and on a
win32 platform by calling FreeLibrary(). For example, the following code for a POSIX
system closes a shared library (the handle) that was opened with dlopen():

```
// only try to close a non-null library
if(handle) dlclose(handle);
```

Now that we have discussed the platform-specific mechanics of opening, using, and closing plugins, we turn our attention to a design strategy that mitigates the inherent complications of working with multiplatform source code.

7.3.3 A Design for Multiplatform Code

Portability across platforms is a laudable goal for any software project. However, achieving this goal while maintaining a readable code base requires significant forethought. In this section, we'll examine some design techniques for achieving platform portability while maintaining readability.

The Obvious Solution: Libraries

The obvious (and preferred) solution to the portability problem is to use a library that abstracts platform dependencies for you. Using a high-quality library for any development scenario always saves you the effort of having to design, implement, test, and maintain functionality required for your project. Using a library for cross-platform development has the additional benefit of hiding platform-specific code behind a platform-independent API. Such an API, of course, allows you to maintain a single code base that works seamlessly across multiple platforms without littering the source code with preprocessor directives. Although we did not explicitly discuss these merits in Chapter 6, Qt's toolkit abstraction provides a platform-independent API for building a GUI, an otherwise platform-dependent task. In pdCalc, we used Qt to build a GUI that compiles and executes on Windows and Linux (and presumably OS X, although I have not verified that fact) without changing a single line of the source code between platforms.

Alas, the obvious solution is not always available. Many reasons exist for not incorporating libraries in a project. First, many libraries are not free, and the cost of a library may be prohibitive, especially if the license has usage fees in addition to development fees. Second, a library's license may be incompatible with a project's license. For example, maybe you are building a closed source code, but the only available library has an incompatible open source license (or vice versa). Third, libraries are frequently shipped without source code. Lacking source code makes extending a library's functionality impossible. Fourth, you might require support for a library, but the vendor might not supply any. Fifth, a library may ship with an upgrade cycle incompatible with your own. Sixth, a library might be incompatible with your toolchain. Finally, a library may not exist at all for the functionality you are seeking. Therefore, while using a library typically is the first choice to achieve portability, enough counterexamples to using a library exist to merit discussing how to achieve portability without one.

Raw Preprocessor Directives

Using raw preprocessor directives is undoubtedly the first method tried when attempting to achieve cross-platform code. Nearly everyone who has written portable code probably started this way. Simply, everywhere platform-dependent code appears, the platform-specific pieces are surrounded by preprocessor #ifdef directives. Let's take, for example, the runtime loading of a shared library in both Linux and Windows:

```
#ifdef POSIX
  void* handle = dlopen("libPlugin.so", RTLD_LAZY);
#elif WIN32
  HINSTANCE handle = LoadLibrary("Plugin.dll");
#endif
```

Don't forget the preprocessor directives surrounding the header files too:

```
#ifdef POSIX
  #include <dlfcn.h>
#elif WIN32
  #include <windows.h>
#endif
```

For a small number of platforms or for a very few instances, using raw preprocessor directives can be tolerable. However, this technique scales poorly. As soon as either the number of platforms or the number of code locations requiring platform-dependent code increases, using raw preprocessor directives quickly becomes a mess. The code becomes difficult to read, and finding all the platform-dependent locations when adding a new platform becomes a nightmare. In even a medium-sized project, sprinkling the code with #ifdefs quickly becomes untenable.

(Slightly) More Clever Preprocessor Directives

Where platform APIs are different in name but identical in function call arguments (more common than you might expect since similar functionality, unsurprisingly enough, requires similar customizations), we can be a little more clever in our usage of the preprocessor. Instead of placing the preprocessor directives at the site of every platform-dependent function call and type declaration, we can instead create platform-dependent macro names and define them in a centralized location. This idea is better explained with an example. Let's look at closing a shared library on Linux and Windows:

```
// some common header defining all platform dependent analogous symbols
#ifdef POSIX
  #define HANDLE void*
  #define CLOSE_LIBRARY dlclose
#elif WIN32
  #define CLOSE_LIBRARY FreeLibrary
  #define HANDLE HINSTANCE
#endif

// in the code, for some shared library HANDLE handle
CLOSE_LIBRARY(handle);
```

This technique is significantly cleaner than the naive approach of sprinkling #ifdefs at every function call invocation. However, it is severely limited by only working for function calls with identical arguments. Obviously, we would still need an #ifdef at the call site for opening a shared library because the POSIX call requires two arguments, while the Windows call requires only one. Certainly, with the abstraction capabilities of C++, we can do better.

A Build System Solution

An interesting idea that seems appealing at first is to separate platform-specific code into platform-specific source files and then use the build system to choose the correct file based on the platform. Let's consider an example. Place all of the Unix-specific code in a file called UnixImpl.cpp, and place all of the Windows-specific code in a file called WindowsImpl.cpp. On each respective platform, code your build scripts to only compile the appropriate platform-specific file. Using this technique, no platform preprocessor directives are required since any given source file only contains source for one platform.

The preceding scheme suffers from two distinct drawbacks. First, the method only works if you maintain identical interfaces (e.g., function names, class names, argument lists) to your own source code across all platform-specific files on all platforms. This feat is easier said than done, especially if you have independent teams working and testing on each platform. Compounding the problem, because the compiler only sees the code for a single platform at any given time, there is no language mechanism (e.g., type system) to enforce these cross-platform interface constraints. Second, the mechanics of achieving cross-platform compatibility are completely opaque to any developer examining the source code on a single platform. On any one platform, only one of the many platform-dependent source files effectively exists, and this source file supplies no hint of the others' existence. Of course, this latter problem exacerbates the former because the lack of cross-platform source transparency coupled with the lack of language support for the technique makes it nearly impossible to maintain interface consistency. For these reasons, a pure build system solution is intractable.

With the downsides of this technique noted, we must be careful not to throw out the baby with the bathwater, for the kernel of our final solution lies in a language-supported mechanism at the juxtaposition of both the preprocessor and the build system solutions. This design technique is examined in the following section.

A Platform Factory Function

Scattering preprocessor macros throughout a code everywhere platform-specific functionality is required is analogous to using integer flags and switch statements to execute type-specific code. Not coincidentally, both problems have the same solution, which is to build an abstract class hierarchy and execute specific functionality via polymorphism.

We'll build our solution to designing a general cross-platform architecture in two steps. First, we'll design a platform hierarchy for handling dynamic loading. Second, we'll extend this specific solution into a framework for abstracting platform dependence into a platform-independent interface. In both steps, we will employ a hybrid solution that utilizes the build system in a type-safe manner through a minimum use of platform-specific preprocessor directives. Along the way, we'll encounter an important design pattern, the abstract factory. Let's start by examining the platform-independent dynamic loading of plugins.

To address our specific problem, we start by first defining a platform-independent abstract interface for a DynamicLoader base class. Our DynamicLoader only needs to do two things: allocate and deallocate plugins. The base class is therefore trivially defined as follows:

```
class DynamicLoader
{
public:
  virtual ~DynamicLoader();

  virtual Plugin* allocatePlugin(const string& pluginName) = 0;
  virtual void deallocatePlugin(Plugin*) = 0;
};
```

The design intent of the preceding base class is that the hierarchy will be specialized by platform.

Notice that the interface itself is platform independent. The platform-dependent allocation and deallocation is an implementation detail handled by the platform-specific derived classes of this interface through the virtual functions. Furthermore, because each platform-specific implementation is wholly contained in a derived class, by placing each derived class in a separate file, we can use the build system to selectively compile only the file relevant for each platform, obviating the need for platform preprocessor directives anywhere within the hierarchy. Even better, once a DynamicLoader has been allocated, the interface abstracts away the platform-specific details of plugin loading, and the consumer of a plugin need not be concerned with plugin loading details. Loading just works. For the implementer of the derived classes of the DynamicLoader, the compiler can use type information to enforce interface consistency across platforms since each derived class must conform to the interface specified by the abstract base class, which is common to all platforms. The design is summarized pictorially in Figure 7-1. The included source code for pdCalc implements platform-specific loaders for a POSIX-compliant system and for Windows.

The preceding design hides platform-specific details behind an abstract interface, alleviating the need for a plugin consumer to understand how a plugin is loaded. That is, of course, assuming that the plugin consumer instantiates the correct platform-specific derived class, something that cannot be handled automatically by the DynamicLoader hierarchy. Here, we can use a familiar design pattern, the factory function, to solve the problem of instantiating the correct derived class. Recall, the factory function is a pattern that separates type creation from the logical point of instantiation.

Figure 7-1. *The dynamic loader hierarchy for platform-independent plugin allocation and deallocation*

In Chapter 4, we defined a factory function that returned a specific type of Command based on a `string` argument. Here, the factory function is even simpler. Since our hierarchy is specialized by platform, rather than passing in a `string` to choose the appropriate derived class, we simply make the selection by using preprocessor directives:

Listing 7-1. A dynamic loader factory function

```
unique_ptr<DynamicLoader> dynamicLoaderFactory()
{
#ifdef POSIX
  return make_unique<PosixDynamicLoader>();
#elif WIN32
  return make_unique<WindowsDynamicLoader>();
```

```
#else
  return nullptr;
#endif
}
```

By compiling the `dynamicLoaderFactory()` function into its own source file, we can achieve platform-independent plugin creation by isolating one set of preprocessor directives in one source file. The factory function is then called to return the correct type of `DynamicLoader` at the site where plugin allocation or deallocation is needed. By having the factory return a `unique_ptr`, we need not worry about memory leaks. The following code snippet illustrates the platform-independent usage of the `DynamicLoader`:

```
// Question: What platform?
auto loader = dynamicLoaderFactory();
// Answer: Who cares?
auto plugin = (loader ? loader->allocatePlugin(pluginName) : nullptr);
```

For the purposes of pdCalc, we could stop with the `DynamicLoader` hierarchy and our simple factory function. We only have the need to abstract one platform-dependent feature (the allocation and deallocation of plugins), and the preceding code is sufficient for this purpose. However, we've come this far, and it's worth taking one extra step to see a generalized implementation of platform independence applicable to situations calling for a number of different platform-dependent features, even if it is not specifically needed for our case study.

An Abstract Factory for Generalized Platform-Independent Code

As software developers, we are constantly faced with design challenges caused by platform dependence. The following is an incomplete list of common platform-specific programming tasks for a C++ developer: plugin loading, interprocess communication, navigation of the file system (standardized in C++17), graphics, threading (standardized in C++11), persistent settings, binary serialization, `sizeof()` built-in data types, timers (standardized in C++11), and network communication. Most, if not all, of the functionality on this list can be obtained through platform-independent APIs in libraries such as boost or Qt. For me personally, the platform-specific feature that has caused the most aggravation has been the humble directory separator (`'/'` on a POSIX system and `'\'` on a Windows system).

Suppose our calculator had required the ability to read, write, and save persistent custom settings (see Chapter 8 for some reasons why this might be necessary for a calculator). Typically, Linux systems save settings in text files (e.g., on Ubuntu, user settings are saved in files in the .config directory in home), while on Windows systems, persistent settings are saved in the system registry. In practice, the best solution would be to use an existing library that has already implemented this abstraction (e.g., Qt's QSettings class). For instructional purposes, we'll assume that no external libraries are available, and we'll examine a design that adds persistent settings (or any number of platform-dependent functionality) alongside our existing dynamic loader. Our focus will be on the abstraction rather than the specifics of the settings implementation on each platform.

The easy solution is to piggyback on our dynamic loader and simply add the necessary settings interface directly into the DynamicLoader class. Of course, we would need to rename the class to something more generic, such as OsSpecificFunctionality, with derived classes such as LinuxFuntionality and WindowsFunctionality. This method is simple, fast, and quickly intractable; it is antithetical to cohesion. For any sizable code, this technique eventually leads to uncontrollable bloat and, hence, a complete lack of maintainability of the interface. Despite time pressures on projects, I recommend always avoiding this quick solution, as it merely increases your technical debt and causes longer delays in the future than would be experienced in the present with a proper solution.

Instead of bloating our existing DynamicLoader class, we instead take inspiration from its design and create a separate, analogous settings hierarchy as depicted in Figure 7-2.

Again, we have the problem of instantiating a platform-specific derived class on each unique platform. However, instead of adding an additional settingsLoaderFactory() function to mirror the existing dynamicLoaderFactory() function, we instead seek a generalized solution that enables indefinite functional extension while preserving the single code point for platform selection. As expected, we are not the first programmers to encounter this particular problem, and a solution already exists, the abstract factory pattern.

Figure 7-2. *The settings hierarchy for platform-independent persistent settings*

According to Gamma et al. [11], an abstract factory "provides an interface for creating families of related or dependent objects without specifying their concrete classes." Essentially, the pattern can be constructed in two steps:

1. Create independent hierarchies (families) for each of the related objects (e.g., a dynamic loader hierarchy and a settings hierarchy, related by their platform dependence).

2. Create a hierarchy, specializing on the dependent relationship (e.g., the platform), that provides factory functions for each of the families.

I find the preceding abstraction very difficult to comprehend without a concrete example; therefore, let's consider the problem we are trying to solve in pdCalc. As we walk through this example, we'll refer to the (overly complex) class diagram in Figure 7-3. Recall that the overall goal of this abstraction is to create a single source location capable of providing a platform-independent mechanism for creating any number of platform-specific specializations.

As we've already seen, the platform-dependent functionality can be abstracted into parallel, independent hierarchies. These hierarchies enable platform-dependent implementations to be accessed through platform-independent base class interfaces via polymorphism. For pdCalc, this pattern translates into providing platform agnostic Settings and DynamicLoader hierarchies to abstract persistent settings and dynamic loading, respectively. For example, we can allocate and deallocate a plugin polymorphically through the abstract DynamicLoader interface, provided the system instantiates the correct underlying derived class (PosixDynamicLoader or WindowsDynamicLoader) based on the platform. This part of the abstract factory is represented by the DynamicLoader hierarchy in Figure 7-3.

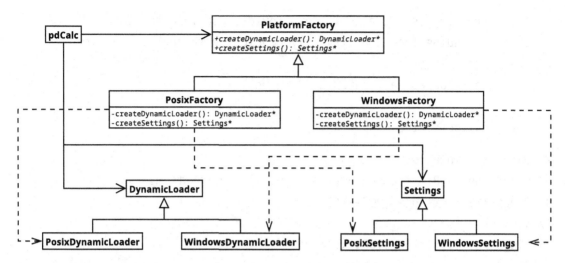

Figure 7-3. *The abstract factory pattern applied to pdCalc*

The problem now reduces to instantiating the correct derived class based on the current platform. Instead of providing separate factory functions to instantiate the DynamicLoader and Settings objects (a decentralized approach requiring separate platform #ifdefs in each factory), we instead create a hierarchy that provides an abstract interface for providing the factory functions necessary to create the DynamicLoader and Settings objects. This abstract factory hierarchy (the PlatformFactory hierarchy in Figure 7-3) is then specialized on the platform so that we have platform-specific derived classes of the factory hierarchy that create platform-specific derived classes of the functional hierarchies. This scheme centralizes the platform dependence into a single factory function that instantiates the correct PlatformFactory specialization. In pdCalc's implementation, I chose to make the PlatformFactory a singleton and thereby "hide" the PlatformFactory's factory function in the Instance() function.

The abstract factory pattern might still not make a lot of sense, so let's look at some sample code, viewing the abstraction in a top-down fashion. Ultimately, the abstract factory pattern enables us to write the following platform-independent, high-level code in pdCalc:

```
// PlatformFactory Instance returns either a PosixFactory or a
// WindowsFactory instance (based on the platform), which in turn
// creates the correct derived DynamicLoader
auto loader = PlatformFactory::Instance().createDynamicLoader();
```

```
// The correctly instantiated loader provides platform specific
// dynamic loading functionality polymorphically through a platform
// independent interface
auto plugin = loader->allocatePlugin(pName);
// ...
loader->deallocatePlugin(plugin);

// Same principle for settings...
auto settings = PlatformFactory::Instance().createSettings();
settings->readSettingsFromDisk();
// ...
settings->commitSettingsToDisk();
```

Drilling down, the first function we'll examine is the PlatformFactory's Instance() function, which returns either a PosixFactory or a WindowsFactory, depending on the platform.

```
PlatformFactory& PlatformFactory::Instance()
{
#ifdef POSIX
  static PosixFactory instance;
#elif WIN32
  static WindowsFactory instance;
#endif

  return instance;
}
```

The preceding function is doing something subtle but clever, and it's a trick worth knowing. From the client's perspective, PlatformFactory looks like an ordinary singleton class. One calls the Instance() function, and a PlatformFactory reference is returned. Clients then use the PlatformFactory's public interface as they would any other singleton class. However, because the Instance() member function returns a reference, we are free to use the instance polymorphically. Since PosixFactory and WindowsFactory both derive from PlatformFactory, the instance variable instantiated is the specialization that matches the platform as defined by the #ifdef in the implementation. We have cleverly disguised an implementation detail, the mechanics of the abstract factory pattern, from the user of the class. Unless the client noticed that the factory functions in the PlatformFactory are pure virtual, they would probably not realize they were consuming an object-oriented hierarchy. Of course, the goal is not to hide anything from the user in a nefarious plot to obscure the implementation. Rather, this use of information hiding is utilized to reduce the cognitive burden on the client of the PlatformFactory.

We next examine the trivial implementations of the createDynamicLoader() functions in the PosixFactory and WindowsFactory classes (note the covariant return type of the functions):

```
unique_ptr<DynamicLoader> PosixFactory::createDynamicLoader()
{
  return make_unique<PosixDynamicLoader>();
}

unique_ptr<DynamicLoader> WindowsFactory::createDynamicLoader()
{
  return make_unique<WindowsDynamicLoader>();
}
```

Previously, we've simply replaced the dynamic loader factory function (see Listing 7-1) by a class hierarchy, replacing the platform #ifdefs with polymorphism. With only one piece of functionality dependent on the platform, the replacement of a factory function with an abstract factory is certainly overkill. However, for our example, we have the independent DynamicLoader and Settings families both dependent on the same platform criterion (in principle, we could have any number of such hierarchies), and the abstract factory pattern allows us to centralize the platform dependency in one location (here, in the PlatformFactory's Instance() function) instead of scattering it through multiple independent factory functions. From a maintenance standpoint, the value proposition is similar to preferring polymorphism to switch statements.

The final piece of the puzzle is the implementations of both the DynamicLoader and Settings hierarchies. Fortunately, these implementations are identical to the ideas outlined in Section 7.3.3, and we need not repeat their implementations here. Using the abstract factory pattern indeed adds no inherent complication to the implementation of platform-dependent functions. The pattern only adds mechanics around the instantiation of these classes via a single factory hierarchy instead of a sequence of factory functions.

In the source code in pdCalc's repository, no Settings hierarchy (or its associated readSettingsFromDisk() and commitSettingsToDisk() functions in PlatformFactory) implementation exists because pdCalc, as written, has no need for a persistent settings abstraction. The Settings hierarchy was merely manufactured as a plausible example to demonstrate concretely the mechanics and relevance of the abstract factory pattern. That said, I did opt to include a full abstract platform factory implementation in pdCalc's code for the DynamicLoader alone just to illustrate a practical implementation of the abstract factory pattern even though a simpler single factory function would have sufficed and been preferred for production code.

7.4 Problem 3: Retrofitting pdCalc

We now turn to the final plugin problem, which is retrofitting the already-developed classes and interfaces to accommodate adding calculator functionality dynamically. This problem is not about plugin management. Rather, the problem we are addressing here is extending pdCalc's module interfaces to accept plugin features. Essentially, where Section 7.2 defined how to discover commands and buttons in a plugin, this section describes how to incorporate these newly discovered commands into pdCalc.

7.4.1 Injecting Commands

Let's begin by creating an interface to enable the injection of newly discovered plugin commands. Recall from Chapter 4 that core commands are loaded into the CommandFactory when the application starts. First, the main application calls the RegisterCoreCommands() function. Second, within this function, the registerCommand() function of the CommandFactory class is called for each core command, registering the command's name and a command prototype with the CommandFactory. In Section 7.2, we developed an interface for exporting command names and command prototypes from plugins. Obviously, to register these plugin commands, we simply need to extend the command dispatcher module's interface to include the existing registerCommand() function so that the code responsible for loading plugins can also register their commands. Since the CommandFactory partition of the commandDispatcher module was already being exported (in order to export the RegisterCoreCommands() function), achieving the needed interface change to the command dispatcher module is accomplished by simply exporting the CommandFactory class from the CommandFactory partition. It really is that easy.

In hindsight, the need to export both the CommandFactory class and the RegisterCoreCommands() function explains why the RegisterCoreCommands() was placed in the CommandFactory partition. Originally, I had implemented the RegisterCoreCommands() in the CoreCommands partition, but I moved it when I realized that the CoreCommands partition would otherwise not need to be exported from the commandDispatcher module.

7.4.2 Adding Plugin Buttons to the GUI

Recall at the outset of this section that we outlined two problems to be solved in retrofitting pdCalc for plugins. The first problem, which we just solved, was how to add plugin commands to the CommandFactory after a plugin is loaded. The solution turned out to be quite trivial since we had already written the necessary function and needed only to extend the module's defined public interface. The second problem involves retrofitting pdCalc to be able to add buttons to the GUI that correspond to plugin commands.

By the design of our command dispatcher, once a command is registered, it can be executed by any user interface raising a commandEntered() event with the command's name as the event's argument. Hence, for the CLI, a plugin command can be executed by the user by typing in its name. That is, plugin commands become immediately accessible to the CLI as soon as they are registered. Making a plugin command accessible in the GUI, of course, is slightly more complicated because a button that can raise a commandEntered() event must be created for each discovered plugin command.

In Section 7.2, we defined an interface for labeling CommandButtons. Each plugin provides a PluginButtonDescriptor that defines the primary command label, the secondary command label, and the underlying commands associated with the labels. Therefore, in order to add a new GUI button corresponding to a plugin command, we must simply extend the interface of the GUI's MainWindow class to include a function for adding buttons based on their labels:

```
class MainWindow : public QMainWindow, public UserInterface
{
public:
  // Existing interface plus the following:
  void addCommandButton(const string& dispPrimaryCmd,
    const string& primaryCmd, const string& dispShftCmd,
    const string& shftCmd);
};
```

Of course, this function will also need to layout the buttons based on some suitable algorithm. My trivial algorithm simply places buttons left to right with four buttons in a row.

Unlike the registerCommand() function of the CommandRegistry, the addCommandButton() was not a preexisting public function of the MainWindow class. Therefore, we must add and implement this new function. In all likelihood, a modular implementation of the GUI would have already had a similar function somewhere in the GUI module, as this functionality was already required to create buttons for core commands. Therefore, implementation of the addCommandButton() function might be as trivial as forwarding this call from the MainWindow to the appropriate internal GUI class, where the function may have already existed. Because of the current limitations of Qt, we were not using C++ modules to encapsulate the GUI. The addition of the addCommandButton() to the pubic section of the MainWindow class is sufficient to extend the logical module.

7.5 Incorporating Plugins

Thus far, we have discussed guidelines for C++ plugins, the plugin interface, plugin command memory management, loading and unloading plugins, design patterns for abstracting platform-dependent code behind interfaces, and retrofitting pdCalc to enable plugin command and GUI injection. However, we are yet to discuss any mechanism for finding plugins, actually loading and unloading plugins from disk, managing the lifetime of plugins, or injecting plugin functionality into pdCalc. These operations are performed by a PluginLoader class and the main() function of the application, both of which are now described.

7.5.1 Loading Plugins

Loading plugins is accomplished by a PluginLoader class. The PluginLoader is responsible for finding plugin dynamic library files, loading the plugins into memory, and serving the concrete Plugin specializations to pdCalc, on demand. The PluginLoader is also responsible for deallocating plugin resources at the appropriate times. As we've seen previously, a good design will implement automatic deallocation via RAII.

The first step in loading plugins is determining which plugins should be loaded and when. Really, only two practical options exist to answer this question. Either plugins are loaded automatically by pdCalc when the program starts (e.g., files specified in a configuration file or all DLLs in a specific directory), or plugins are loaded on demand by direct user requests. Of course, these options are not mutually exclusive, and a PluginLoader class could be designed that incorporates both options, possibly with the ability for the user to direct which manually loaded plugins should be automatically loaded in the future. There is no right or wrong answer to how plugins are loaded. The decision must be addressed by the program's requirements.

For simplicity, I chose to implement a plugin loader that automatically loads plugins during pdCalc's startup. The PluginLoader finds these plugins by reading an ASCII configuration file comprised of lines of text each individually listing the file name of a plugin. The configuration file is arbitrarily named plugins.pdp, and this file must be located in the current executable path. Plugin files listed in plugins.pdp can be specified using either a relative or absolute path. A more sophisticated plugin loader implementation would probably store the location of the plugin file in an operating system–specific configuration location (e.g., the Windows registry) and use a better file format, such as XML or JSON. A good library, like Qt, can help you parse files and find system-specific configuration files using a platform-independent abstraction.

As was previously mentioned in Section 7.1.1, plugins traditionally have different naming conventions on different platforms. For pdCalc, I chose to require the user to specify the platform-dependent file name of each plugin in the plugins.pdp file. An alternative would have been to require users to specify a platform-independent root name for each plugin and have pdCalc reconstruct the platform-dependent name on each platform. Had we chosen this latter route, we would have been able to cleanly implement this feature by extending the abstract platform factory with a plugin name builder hierarchy.

With the preceding plugin loader design constraints in mind, the PluginLoader interface is quite trivial:

```
export module pdCalc.pluginManagement;

export class PluginLoader
{
public:
  void loadPlugins(UserInterface& ui, const string& pluginFileName);
  const vector<const Plugin*> getPlugins();
};
```

The loadPlugins() function takes the name of the configuration file as input, loads each library into memory, and allocates an instance of each library's Plugin class. The UserInterface reference is solely for error reporting. When the main() function is ready to inject the plugins' commands, the getPlugins() function is called to return a collection of loaded Plugins. Of course, the loadPlugins() and getPlugins() functions could be combined, but I prefer a design that enables the programmer to retain finer-tuned control over the timing of plugin loading vs. plugin usage. My implementation of the PluginLoader makes use of a few clever techniques for using RAII to manage the automatic deallocation of the plugins. As the implementation here is orthogonal to the design, the interested reader is referred to the PluginLoader.m.cpp source file for details.

7.5.2 Injecting Functionality

Having decided that plugins should be loaded automatically from a configuration file, the most logical placement for plugin loading is somewhere in the main() function (or a helper function called by main()). Essentially, this loadPlugins() function simply puts together all of the pieces we have previously discussed: loading plugin libraries, loading plugins, extracting commands and buttons from the plugin descriptors, and injecting these commands and buttons into pdCalc. Of course, a proper implementation will also perform error checking on the plugins. For example, error checking might include checking the plugin API version, ensuring the commands have not already been registered, and ensuring the GUI buttons correspond to commands in the command factory. The following code snippet is a skeleton of a function for loading plugins. Its inputs are a UserInterface reference for reporting errors and a PluginLoader reference.

```
void setupPlugins(UserInterface& ui, PluginLoader& loader)
{
  loader.loadPlugins(ui, "plugins.pdp");
  auto plugins = loader.getPlugins();

  for(auto p : plugins)
  {
    auto apiVersion = p->apiVersion();
    // verify plugin API at correct level

    // inject plugin commands into CommandFactory - recall
```

```
// the cloned command will auto release in the plugin
auto descriptor = p->getPluginDescriptor();
for( auto i : views::iota(0, descriptor.nCommands) )
{
  registerCommand(ui, descriptor.commandNames[i],
    MakeCommandPtr(descriptor.commands[i]->clone()) );
}

// if gui, setup buttons
auto mw = dynamic_cast<MainWindow*>(&ui);
if(mw)
{
  auto buttonDescriptor = p->getPluginButtonDescriptor();
  if(buttonDescriptor)
  {
    for( auto i : views::iota(0, buttonDescriptor->nButtons) )
    {
      auto b = *buttonDescriptor;
      // check validity of button commands
      mw->addCommandButton(b.dispPrimaryCmd[i], b.primaryCmd[i],
        b.dispShftCmd[i], b.shftCmd[i]);
    }
  }
}

return;
}
```

After a long chapter describing how to implement C++ plugins, the denouement is somewhat anticlimactic, as most of the mechanics are handled at deeper layers of the abstraction. Of course, this "boringness," as we've learned in this book, is only achieved through meticulous design. Simplicity is always more difficult to achieve than the code itself indicates. Had any complications leaked through at this high-level abstraction, it would surely have implied an inferior design.

7.6 A Concrete Plugin

After a long discussion explaining how to incorporate native C++ plugins into pdCalc, we've finally reached the point where we can implement a concrete plugin. Based on our requirements from Chapter 1, we need to write a plugin that adds commands for the natural logarithm, its inverse exponentiation algorithm, and the hyperbolic trigonometric functions. Of course, you should feel free to add plugins encompassing any functionality you might like. For example, two interesting plugins might be a probability plugin and a statistics plugin. The probability plugin could compute permutations, combinations, factorials, and random numbers, while the statistics plugin could compute mean, median, mode, and standard deviation. For now, however, we'll simply consider the design and implementation of our hyperbolic, natural log plugin.

7.6.1 Plugin Interface

The implementation of the HyperbolicLnPlugin is actually quite straightforward. We'll begin with the interface for the class and then, uncharacteristically, examine a few implementation details. The code chosen for further examination highlights particular details relevant to native C++ plugins.

The interface for HyperbolicLnPlugin is given by the class definition specializing the Plugin class and the required plugin allocation and deallocation functions:

```
class HyperbolicLnPlugin : public pdCalc::Plugin
{
public:
  HyperbolicLnPlugin();
  ~HyperbolicLnPlugin();

private:
  const PluginDescriptor& getPluginDescriptor() const override;
  const PluginButtonDescriptor* getPluginButtonDescriptor()
    const override;
  pdCalc::Plugin::ApiVersion apiVersion() const;

};

extern "C" void* AllocPlugin();
extern "C" void DeallocPlugin(void*);
```

As expected, the class implements the three pure virtual functions in the Plugin class. The AllocPlugin() and DeallocPlugin() functions have their obvious implementations. The AllocPlugin() simply returns a new HyperbolicLnPlugin instance, while the DeallocPlugin() function casts its void* argument to a Plugin* and subsequently calls delete on this pointer. Note that plugins are, by definition, not part of the main program and should therefore not be part of the pdCalc namespace. Hence, the explicit namespace qualification in a few locations.

The responsibility of the HyperbolicLnPlugin class is simply to serve plugin descriptors on demand and manage the lifetime of the objects needed by the descriptors. The PluginDescriptor provides command names and the corresponding Commands implemented by the plugin. These Commands are described in Section 7.6.3. The PluginButtonDescriptor for the plugin simply lists the names of the Commands as defined by the PluginDescriptor and the corresponding labels to appear on the GUI buttons. Because the commands in the HyperbolicLnPlugin all have natural inverses, we simply label each button with a forward command and attach the secondary (shifted) command to the inverse. I used the obvious labels for the commands provided by the plugin: sinh, asinh, cosh, acosh, tanh, atanh, ln, and exp. Whether you choose ln for the primary and exp as the secondary or vice versa is simply a matter of preference.

For reasons already discussed, plugin descriptors transfer content without using STL containers. Where we would normally prefer to use vectors and unique_ptrs in the interface to manage resources, we are forced instead to use raw arrays. Of course, the encapsulation provided by our class enables us to use whatever memory management scheme we desire in the implementation. For the HyperbolicLnPlugin, I chose a complicated scheme of automatic memory management using strings, unique_ptrs, and vectors. The advantage of using an RAII memory management scheme is that we can be assured that the plugin will not leak memory in the presence of exceptions (namely, an out of memory exception thrown during construction). Realistically, I would not expect the calculator to be executed in a low-memory environment, and even if it were, it's unclear leaking memory during plugin allocation would matter much since the user's likely next action in this situation would be to reboot their computer. Therefore, in retrospect, a simpler memory management scheme with naked news in the constructor and deletes in the destructor would probably have been more pragmatic.

7.6.2 Source Code Dependency Inversion

Surprisingly, the preceding class declaration for `HyperbolicLnPlugin` is indeed the complete interface to the plugin. I say surprisingly because, at first glance, one might be surprised that the plugin's interface bears no relationship to the functionality the plugin provides. Of course, this situation is exactly as it should be. The calculator functionality that the plugin provides is indeed merely an implementation detail and can be contained entirely within the plugin's implementation file.

The preceding subtlety, namely, that pdCalc knows only the interface to a plugin and nothing about the functionality itself, should not be overlooked. As a matter of fact, this source code dependency inversion is the entire point of plugin design. What exactly is source code dependency inversion and why is it important? To answer this question, we must first embark on a short history lesson.

Traditionally (think 1970s Fortran), code was extended by simply writing new functions and subroutines. The primary design problem with this approach was that requiring the main program to call new functions bound the main program to the concrete interface of any extension. Thus, the main program became dependent on interface changes defined by the whims of extension authors. That is, every new extension defined a new interface to which the main program had to conform. This setup was extremely brittle because the main program required constant modification to keep pace with the changes to its extensions' interfaces. Since each new extension required unique modifications to the main program's source code, the complexity of the main program's code for handling extensions grew linearly with the number of extensions. If that wasn't bad enough, adding new functionality always required recompiling and relinking the main program. In concrete terms, imagine a design for pdCalc that would require modifying, recompiling, and relinking pdCalc's source code every time a new plugin command was added.

The preceding problem can be solved without object-oriented programming via function pointers and callbacks, albeit in a somewhat inelegant and cumbersome fashion. However, with the rise of object-oriented programming, specifically, inheritance and polymorphism, the solution to the dependency problem was solved in a type-safe manner with language support. These techniques enabled the popularization of source code dependency inversion. Specifically, source code dependency inversion states that the main program defines an interface (e.g., the plugin interface we've studied in this chapter) to which all extensions must conform. Under this strategy, the extensions become subservient to the main program's interface rather than the reverse. Hence, the main program can be extended via plugins without modifying, recompiling, or relinking the main program's source code. More importantly, however, the interface for extensibility is dictated by the application rather than its plugins. In concrete terms, pdCalc provides the Plugin interface class to define the addition of new functionality, but pdCalc is never aware of the implementation details of its extensions. A plugin that does not conform to pdCalc's interface is simply unable to inject new Commands.

7.6.3 Implementing HyperbolicLnPlugin's Functionality

By this stage in the game, we know that the HyperbolicLnPlugin will provide its functionality by implementing a command class for each operation. After implementing a few of these classes, one would quickly notice that all of the commands in the plugin are unary commands. Unfortunately, based on our third rule of C++ plugins (assume incompatible alignment), we cannot inherit from the UnaryCommand class and instead must inherit from the PluginCommand class. Note that our alignment assumption even precludes using the UnaryCommand class via multiple inheritance, and we must reimplement the unary command functionality in our HyperbolicLnPluginCommand base class. While this does feel a bit duplicative, the rules for C++ plugins leave us with no alternatives (although we could provide source code for a UnaryPluginCommand and a UnaryBinaryCommand, but these would have to be separately compiled with each plugin).

We, therefore, finally arrive at the interface class from which all commands within the HyperbolicLnPlugin derive:

```
class HyperbolicLnPluginCommand : public pdCalc::PluginCommand
{
public:
  HyperbolicLnPluginCommand() = default; // ???? see sidebar
  explicit HyperbolicLnPluginCommand(const HyperbolicLnPluginCommand&
    rhs);
  virtual ~HyperbolicLnPluginCommand() = default;
  void deallocate() override;

protected:
  const char* checkPluginPreconditions() const noexcept override;
```

```
private:
  void executeImpl() noexcept override;
  void undoImpl() noexcept override;
  HyperbolicLnPluginCommand* clonePluginImpl() const noexcept override;

  virtual HyperbolicLnPluginCommand* doClone() const = 0;
  virtual double unaryOperation(double top) const = 0;

  double top_;
};
```

As with the UnaryCommand class, the HyperbolicLnPluginCommand class implements the pure virtual executeImpl() and undoImpl() commands, delegating the command operation to the pure virtual unaryOperation() function. Additionally, the HyperbolicLnPluginCommand class implements the checkPluginPreconditions() function to ensure at least one number is on the stack before the command is called. The function is protected so that a subclass can directly override the precondition function if it must implement any additional preconditions yet still call the base class's checkPluginPreconditions() to make the unary command precondition check.

The deallocate() and clonePluginImpl() functions have obvious implementations but play critical roles in the plugin. The deallocate() function is simply implemented as

```
void HyperbolicLnPluginCommand::deallocate()
{
  delete this;
}
```

Recall that the point of the deallocate() function is to force memory deallocation of the plugin's commands in the plugin's compilation unit. It is called via the CommandDeleter() function when the unique_ptr holding a command is destroyed.

The clonePluginImpl() function is given by

```
HyperbolicLnPluginCommand*
HyperbolicLnPluginCommand::clonePluginImpl() const noexcept
{
  HyperbolicLnPluginCommand* p;
  try
```

```
  {
    p = doClone();
  }
  catch(...)
  {
    return nullptr;
  }

  return p;
}
```

The sole purpose of this function is to adapt the cloning of a plugin command to ensure that exceptions do not cross the memory boundary between the plugin and the main application.

All that remains to complete the `HyperbolicLnPlugin` is to subclass `HyperbolicLnPluginCommand` for each mathematical operation required in the plugin and implement the few remaining pure virtual functions (`unaryOperation()`, `doClone()`, and `helpMessageImpl()`). Once we have gotten to this point, the implementation of these functions is no different than the implementation of the unary functions of Chapter 4. The interested reader is referred to the source code in `HyperbolicLnPlugin.cpp` for details.

MODERN C++ DESIGN NOTE: DEFAULTING SPECIAL FUNCTIONS

Some member functions are special in that if you don't provide an implementation, the compiler is able to provide one for you. The only member functions for which this is permitted are the default constructor, the copy constructor, the move constructor, the default destructor, the copy assignment, the move assignment, and the comparison operations. Why do we need the = `default` syntax when the compiler can provide these operations automatically? Really, there are two primary reasons. First, sometimes default implementation is suppressed. For example, the default constructor is only automatically generated if no other constructor is provided. Therefore, if you provide an alternative constructor but still want the compiler to automatically generate a default constructor for you, you must manually instruct it to do so. The second reason the `default` keyword is useful is for clarity. Formerly, in instances where the compiler would implement a special member function for you, you could either allow it to do so silently (possibly confusing novices) or implement it manually, unnecessarily writing the same code the compiler could have written for you. The new syntax affords you the ability to be explicit by declaring the existence of a special function but also efficient by "implementing" it via = `default`.

7.7 Next Steps

After a rather long discussion about C++ plugins and with the implementation of the hyperbolic trigonometric and natural logarithm plugin, we have completed the requirements for pdCalc set forth in Chapter 1. The calculator, as originally described, is complete, and we're ready to release! However, as experienced software developers, we know that any "finished" product is just a temporary milestone before the customer requests new features. The next chapter handles this exact situation, where we'll modify our design to incorporate unplanned extensions.

New Requirements

It's a beautiful Monday morning, and you just stepped into work after a relaxing weekend. After all, you just finished pdCalc on Friday, and now you are ready to ship. Before you can sit down and have your morning cup of coffee, your project manager steps into your office and says, "We're not done. The client requested some new features."

The preceding scenario is all too common in software development. While new features probably won't be requested on the go-live date, new features will almost inevitably be requested well after you have completed large parts of both your design and your implementation. Therefore, one should develop as defensively as practical to anticipate extensibility. I say as defensively as practical rather than as defensively as possible because overly abstract code can be as much of a detriment to development as overly concrete code. Often, it is easier to simply rewrite an inflexible code if the need arises than it is to maintain a highly flexible one for no reason. In practice, we seek to strike a balance for code to be both simple and maintainable yet somewhat extensible.

In this chapter, we'll explore modifying our code to implement features beyond the design of the original requirements. The discussion of the new features introduced in this chapter ranges from full design and implementation to design only to suggestions merely for self-exploration. Let's begin with two extensions that we'll take from requirements all the way through implementation.

8.1 Fully Designed New Features

In this section, we'll examine two new features: batch operation of the calculator and execution of stored procedures. We'll begin with batch operation.

© Adam Singer 2022
A. B. Singer, *Practical C++ Design*, https://doi.org/10.1007/978-1-4842-7407-1_8

8.1.1 Batch Operation

For those few unfamiliar with the term, let's define batch operation. Batch operation of any program is simply the execution of the program, from beginning to end, without interaction from the user once the program is launched. Most desktop programs do not run in batch mode. However, batch operation is still very important in many branches of programming, such as scientific computing. Perhaps of greater interest, for those of you employed by large corporations, your payroll is probably run by a program operating in batch mode.

Let's be honest. Batch operation for pdCalc, other than maybe for testing, is not a very useful extension. I've included it mainly because it demonstrates how trivially a well-designed CLI can be extended to add a batch mode.

Recall from Chapter 5 that pdCalc's CLI has the following public interface:

```
class Cli : public UserInterface
{
public:
  Cli(istream& in, ostream& out);
  ~Cli();

  void execute(bool suppressStartupMessage = false, bool echo = false);
};
```

To use the CLI, the class is constructed with cin and cout as the arguments, and execute() is called with empty arguments:

```
Cli cli{cin, cout};
// setup other parts of the calculator
cli.execute();
```

How do we modify the Cli class to enable batch operation? Amazingly, we do not need to modify the class's code at all! By design, the CLI is essentially a parser that simply takes space-separated character input from an input stream, processes the data through the calculator, and generates character output to an output stream. Because we had the forethought not to hard-code these input and output streams as cin and cout, we can convert the CLI to a batch processor by making the input and output streams to be file streams as follows:

```
ifstream fin{inputFile};
ofstream fout{outputFile};
Cli cli{fin, fout};
// setup other parts of the calculator
cli.execute(true, true);
```

where `inputFile` and `outputFile` are file names that could be acquired through command line arguments to pdCalc. Recall that the arguments to the `execute()` function simply suppress the startup banner and echo commands to the output.

Yes, that really is it (but see `main.cpp` for a few implementation tricks). Our CLI was built originally so that it could be converted to a batch processor simply by changing its constructor arguments. You could, of course, argue that I, as the author, intentionally designed the `Cli` class this way because I knew the calculator would be extended in this manner. The reality is, however, that I simply construct all of my CLI interfaces with stream inputs rather than hard-coded inputs because this design makes the CLI more flexible with nearly no additional cognitive burden.

Before leaving this section, I'll quickly note that the reality is that pdCalc's CLI, with an assist from the operating system, already had a batch mode. By redirecting input and output at the command line, we can achieve the same results:

```
my_prompt> cat inputFile | pdCalc --cli > outputFile
```

For Windows, simply replace the Linux `cat` command with the Windows `type` command.

8.1.2 Stored Procedures

Adding a batch mode to pdCalc was, admittedly, a somewhat contrived example. The added functionality was not terribly useful, and the code changes were trivial. In this section, we'll examine a more interesting feature extension, stored procedures.

What is a stored procedure? In pdCalc, a stored procedure is a stored, repeatable sequence of operations that operate on the current stack. Stored procedures provide a technique to expand the calculator's functionality by creating user-defined functions from existing calculator primitives. You can think of executing a stored procedure as being analogous to running a very simple program for the calculator. The easiest way to understand the concept is to consider an example.

Suppose you need to frequently calculate the hypotenuse of a triangle. For the right triangle depicted in Figure 8-1, we can compute the length of the hypotenuse, *c*, using the Pythagorean formula: $c = \sqrt{a^2 + b^2}$.

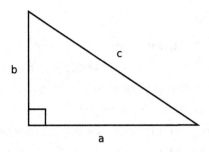

Figure 8-1. *A right triangle*

Suppose we had a triangle with sides *a* = 4, *b* = 3, and these values were entered onto pdCalc's stack. In the CLI, you would see the following:

```
Top 2 elements of stack (size = 2):
2:      3
1:      4
```

In order to compute *c* for this triangle, we would implement the following sequence of instructions: dup * swap dup * + 2 root. After hitting enter, the final result would be

```
Top element of stack (size = 1):
1:      5
```

If the commands were entered one at a time, we would see the intermediate results stack every time we pressed enter. Had we entered all of the commands on a single line and then pressed enter, pdCalc would display each intermediate stack before showing the final result. Note, of course, that this command sequence is not unique. The same result could have been achieved using, for example, the command sequence 2 pow swap 2 pow + 2 root.

If you are anything like me, if you had to compute hypotenuses with pdCalc repeatedly, you would probably want to automate the operation after the first manual computation. That is precisely what stored procedures allow. Not only does automation save time, but it is also less error prone since stored procedures that encapsulate many consecutive commands can be written, tested, and subsequently reused. Provided the operation can be assembled from pdCalc primitives (including plugin functions), stored procedures enable extending the calculator's functionality to compute simple formulas without needing to write any C++ code. Now we just need to design and implement this new feature.

The User Interface

pdCalc has both a GUI and a CLI, so adding any user facing feature will require some modification to both user interface components. For stored procedures, the modifications to the user interfaces are remarkably minor. First, a stored procedure is simply a text file containing an ordered sequence of pdCalc instructions. Therefore, a user can create a stored procedure using any plain text editor. Thus, unless you want to provide a stored procedure text editor with syntax highlighting, the user interface for stored procedures reduces to enabling their execution from the CLI and the GUI.

Let's first address incorporating stored procedures in the CLI. As previously stated, stored procedures are simply text files in the file system. Recall that the CLI works by tokenizing space-separated input and then passing each token individually to the command dispatcher by raising an event. Therefore, a trivial method for accessing a stored procedure is simply to pass the name of the stored procedure file to the CLI. This file name will then be tokenized like any other command or number and passed to the command dispatcher for processing. To ensure that the file name is interpreted by the command dispatcher as a stored procedure rather than a command, we simply prepend the symbol `proc:` to the file name and change the command dispatcher's parser. For example, for a stored procedure named `hypotenuse.psp`, we would issue the command `proc:hypotenuse.psp` to the CLI. I adopted the file extension `psp` as a shorthand for pdCalc stored procedure. Naturally, the file itself is an ordinary ASCII text file containing a sequence of commands for calculating the hypotenuse of a right triangle, and you can use the `txt` extension if you prefer.

Recall that the GUI is designed to pass commands to the command dispatcher identically to the CLI. Therefore, to use a stored procedure, we add a button that opens a dialog to navigate the file system to find stored procedures. Once a stored procedure is selected, we prepend `proc:` to the file name and raise a `CommandEntered` event. Obviously, you can make your stored procedure selection dialog as fancy as you would like. I opted for a simplistic design that permits typing the name of the file into an editable combo box. For ease of use, the combo box is prepopulated with any files in the current directory with a `.psp` extension.

Changes to the Command Dispatcher Module

The following is an abbreviated listing of CommandInterpreter's executeCommand()
function including the logic necessary for parsing stored procedures. The omitted
portions of the code appear in Section 4.5.2.

```
void CommandInterpreter::CommandInterpreterImpl::executeCommand(const
string& command)
{
  string_view sv{command};
  // handle numbers, undo, redo, help in nested if
  // ...
  else if( command.size() > 6 && sv.starts_with("proc:") )
  {
    string filename{sv.substr(5, command.size() - 5)};
    handleCommand( MakeCommandPtr<StoredProcedure>(ui_, filename) );
  }
  // else statement to handle Commands from CommandFactory
  // ...

  return;
}
```

From the preceding code listing, we see that the implementation simply peels off the
proc: from the string command argument to create the stored procedure file name,
creates a new StoredProcedure class, and executes this class. For now, we'll assume
that making the StoredProcedure class a subclass of the Command class is the optimal
design. We'll discuss why this strategy is preferred and examine its implementation in
the following sections. However, before we get there, let's discuss this new overload of
the MakeCommandPtr() function.

In Section 7.2.1, we first saw a version of MakeCommandPtr given by the following
implementation:

```
inline void CommandDeleter(Command* p)
{
  if(p) p->deallocate();
  return;
}
```

```
using CommandPtr = std::unique_ptr<Command, decltype(&CommandDeleter)>;

inline auto MakeCommandPtr(Command* p)
{
  return CommandPtr{p, &CommandDeleter};
}
```

The preceding function is a helper function used to create CommandPtrs from raw Command pointers. This form of the function is used to create a CommandPtr from the cloning of an existing Command (e.g., as in CommandFactory::allocateCommand()):

```
auto p = MakeCommandPtr( command->clone() );
```

Semantically, however, in CommandInterpreterImpl::executeCommand(), we see a completely different usage, which is to construct a named instance of a class derived from Command. Certainly, we can meet this use case with the existing MakeCommandPtr prototype. For example, we could create a StoredProcedure as follows:

```
auto c = MakeCommandPtr(new StoredProcedure{ui, filename});
```

However, whenever possible, we would prefer not to pollute high-level code with naked news. We therefore seek to implement an overloaded helper function that can perform this construction for us. Its implementation is given by the following:

Listing 8-1. Generic perfect forwarding constructor

```
template<typename T, typename... Args>
auto MakeCommandPtr(Args&&... args)
requires std::derived_from<T, Command>
{
  return CommandPtr{new T{std::forward<Args>(args)...}, &CommandDeleter};
}
```

Prior to C++11, no simple and efficient technique existed for constructing generic types with variable numbers of constructor arguments, as is necessary to create any one of the possible classes derived from the Command class, each having different constructor arguments. Modern C++, however, provides an elegant solution to this problem using variadic templates and perfect forwarding. This construct is the subject of the following sidebar.

MODERN C++ DESIGN NOTE: VARIADIC TEMPLATES AND PERFECT FORWARDING

Variadic templates and perfect forwarding each solve different problems in C++. Variadic templates enable type-safe generic function calls with unknown numbers of typed arguments. Perfect forwarding enables correct type forwarding of arguments to underlying functions inside of template functions. The mechanics of each of these techniques can be studied in your favorite C++11 reference text (e.g., [30]). In this sidebar, we'll examine a type-safe, generic design technique for constructing concrete objects that require different numbers of constructor arguments. This technique is enabled by the combination of variadic templates and perfect forwarding. Due to a lack of naming creativity, I named this pattern the generic perfect forwarding constructor (GPFC). Let's begin by presenting the underlying problem that GPFC solves.

Let's consider every author's favorite overly simplified object-oriented programming example, the shapes hierarchy:

```cpp
class Shape
{
public:
  virtual double area() const = 0;
};

class Circle : public Shape
{
public:
  Circle(double r) : r_{r} {}
  double area() const override { return 3.14159 * r_ * r_; }

private:
  double r_;
};

class Rectangle : public Shape
{
public:
  Rectangle(double l, double w) : l_{l}, w_{w} {}
  double area() const override { return l_ * w_; }
```

```
private:
  double l_, w_;
};
```

In C++, substitutability, implemented as virtual dispatch, solves the problem of needing to call a derived type's specific implementation via a base class pointer using an interface guaranteed by the base class. In the shapes example, substitutability implies the ability to compute the area as follows:

```
double area(const Shape& s)
{
  return s.area();
}
```

for any class derived from Shape. The exact interface for the virtual function is fully prescribed, including the number and type of any function arguments (even in the vacuous case as in the area() function in this example). The problem, however, is that object construction can never be "virtualized" in this manner, and even if it could, it wouldn't work since the information necessary to construct an object (its arguments) is very frequently different from one derived class to the next.

Enter the generic perfect forwarding constructor pattern. In this pattern, we use variadic templates to provide a type-safe interface that can take any number of constructor arguments with different types. The first template argument is always the type we want to construct. Then, perfect forwarding is used to guarantee the arguments are passed to the constructor with the correct types. Precisely why perfect forwarding is necessary in this situation derives from how types are deduced in templates and is beyond the scope of this discussion (see [24] for details). For our shapes example, applying the GPFC pattern results in the following implementation:

```
template<typename T, typename... Args>
auto MakeShape(Args&&... args)
{
  return make_unique<T>(forward<Args>(args)...);
}
```

The following code illustrates how the MakeShape() function can be used to create different types with different numbers of constructor arguments:

```
auto c = MakeShape<Circle>(4.0);
auto r = MakeShape<Rectangle>(3.0, 5.0);
```

Note that the GPFC pattern also works for creating classes not related to each other in an inheritance hierarchy. The GPFC pattern, in fact, is used by the make_unique() function in the standard library for making unique_ptrs in an efficient, generic manner without requiring a naked new. While they are, strictly speaking, distinct, I like to think of the GPFC pattern as the generic analogue of the factory method.

The astute reader will have noticed the peculiar requires clause following the function declaration in Listing 8-1. New to C++20, the requires clause introduces a constraint that specifies a compile time requirement on a template parameter. In the case of Listing 8-1, we are requiring that the type T must be derived from Command. Constraints are a component of concepts, a new language feature of C++20. Concepts are briefly addressed in the following sidebar.

MODERN C++ DESIGN NOTE: CONCEPTS

Concepts, a very prominent new feature of C++20, are used for adding requirements to template types. Concepts do not feature prominently in this book because pdCalc does not incorporate many templates in its implementation. However, because of the significance of concepts in the new standard, I've chosen to mention them briefly in a sidebar to illustrate why you might use them.

Templates have existed in the C++ language for decades, and during their entire existence, programmers have all had the same complaint: template errors result in long, indecipherable compiler error messages. Why were poor error messages uniform across compilers? The answer is essentially because type errors are generally found deep in the call stack and not at the first line where the type is used. At the point where the error occurs, too much context is lost to give a succinct message.

Concepts fix the preceding problem by constraining the acceptable template type at the point of use. These requirements can either be added as a constraint via a requires clause or by using a requires clause (or conjunctions thereof) to build a restricted template type called a concept. If you choose to use concepts in your template code (and you probably should), don't start from scratch. The C++20 concepts library predefines many concepts, such as the `derived_from` concept used in Listing 8-1.

Let's reexamine the code in Listing 8-1 from the context of concepts and the `requires` clause. In the first edition of this book, because concepts were not yet a language feature, the exact same function was presented unconstrained. That is, Listing 8-1 was identical except the `requires` clause was not present. For both versions of the source code, when a class derived from `Command` is passed to `MakeCommandPtr()`, the same compiled code is generated. The real benefit of concepts is when errors are made.

Consider a default constructible dummy class A that does not derive from `Command`, and further consider the following erroneous function call:

```
auto p = MakeCommandPtr<A>();
```

Using gcc, calling the constrained version of `MakeCommandPtr()` results in the following "friendly" error:

```
note: 'pdCalc::Command' is not a base of 'A'
```

I wrote friendly in quotes because gcc gives a huge template expansion error but at least contains the useful comment that `Command` is not a base of A as a note at the end of the error, which is precisely why this code does not compile. Now let's contrast that with the same call but to the unconstrained version of `MakeCommandPtr()`. This time, the final error appearing is

```
note: candidate expects 0 arguments, 2 provided
return CommandPtr{new T{std::forward<Args>(args)...}, &CommandDeleter};
```

which really does not explain why this function call failed. Before the introduction of concepts to the language, experienced programmers simply got used to bad template error messages. My personal strategy for diagnosing template errors was to use the compiler to find the offending line of source code, ignore all messages the compiler produced, and just think hard about why that line caused an error. Such techniques are impossible for novices; concepts are a big improvement.

Before concluding this sidebar, it is worth noting that instead of using the `requires` clause in Listing 8-1, we could have created a concept and constrained the template parameter to `MakeCommandPtr()` instead. This strategy would have resulted in the following alternative code:

```
template<typename T>
concept PdCalcCommand = std::derived_from<T, Command>;

template<PdCalcCommand T, typename... Args>
auto MakeCommandPtr(Args&&... args)
{
  return CommandPtr{new T{std::forward<Args>(args)...}, &CommandDeleter};
}
```

I chose to use the `requires` clause directly instead of creating a concept because the concept was not used anywhere else in the code. That is, the code did not benefit conceptually from a `PdCalcCommand`; it only needed a single constraint on `MakeCommandPtr`. The use of the `requires` clause therefore seemed simpler, deferring once again to design by Occam's razor.

Designing the StoredProcedure Class

We now return to the thorny problem of designing the `StoredProcedure` class. The first question we ask is, do we need a class at all? We already have a design for parsing individual commands, executing them, and placing them on an undo/redo stack. Maybe the correct answer is to treat a stored procedure in a manner similar to the treatment of batch input. That is, during an interactive session (either GUI or CLI), handle stored procedures by reading the stored procedure file, parsing it, and executing the commands in batch (as we would a long line with multiple commands in the CLI) without introducing a new `StoredProcedure` class.

The aforementioned design can be dismissed almost immediately after considering the following very simple example. Suppose you implemented a stored procedure for computing the area of a triangle. The stored procedure's input would be the base and height of the triangle on the stack. `triangleArea.psp` is given by the following:

```
*

0.5
*
```

If we did not have a StoredProcedure class, then each of the commands in triangleArea.psp would be executed and entered, in order, on the undo/redo stack. For the values 4 and 5 on the I/O stack, forward execution of the stored procedure would yield the correct result of 10, and an undo stack as depicted in Figure 8-2. Based on this undo stack, if the user tried to undo, rather than undoing the triangle area stored procedure, the user would undo only the top operation on the stack, the final multiply. The I/O stack would read

Figure 8-2. *The undo stack without a StoredProcedure class*

4
5
0.5

(and the undo stack would have a * between the 5 and 0.5) instead of

4
5

To fully undo a stored procedure, the user needs to press undo n times, where n is equal to the number of commands in the stored procedure. The same deficiency is present for the redo operation. In my opinion, the expected behavior for undoing a stored procedure should be to undo the entire procedure and leave the I/O stack in its state prior to executing the stored procedure. Hence, the design for handling stored procedures not employing a StoredProcedure class fails to implement undo and redo properly and must therefore be discarded.

The Composite Pattern

Essentially, in order to solve the undo/redo problem with stored procedures, we need a special command that encapsulates multiple commands but behaves as a single command. Fortunately, the composite pattern solves this dilemma. According to Gamma et al. [11], the composite pattern "lets clients treat individual objects and compositions of objects uniformly." Typically, the composite pattern refers to treed data structures. I prefer a looser definition where the pattern may be applied to any data structure admitting uniform treatment of composite objects.

Figure 8-3 illustrates the composite pattern in its general form. The Component class is an abstract class that requires some action to be performed. This action can be performed individually by a Leaf node or by a collection of Components known as a Composite. Clients interact with objects in the component hierarchy polymorphically through the Component interface. Both Leaf nodes and Composite nodes handle doSomething() requests indistinguishably from the client's point of view. Usually, Composites implement doSomething() by simply calling the doSomething() command for Components (either Leafs or nested Composites) it holds.

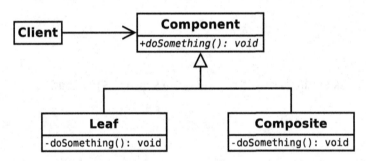

Figure 8-3. *General form of the composite pattern*

In our particular concrete case, the Command class takes the role of the Component, concrete commands such as Add or Sine take the role of Leaf nodes, and the StoredProcedure class is the composite. The doSomething() command is replaced by the executeImpl() and undoImpl() pair of pure virtual functions. I suspect combining the command and composite patterns in this fashion is rather common.

Previously, we learned that in order to properly implement the undo/redo strategy for stored procedures, a class design was necessary. Application of the composite pattern, as described previously, motivates subclassing the StoredProcedure class from the Command class. Let's now design a StoredProcedure class and examine its implementation as a concrete application of the composite pattern.

A First Attempt

A common approach to implementing the composite pattern is via recursion. The Composite class holds a collection of Components, often either via a simple vector or perhaps something more complex such as nodes in a binary tree. The Composite's doSomething() function simply iterates over this collection calling doSomething() for each Component in the collection. The Leaf nodes' doSomething() functions actually *do something* and terminate the recursion. Although not required, the doSomething() function in the Component class is often pure virtual.

Let's consider the preceding approach for implementing the composite pattern for StoredProcedures in pdCalc. We have already established that pdCalc's Command class is the Component and that the concrete command classes, such as Add, are the Leaf classes. Therefore, we need only to consider the implementation of the StoredProcedure class itself. Note that since the current implementation of the Component and Leaf classes can be used as is, the composite pattern can be trivially applied to extend the functionality of an existing code base.

Consider the following skeletal design for the StoredProcedure class:

```
class StoredProcedure : public Command
{
private:
  void executeImpl() noexcept override;
  void undoImpl() noexcept override;

  vector<unique_ptr<CommandPtr>> components_;
};
```

The executeImpl() command would be implemented as follows:

```
void StoredProcedure::executeImpl()
{
  for(auto& i : components_)
    i->execute();

  return;
}
```

undoImpl() would be implemented analogously but with a reverse iteration over the component_ collection.

Does the preceding design solve the undo/redo problem previously encountered when entering stored procedure commands directly onto the undo/redo stack without a StoredProcedure class? Consider the undo stack shown in Figure 8-4 for the triangleArea.psp example that we previously examined. The stored procedure, shown as SP in the figure, appears as a single object in the undo stack rather than as individual objects representing its constituent commands. Hence, when a user issues an undo command, the CommandManager will undo the stored procedure as a single command by calling the stored procedure's undoImpl() function. This stored procedure's undoImpl() function, in turn, undoes the individual commands via iteration over its container of Commands. This behavior is precisely what was desired, and this application of the composite pattern indeed solves the problem at hand.

Figure 8-4. *The undo stack using a StoredProcedure class*

To complete the implementation of the StoredProcedure class, we need to parse the stored procedure file's string commands (with error checking) and use them to populate the StoredProcedure's components_ vector. This operation could be written in the StoredProcedure's constructor, and the implementation would be both valid and complete. We would now have a StoredProcedure class that could transform string commands into Commands, store them in a container, and be able to execute and undo these stored Commands on demand. In other words, we would have essentially rewritten the CommandInterpreter! Instead, let's consider an alternative design that implements the StoredProcedure class by reusing the CommandInterpreter class.

A Final Design for the **StoredProcedure** Class

The goal in this design is to reuse the CommandInterpreter class as is. Relaxing this constraint and modifying the CommandInterpreter's code can clean up the implementation slightly, but the essence of the design is the same either way. Consider the following modified skeletal design of the StoredProcedure class:

```
class StoredProcedure : public Command
{
private:
  void executeImpl() noexcept override;
  void undoImpl() noexcept override;

  std::unique_ptr<Tokenizer> tokenizer_;
  std::unique_ptr<CommandInterpreter> ci_;
  bool first_ = true;
};
```

The present design is almost identical to our previous design except the components_ vector has been replaced by a CommandInterpreter and the need for a tokenizer has been made explicit. Good thing we wrote our tokenizer to be reusable in Chapter 5!

We are now prepared to see the complete implementations of executeImpl() and undoImpl(). Note that while the following implementation does not use the canonical version of the pattern seen previously, this implementation of the StoredProcedure class is still simply an application of the composite pattern. First, let's examine executeImpl():

```
void StoredProcedure::executeImpl() noexcept
{
  if(first_)
  {
    ranges::for_each( *tokenizer_,
      [this](auto c){ci_->commandEntered(c);} );
    first_ = false;
  }
```

```
  else
  {
    for(auto i = 0u; i < tokenizer_->nTokens(); ++i)
      ci_->commandEntered("redo");
  }

  return;
}
```

The first time that executeImpl() is called, the tokens must be extracted from
the tokenizer and executed by the StoredProcedure's own CommandInterpreter.
Subsequent calls to executeImpl() merely request the StoredProcedure's
CommandInterpreter to redo the forward execution of each of the StoredProcedure's
commands. Remember, StoredProcedure's executeImpl() function will itself
be called by pdCalc's CommandInterpreter; hence, our design calls for nested
CommandInterpreter's. Figure 8-5 shows this design for the triangle area stored
procedure example, where CI represents the CommandInterpreter.

Figure 8-5. *The undo stack using nested* CommandInterpreters

The implementation of StoredProcedure's undoImpl() is trivial:

```
void StoredProcedure::undoImpl() noexcept
{
  for(auto i = 0u; i < tokenizer_->nTokens(); ++i)
    ci_->commandEntered("undo");

  return;
}
```

Undo is implemented by requesting the underlying `CommandInterpreter` to undo the number of commands in the stored procedure.

Before concluding our discussion of the final `StoredProcedure` class, we should consider tokenization of the commands within the `StoredProcedure` class. The tokenization process for a `StoredProcedure` involves two steps. The stored procedure file must be opened and read followed by the actual tokenization of the text stream. This process needs to be performed only once per `StoredProcedure` instantiation, at initialization. Therefore, the natural placement for tokenization is in the `StoredProcedure`'s constructor. However, placement of tokenization in the `StoredProcedure`'s constructor creates an inconsistency with pdCalc's error handling procedure for commands. In particular, pdCalc assumes that commands can be constructed, but not necessarily executed, without failure. If a command cannot be executed, the expectation is that this error is handled by checking a command's preconditions. Can tokenization fail? Certainly. For example, tokenization would fail if the stored procedure file could not be opened. Therefore, in order to maintain consistency in error handling, we implement tokenization in `StoredProcedure`'s `checkPreconditionsImpl()` function, which will be called when pdCalc's `CommandInterpreter` first attempts to execute the stored procedure. Since tokenization needs to be performed once, we only perform the operation on the first execution of the `checkPreconditionsImpl()` function. The complete implementation can be found in the `StoredProcedure.cpp` file.

8.2 Designs Toward a More Useful Calculator

Up until now, all of the discussion about pdCalc has focused on the design and implementation of a completed code available for download from GitHub. The remainder of this chapter, however, marks a departure from this style. Henceforth, we will discuss only ideas for extensions and suggestions for how pdCalc might be modified to accommodate new features. Not only is working code not provided, but working code was not created before writing these sections. Therefore, the designs we're about to discuss have not been tested, and the adventurous reader choosing to complete these extensions may discover the ideas to be discussed are suboptimal, or, dare I say, wrong. Welcome to the wild west of designing features from a blank slate! Experimentation and iteration will be required.

8.2.1 Complex Numbers

The original design specification for the calculator called for double-precision numbers, and we designed and implemented the calculator explicitly to handle only double-precision numbers. However, requirements change. Suppose your colleague, an electrical engineer, drops by your office, falls in love with your calculator, but requires a calculator that handles complex (imaginary) numbers. That's a reasonable request, so let's look at how we might refactor our calculator to satisfy this new feature.

Adding complex numbers requires four main modifications to pdCalc: using a complex number representation internally instead of representing numbers as `doubles`, changing input and output (and, by extension, parsing) to accommodate complex numbers, modifying pdCalc's stack to store complex numbers instead of `doubles`, and modifying commands to perform their calculations on complex numbers instead of real valued inputs. The first change, finding a C++ representation for complex numbers, is trivial; we'll use `std::complex<double>`. A number with only a real part will simply be stored as a `complex<double>` with its imaginary part set to 0. The other three changes are less trivial. Let's now look in more depth at some design options capable of accommodating these changes.

Modifying Input and Output

Of all the required changes, modifying the I/O routines is actually the easiest. The first item to be addressed is how will complex numbers be interpreted and presented. For example, do we want a complex number, `c`, to be represented as `c = re + im * i` (maybe the imaginary number should be `j` since the feature request came from an electrical engineer)? Perhaps we prefer using `c = (re, im)` or a variant that uses angle brackets or square brackets instead. There is no correct answer to this question. Although some choices might be easier to implement than others, since this choice is merely a convention, in practice, we would defer resolution to our customer. For our case study, we'll simply adopt the convention `c = (re, im)`.

We'll only discuss modifying the command line version of the I/O. Once the infrastructure to handle complex numbers is in place for the CLI, adapting the GUI should be reasonably straightforward. The first problem that we encounter is the `Tokenizer` class. The original design for this class simply tokenized by splitting input on whitespace. However, for complex numbers, this scheme is insufficient. For example, complex numbers would be tokenized differently based on whether or not a space was inserted after the comma.

At some point, input becomes sufficiently complex that you'll need to employ a language grammar and migrate the simple input routines to a "real" scanner and parser (possibly using libraries such as lex and yacc). Some might argue that by adding complex numbers, we have reached this level of complexity. However, I think that we can probably scrape by with our existing simple input tokenizer if we modify the `tokenize()` routine to scan for the '(' token and create one "number" token for anything between and including the opening and closing parenthesis. Obviously, we would need to perform some basic error checking to ensure correct formatting. Another alternative would be to decompose the input stream based on regular expression matching. This is essentially how lex operates, and I would investigate using lex or a similar library before writing a sophisticated scanner from scratch.

The next input problem we encounter is parsing of numbers in `CommandInterpreterImpl`'s `executeCommand()` function. Currently, a string argument (the token) is passed to this function, and the string is parsed to determine if it is a number or a command. Upon inspection, we can see that `executeCommand()` will work for complex numbers if we modify `isNum()` to identify and return complex numbers instead of floating-point numbers. Finally, the `EnterNumber` command will need to be updated to accept and store a `complex<double>`.

That takes care of modifying the input routines, but how do we modify the output routines? Recall that the `Cli` class is an (indirect) observer of the `Stack`'s `stackChanged()` event. Whenever the `Stack` raises this event, the `Cli`'s `stackChanged()` function will be called to output the current stack to the command line. Let's examine how `Cli::stackChanged()` is implemented. Essentially, the CLI calls back to the stack to fill a container with the top `nElements` using the following function call:

```
auto v = Stack::Instance().getElements(nElements);
```

A `string`, s, and corresponding `back_inserter`, bi, are then created and filled first with some stack metadata and then with the stack elements using the following code:

```
for( auto j = v.size(); auto i : views::reverse(v) )
{
  std::format_to(bi, "{}:\t{:.12g}\n", j--, i);
}
```

Finally, s is posted to the CLI's output routine, which outputs it to the CLI's output stream. Once Stack's getElements() function is modified to return a vector<complex<double>> and the output formatting is changed accordingly, Cli's stackChanged() function will work as expected. Very few changes are actually required – that's the beauty of well-designed and well-implemented code.

Modifying the Stack

In Chapter 3, we originally designed the calculator's stack to operate only on double-precision variables. Clearly, this limitation means the Stack class must now be refactored in order to handle complex numbers. At the time, we questioned the logic of hard-coding the target data type for the stack, and I recommended not designing a generic Stack class. My suggestion was, in general, to not design generic interfaces until the first reuse case is clearly established. Designing good generic interfaces is generally harder than designing specific types, and from my personal experience, I've found that serendipitous reuse of code infrequently comes to fruition. However, for our Stack class, the time to reuse this data structure for another data type has come, and it is prudent, at this point, to convert the Stack's interface into a generic interface rather than merely refactor the class to be hard-coded for complex numbers.

Making the Stack class generic is almost as easy as you might expect. The first step is to make the interface itself generic by replacing explicit uses of double with our generic type T. The interface becomes

```
template<typename T>
class Stack : private Publisher
{
public:
  static Stack& Instance();
  void push(T, bool suppressChangeEvent = false);
  T pop(bool suppressChangeEvent = false);
  void swapTop();

  std::vector<T> getElements(size_t n) const;
  void getElements(size_t n, std::vector<T>&) const;

  using Publisher::attach;
  using Publisher::detach;
};
```

In general, the required implementation changes are straightforward. Uses of double are replaced with T, and the uses of the Stack class within pdCalc obviously must be refactored to use the generic rather than the nontemplated interface.

The last part of the interface that requires modification is the five global extern "C" helper functions added in Chapter 7 for exporting stack commands to plugins. Because these functions must have C linkage, we cannot make them templates nor can they return the C++ complex type in place of a double. The first problem is not quite as dire as it may appear at first glance. While our goal is to make the Stack class generic and reusable, the stack's plugin interface does not need to be generic. For any particular version of pdCalc, either one that operates on real numbers or one that operates on complex numbers, only one particular instantiation of Stack<T> will exist in the system, and this one instantiation will have a particular realization for T. Therefore, the C linkage interface to the stack for pdCalc needs to only reflect the choice of T used in the calculator. That is, the container is designed to be generic and reusable, but the interface for plugins does not require this flexibility since it is not reused once a data format for the calculator has been chosen.

Replacing the complex<double> representation in the C linkage interface to the stack is straightforward. We have several options. First, we could replace each double with a sequence of two doubles: one representing the real part and one representing the complex part. Of course, since a C function cannot natively return two doubles, we would have to modify the functions returning a stack value. One option would be to use pointer parameters in argument lists to "return" complex values through these parameters. A second option would be to return complex numbers through an array. Another solution, and my preferred choice, would be to simply define a struct:

```
struct Complex
{
  double re;
  double im;
};
```

to complement the interface functions, replacing the current use of double with Complex. While this new Complex struct does duplicate the storage of the standard complex class, we cannot use the standard complex class in a pure C interface.

Modifying Commands

Modifying commands to work with complex numbers is really quite easy since the C++ library provides overloads for all of the mathematical operations required by our calculator. Minus the syntactic changes of replacing `Stack` with `Stack<complex<double>>` (hopefully we've aliased that somewhere) and swapping `complex<double>` for `double` in `BinaryCommand` and `UnaryCommand`, most of the commands remain unchanged. For example, clearing a stack of real numbers vs. clearing a stack of complex numbers is identical. Adding two complex numbers vs. adding two real numbers is identical, given operator overloading. Of course, we might want to add additional commands such as complex conjugate, but even that functionality is provided by the C++ `complex` class. In the event that a command you've created uses an algorithm not supported natively by the `complex` class, you are likely to encounter more mathematical difficulties than programmatic ones in modifying commands to support complex numbers.

8.2.2 Variables

Earlier in this chapter, we implemented stored procedures as a method for storing a simple instruction sequence. While stored procedures work fine for trivial operations that only use each input once (e.g., the Pythagorean theorem), you'll very quickly run into problems trying to implement more complicated formulas that use each input more than once (e.g., the quadratic formula). To overcome this difficulty, you'll need to implement the ability to store arguments in named variables.

Implementing variables in pdCalc will require several modifications to existing components, including the addition of one prominent new component, a symbol table. For simplicity in example code, I have reverted to using a real number representation for pdCalc. However, using complex numbers would add no additional design complexity. Let's now explore some possible design ideas for implementing variables.

Input and New Commands

Obviously, using variables will require some means of providing symbolic names. Currently, our calculator only accepts numbers and commands as input. Inputting any string that cannot be found in the `CommandFactory` results in an error. Recall, however, that this error is generated in the `CommandInterpreter`, not in the tokenizer. Therefore, we need to modify the `CommandInterpreter` to not reject strings but instead to somehow place them on the stack. For now, we'll assume that the stack can accept strings in addition to numbers. We'll discuss the necessary modifications to the `Stack` class in the upcoming sections. Again, we'll restrict our discussion to the command line interface. The only additional complication posed by the graphical user interface is providing a mechanism to input character strings in addition to numbers (perhaps a virtual keyboard to accompany the virtual numeric keypad).

Technically, we could allow any string to represent a variable. However, we are probably better served by restricting the allowable syntax to some subset of strings, possibly delimited by a symbol to differentiate variable names from commands. Because this choice is merely convention, you are free to choose whatever rules suit yours or your users' tastes. Personally, I would probably choose something like variable names must begin with a letter and can contain any combination of letters, numbers, and possibly a few special symbols such as the underscore. To eliminate confusion between variable names and commands, I would enclose variables in either single or double quotation marks.

Now that we've established the syntax for variables, we'll still need a mechanism for taking a number from the stack and storing it into a variable. The simplest method for accomplishing this task is to provide a new binary command, `store`, that removes a number and a string from the stack and creates a symbol table entry linking this variable name to this number. For example, consider the stack

```
4.5
2.9
"x"
```

Issuing the `store` command should result in an entry of $x \rightarrow 2.9$ in the symbol table and a resultant stack of

```
4.5
```

Implicitly, variables should be converted to numbers for use during calculations but appear as names on the stack. We should also provide an explicit command, `eval`, to convert a symbolic name into a number. For example, given the stack

```
"x"
```

issuing the `eval` command should result in the stack

```
2.9
```

Such a command should have a fairly obvious implementation: replace the variable on the top of the stack with its value from the symbol table. Obviously, requesting the evaluation of a variable not in the symbol table should result in an error. Evaluating a number can either result in an error or, preferably, just return the number. You can probably think of any number of fancy commands for working with variables (e.g., list the symbol table). However, store and eval commands comprise the minimum necessary command set to use variables.

Number Representation and the Stack

Until now, our stack has only needed to represent a single, unique type, either a real or complex number. However, since variables and numbers can both be stored on the stack, we need the ability for the stack to store both types simultaneously. We dismiss immediately the notion of a stack that could handle two distinct types simultaneously as this would lead quickly to chaos. Instead, we seek a uniform representation capable of handling both number and variable types through a single interface. Naturally, we turn to a hierarchy.

Consider the design expressed in the class diagram in Figure 8-6. This hierarchy enables both Variables and Numbers to be used interchangeably as Values. This polymorphic design solves three problems that we've already encountered. First, Variables and Numbers can both be stored uniformly in a Stack<Value*> (likely using a more appropriate smart pointer storage scheme). Second, when commands such as Add or Sine need a number to perform an operation, they can pop Values from the stack and request doubles through the virtual evaluate() function. Obviously, a Number directly stores the double that it represents, while a Variable stores the variable's name, which can be converted to a numeric value via lookup in the variable symbol table. Finally, subclasses of Value can return a string representation of their underlying value (either a Number's numeric value or a Variable's name). This string conversion is necessary for display on the I/O stack.

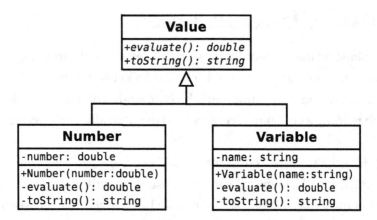

Figure 8-6. *A hierarchy capable of representing both numbers and variables uniformly*

The Symbol Table

At its core, a symbol table is merely a data structure that allows symbolic lookup by pairing a key to a value (an associative array). In this case, the name of the variable serves as the key, and the numeric value serves as the value. The C++ standard library provides this service directly through either a map or an unordered_map, depending on the desired underlying data structure. However, as in Chapter 3, I highly recommend against directly using a standard library container as an external facing interface within a program. Instead, one should employ the adapter pattern to encapsulate the library container behind an interface defined by the application itself. This pattern adds no restrictions to the users of a class, but it does permit the designer to restrict, expand, or later modify the component's interface independent of the interface of the underlying library container.

Therefore, the recommended design for a symbol table is to create a SymbolTable class to wrap an unordered_map<string, double>. This underlying hash table provides a storage type to map between the variable name as a string and the underlying numeric value. The public interface for the SymbolTable class provides member functions for adding and, optionally (we did not specify a command for clearing variables), removing variables from the symbol table. The SymbolTable should probably be implemented as a singleton since we only need one symbol table in the calculator.

A Trivial Extension: Numeric Constants

Once we've established the mechanics for storing user-defined variables, we can make a trivial extension to provide user-defined constants. Constants are simply variables that cannot be altered once set. Constants could be hard-coded in pdCalc, added at program launch through reading a constants file, or added dynamically during calculator execution.

Obviously, in order to store a constant, we will need to add a new command; let's call it cstore. cstore works identically to store except that the command informs the symbol table that the variable being stored cannot be changed. We have two obvious options for implementation. First, inside the SymbolTable class, we add a second map that indicates whether a given name represents a variable or a constant. The advantage of this approach is that adding an additional map will require minimal implementation changes to the existing code. The disadvantage is that this approach requires two independent lookups for each call to the symbol table. The better approach is to modify the original map to store the value type as an Entry instead of a double, where an Entry is defined as

```
struct Entry
{
  double val;
  bool isConst;
};
```

Of course, to avoid hard-coding the double type, we could, of course, template both SymbolTable and Entry.

Functionality Enabled by Variables

Let's examine what variables enable us to do. Consider the quadratic equation $ax^2 + bx + c = 0$ with roots given by

$$r = \frac{-b \pm \sqrt{b^2 - 4ac}}{2a}$$

Where we formerly could not write a stored procedure for computing both roots, we can now write the stored procedure:

```
"c" store "b" store "a" store "b" 2 pow 4 "a" "c" * * - sqrt "root" store
"b" neg "root" + 2 a * / "b" neg "root" - 2 a * /
```

which will take three entries from the stack representing the coefficients a, b, c and return two entries representing the roots of the quadratic equation. Now, our calculator is getting somewhere!

8.3 Some Interesting Extensions for Self-Exploration

This chapter concludes with a section listing a few interesting extensions to pdCalc that you might consider trying on your own. In contrast to the previous section, I offer no design ideas to get you started. I have provided merely a brief description of each challenge.

8.3.1 High DPI Scaling

Monitors with extremely high pixel resolutions are becoming increasingly the norm. Consider how you would modify the GUI for pdCalc to properly handle scaling for such displays. Is this feature operating system independent or do we have another use for the PlatformFactory from Chapter 7? Since version 5.6, Qt helps you out with this task via an interface for high DPI scaling.

8.3.2 Dynamic Skinning

In Chapter 6, a class was introduced to manage the look-and-feel of the GUI. However, the provided implementation only centralized the look-and-feel. It did not permit user customization.

Users often want to customize the look-and-feel of their applications. Applications that permit such changes are considered "skinable," and each different look-and-feel is called a skin. Consider an interface and the appropriate implementation changes necessary to the LookAndFeel class to enable skinning of pdCalc. Some possible options include a dialog for customizing individual widgets or a mechanism to choose skins from skin configuration files. Having a centralized class to handle the look-and-feel for the application should make this change straightforward. Don't forget to add a signal to LookAndFeel so the other GUI elements will know when they need to repaint themselves with a new appearance!

8.3.3 Flow Control

With variables, we greatly enhanced the flexibility of stored procedures. For computing most formulas, this framework should prove sufficient. However, what if we wanted to implement a recursive formula such as computing the factorial of a number. While we have the ability to perform such complex computations via plugins, it would be nice to extend this functionality to users of the calculator who are not also experienced C++ programmers. To accomplish this task, we would need to devise a syntax for flow control. The simplest design would at least be able to handle looping and conditional operations. Adding flow control to pdCalc would be a fairly significant enhancement in terms of both added capability and implementation effort. It might be time to move to a real scanner and parser!

8.3.4 An Alternative GUI Layout

The pdCalc GUI currently has a vertical orientation inspired by the HP48S calculator. However, modern screen resolutions tend to be wider than they are tall, making the vertical orientation suboptimal. Hard-coding a horizontal orientation is no more challenging than the original vertical orientation. Consider instead how to redesign pdCalc to be able to switch between orientations at runtime. Maybe vertical orientation is simply a different skin option?

8.3.5 A Graphing Calculator

The HP48 series of calculators were not merely scientific calculators; they were graphing calculators. Although it might not be practical to implement a graphing calculator for a computer when sophisticated stand-alone graphing programs exist, the exercise might prove to be a lot of fun. Starting with version 5.7, Qt now includes a graphing module to make this task significantly easier than it would have been previously. Given this graphing widget set, the biggest challenge might simply be devising a method for graphical input. If you're in the mood for a silly throwback to the 1970s, consider implementing an ASCII graphing calculator for the CLI!

8.3.6 A Plugin Management System

Currently, plugins are loaded during pdCalc's startup, and which plugins to load are determined by reading shared library names from a text file. Plugins, once loaded, cannot be unloaded. Consider implementing a dynamic plugin management system so that plugins can be selected, loaded, and unloaded at runtime. You could even extend the plugin interface to enable dynamic querying of plugin descriptions. I think the real gotcha here will be in figuring out how to handle the unloading of a plugin that has one of its commands currently on the undo/redo stack.

8.3.7 A Mobile Device Interface

In my original machinations for creating this book, I envisioned a chapter describing how to extend pdCalc to an iOS or Android tablet. The Qt library can once again help you with this task. The reason I did not include such a chapter in this book is that I do not have any practical experience with tablet programming. I felt it would be disingenuous to try to teach others how to design a tablet interface from my first ever foray into that design space. Well, it might have been an excellent example of a bad design! Nonetheless, extending pdCalc to a tablet or smartphone interface is a worthy challenge.

8.3.8 pdCalc in the Cloud

Suppose you wanted to extend pdCalc to execute in the cloud. The design of pdCalc presented in this book would probably be classified as a modular monolith. Most large-scale cloud programs are designed as distributed services. Therefore, the first design change I would propose would be to restructure pdCalc into a microservices architecture. Instead of constructing modules as shared libraries, we would instead implement modules as separate services, each running in its own container. Modules would then communicate via RESTful APIs instead of function calls. Designing RESTful APIs from the existing C++ APIs should be a straightforward task. Depending on the expected load on the program, you could add dynamic scaling via a container orchestration service such as Kubernetes. However, I suspect our lowly calculator would unlikely ever see a load requiring more than a single container per service. A proper build system would even include an automated test suite and a pipeline for continuous integration and continuous deployment.

A convenient feature of a microservice architecture is that since different components communicate through APIs, it is trivial to write different modules in different programming languages. Likely, the GUI for a cloud-based pdCalc would be a web page, and we'd probably want to write that component in JavaScript (or TypeScript), potentially using a library such as Angular. The backend could be designed with C++, but Python might be a more suitable language. Depending on the design for session state and the stack, pdCalc might even need a database.

Porting pdCalc to the cloud sounds like more than a minor design modification. In fact, its design might be sufficiently distinct to warrant its own book – feel free to email me if you want to cowrite it. Now that you're done with this book, you and I will both need a new project!

APPENDIX A

Acquiring, Building, and Executing pdCalc

This appendix explains how to acquire and build pdCalc, the program described in this book.

A.1 Getting the Source Code

The source code for pdCalc is hosted on Apress's GitHub repository:

`https://github.com/Apress/practical-cplusplus-design-2e`

From the GitHub site, you have two options for downloading the source code. The first option is to use a git client (`https://git-scm.com/`) and clone the repository to your local computer. For those familiar with managing source code with git, this is the preferred source code acquisition method. Using git to clone the repository will enable you to pull periodic bug updates from the online repository. Maybe you'll even decide to contribute a bug fix to pdCalc yourself! The second option for acquiring the source code is to download a single zip file of pdCalc from GitHub. Obviously, downloading a single zip file makes updating the source code significantly more challenging than using git if you have made any local changes.

© Adam Singer 2022
A. B. Singer, *Practical C++ Design*, https://doi.org/10.1007/978-1-4842-7407-1

A.2 Dependencies

Now that you have the source code, you'll probably want to build and execute pdCalc and its unit test suite. Before that can be accomplished, however, you'll need to ensure that you have an appropriate toolchain. Intentionally, pdCalc requires very few external dependencies, all of which can be obtained for Linux, Windows, or Mac OS X at no cost. In order to build pdCalc, you will need a modern C++ compiler (C++20 compliant), Qt (version 5 or 6), and CMake.

As someone willing to have read this book, you probably already have or know how to get a C++ compiler. Unfortunately, at the time of writing, only one major compiler, Microsoft's Visual C++ (MSVC), sufficiently supports the C++20 standard to build pdCalc. Fortunately, however, Microsoft provides a free version of Visual Studio (VS), Community Edition, which is downloadable from their website (`https://visualstudio.microsoft.com`). The current version of Visual Studio is 2019, with version VS 2022 currently in preview. For Visual Studio 2019, you'll need at least version 16.10 to build the code as is.

On the Windows platform, Qt and its IDE, Qt Creator, can be downloaded from `www.qt.io/download`. Once you are on the website, select the version that is licensed appropriately for your use. pdCalc is distributed under the GPL version 3, so the open source edition of Qt is compatible. From there, download and execute the Qt Online Installer. If you don't already have a Qt account, you'll need to create one first. When you're ready to install Qt, ensure you select the MSVC 2019 (32 or 64 bit, as appropriate) binaries for installation. While not strictly necessary, I highly recommend also installing Qt Creator. Please be patient with the download. Qt, with its many modules, is a powerful but very sizable package.

If you've written a lot of cross-platform C++ code, you've probably already encountered CMake. If it is not already installed on your system, it can be acquired from the CMake website: `https://cmake.org`. Building pdCalc with CMake is described in Section A.3.

For the first edition of this book, pdCalc was built with Qt's own qmake tool. While qmake is still supported in Qt 6, the preferred build system for Qt 6 is CMake. I therefore chose to "upgrade" pdCalc's build system from qmake to CMake. Additionally, even though CMake did not support automatic detection of C++ modules when this book was written, I found CMake to be more accommodating than qmake in compiling C++ modules. Admittedly, this ease of use may reflect more on my experience with each tool than with each tool's actual flexibility.

A.3 Building pdCalc

pdCalc uses CMake for its build system and QTest for its unit test framework. Other good alternatives for unit testing are boost test, cppunit, or Google Test. QTest was used to avoid adding any additional dependencies. To build pdCalc, you can either configure and compile at the command line or use Qt Creator. Both build methods rely on CMake. Therefore, before discussing how to build pdCalc, a brief explanation of how CMake operates is warranted.

Using CMake to build a solution is a two-step process involving both CMake and a build tool such as ninja or make. CMake itself does not directly call the compiler and linker. Rather, CMake is simply a cross-platform build file generator. Therefore, in the first step of the build process, CMake reads its `CMakeLists.txt` configuration files and produces files native to the build tool you specified. This step needs to be performed before the first build and subsequently only after changes requiring modification to configuration files (e.g., the addition of a new source file). In the second step, the object code is built using your specified build tool, which, in turn, calls the compiler and linker. For pdCalc, on a Windows system, I set up the CMake configuration files to use Visual Studio's nmake, which will, in turn, use the MSVC compiler and linker. Alternatively, it should be fairly easy to modify the `CMakeLists.txt` files to build with Visual Studio directly or with its command line build tool, msbuild. The main problems you will likely encounter are in the post build steps required to copy files (e.g., the plugin file and some testing files) to the proper build directories.

Now that you understand how CMake works, let's examine how to build pdCalc using either Qt Creator or the command line. Since MSVC is the only compiler currently capable of building pdCalc, only Windows instructions are given. Once they reach a level of maturity capable of compiling pdCalc, the build processes using GCC and clang should be similar. In particular, though, you will need to modify the `CMakeLists.txt` files to manually account for module interface files and compiler options. I've provided an initial framework for working with both GCC and clang in the top-level CMake configuration file.

A.3.1 Using Qt Creator

If your preference is to use Qt Creator, most of the complexity of using CMake will be hidden from you. First, you need to ensure that Qt Creator is configured to use nmake (make if you are attempting to use GCC or clang). To begin, simply launch the IDE and click Tools->Options... from the menu. This will display the Qt Creator options dialog. If it is not already selected, select the Kits tab. If you have a valid C++ compiler and Qt installed, you should see at least one desktop kit in the auto-detected list. Highlight the kit you intend to use. Toward the bottom of this kit's options, you should see the ability to set the CMake Generator. If it is not already set to NMake Makefiles, click Change... and select NMake Makefiles as your generator and click Ok. You are now ready to open pdCalc's project.

Go to the File menu and open the CMakeLists.txt file located at the top level of pdCalc's source tree. The first time you open a CMake project file with Qt Creator, you will be presented with a configuration list asking you which kit to target (you may only have one option). Select a kit that is configured to use either Qt 5 or 6, a C++20-conforming compiler, and a properly configured CMake generator. If you expand the Details button for your selected Qt version, you will be given the option to configure pdCalc for Debug, Release, and a few other configurations. Select the configurations you wish to build, and, optionally, modify the default location for your out-of-source build. Once you have selected your configuration options, click the Configure Project button. Qt Creator will then configure your project. You can always change both your build and execute configuration options later through the Projects tab on the left (the wrench icon) in Qt Creator.

After Qt Creator configures your project, you will be presented with the edit mode for the project. The edit mode of Qt Creator is a good tool for exploring the source code. The complete source tree will appear in an expandable tree control on the left side of the display, and individual files can be opened by clicking on them. The source tree for pdCalc is described in Appendix B.

Qt Creator works similarly to any other fully featured IDE you have probably used, and a complete description of its usage is beyond the scope of this appendix (see http://doc.qt.io/qtcreator for its full manual). However, I will highlight a few quick features to help get you started. If you don't like Qt Creator, pdCalc should work with any IDE that can understand CMake projects. You also have the option of using any IDE or text editor to view and modify the source code and then using the command line for compiling and debugging.

The first shortcut to learn is choosing which configuration of your project you want to build and run. These options are selected by the monitor icon in the lower left corner of the display. It will currently be labeled with the active project (pdCalc if it's the only project loaded) and the current configuration (e.g., Debug or Release). If you click this monitor icon, a pane will open, allowing you to select which configuration you wish to build and which executable you wish to run. For pdCalc, you'll have four executable options: pdCalc, pdCalc-simple-cli, pdCalc-simple-gui, and testDriver. pdCalc runs the full version of pdCalc (the GUI by default), pdCalc-simple-cli runs the simple CLI constructed at the end of Chapter 5, pdCalc-simple-gui runs the simple GUI constructed at the end of Chapter 6, and testDriver runs the unit test suite. If you want to change the build or run configuration options, you can click the Projects button (folder icon) on the left side of the display to open the configuration panel. Clicking the Edit button will bring you back to edit mode.

pdCalc can be built either through the Build menu or by clicking the hammer icon (at least that's what it looks like to me) on the lower left side of the display. If you want to watch the compiler output as it builds, click the Compile Output button on the bottom of your screen. If you have any build issues, they can be found on the Issues tab of the same information panel. Clicking on one of these issues should take you to the offending line of source code. Hopefully, pdCalc will build for you with no issues, no warnings, and no errors. If you have build problems, see the "Troubleshooting" section.

A.3.2 Using the Command Line

If Qt Creator is not for you, pdCalc can be built directly at the command line. The first step in building at the command line is, of course, launching the command shell. While this may seem obvious, what might not be obvious is that you need to specifically launch the Visual Studio command shell, usually located in the start menu with a name like "x64 Native Tools Command Prompt for VS 2019." I always build in 64-bit mode, but I suspect pdCalc will build correctly if you choose the 32-bit shell and have all of the appropriate 32-bit libraries installed.

Once you have launched a VS command shell, you are ready to configure CMake and then compile. CMake supports out-of-source builds, which is the recommended strategy. Simply create a build directory for each configuration of pdCalc that you wish to build, change your path to the build directory, and issue the following command:

```
CMake -G"NMake Makefiles" $PATH_TO_PDCALC
```

where $PATH_TO_PDCALC must be replaced by the path to the CMakeLists.txt file in pdCalc's root directory. If Qt is in your environment path variable, CMake should produce all the files needed to build pdCalc. If you receive an error indicating that CMake could not find Qt, you will need to either add the Qt bin directory to your path or manually specify how to find Qt by setting the CMAKE_PREFIX_PATH variable. For example, on my Windows machine, to use 64-bit Qt 5, I would instead call CMake as follows:

```
cmake -G"NMake Makefiles" -DCMAKE_PREFIX_PATH="c:\Qt\5.15.2\msvc2019_64"
$PATH_TO_PDCALC
```

You can also issue additional options to CMake during this initial configuration phase, or you can reconfigure CMake later. CMake configuration options are issued using the -D switch. For example, to use Qt 6 (the configuration defaults to Qt 5), you would issue the following command:

```
cmake -G"NMake Makefiles" -DPDCALC_QT_VERSION=6 $PATH_TO_PDCALC
```

The other option you may wish to specify at the command line is which configuration you want to build. By default, CMake will configure the project to build the Debug configuration. If instead you wanted to configure CMake to build Release, you would issue the following command:

```
cmake -G"NMake Makefiles" -DCMAKE_BUILD_TYPE=Release $PATH_TO_PDCALC
```

If it's not obvious, you can combine multiple CMake options on one line, and you can reissue separate options on successive calls to CMake. Your configuration options are saved in a CMake cache file in the build tree.

The preceding command triggers CMake to descend the pdCalc directory tree recursively reading each configuration file and writing a corresponding makefile. If everything executes normally, the output from the preceding command should be a sequence of lines informing you about detected compiler configurations and features ending with a statement informing you that build files have been written. After these makefiles are written, pdCalc can be built by issuing the build command nmake in the same top-level directory from which the CMake command was issued. The code should build cleanly without errors.

A.4 Executing pdCalc

pdCalc, pdCalc-simple-cli, and pdCalc-simple-gui and the unit test suite can be executed from Qt Creator, the command line, or double-clicking the executable (if all of your executable paths are correctly set). Let's look at the details for the first two options. Hopefully, double-clicking is self-explanatory.

A.4.1 Using Qt Creator

Using Qt Creator, the currently selected executable can be started by pressing the green triangular run button in the lower left corner. The green triangle with the magnifying glass will start the executable in Qt Creator's interactive debugger. If the source code is out of date, the project will be built before execution begins. If you currently have the testDriver executable selected, the unit test suite will execute, and its output will appear in the Application Output information panel. Hopefully, you will see details of individual tests passing with a final message of "All tests passed." If you currently have either the pdCalc or pdCalc-simple-gui executable selected, the GUI should launch. If you have the pdCalc-simple-cli executable selected, the CLI will launch in the Application Output information panel. However, you cannot interact with the CLI using this panel, making this mode of executing the CLI rather useless.

A.4.2 Using the Command Line

pdCalc is configured to build all executables in the bin directory and all shared libraries in the lib directory. Therefore, in Windows, pdCalc's lib directory must be added to the path before the executables are launched. For example, for a command line execution of pdCalc on Windows, one must first issue the following command:

```
path=%path%;$PATH_TO_PDCALC_LIB
```

where $PATH_TO_PDCALC_LIB must be replaced by the relative or absolute path to the pdCalc lib directory. As an example, $PATH_TO_PDCALC_LIB can be set to ..\lib for the relative path if executing pdCalc from the bin directory. Of course, an alternative is to simply copy the DLLs into the same location as the executables.

A build of pdCalc creates four executables: pdCalc, pdCalc-simple-cli, pdCalc-simple-gui, and testPdCalc (all have an .exe extension in Windows).

testPdCalc runs the unit test suite; it is a command line only program. As each unit test runs, you will see the names of the individual tests, the passage or failure of each test, and some statistics for each unit test suite. If all of the tests pass, an "All tests passed" message will be issued as the final output.

The pdCalc executable launches the complete calculator. It can be launched with the --gui option to run the graphical user interface, the --cli option to run the command line interface, or the --batch option to run the calculator in batch mode. Batch operation requires an input file and, optionally, an output file. pdCalc can also be given the --help option to see a listing of the various modes of operation. If no command line option is given, pdCalc defaults to launching the GUI.

The pdCalc-simple-cli executable launches the simple CLI built at the end of Chapter 5. The pdCalc-simple-gui executable launches the simple GUI built at the end of Chapter 6. Strictly speaking, both of these executables are unnecessary. They are provided merely as a convenience to the reader to be able to run pdCalc before it reaches feature complete status. In agile terms, these feature-incomplete executables provide stages of a minimum viable product.

A.5 Troubleshooting

Despite considerable effort to ensure trouble-free building of pdCalc, I still find that every different combination of Qt, CMake, environment variables, operating system, and probably the weather manages to create some new, wonderful build error. If you encounter build or runtime errors, I encourage you to make an effort to diagnose and correct them yourself. Diagnosing and correcting build errors is a skill worth acquiring. It will also give you a greater appreciation for the thankless soul on your team tasked with maintaining your cross-platform build system. Often, the problem is as trivial as conflicting compiler versions or incorrect/missing paths.

Finally, I do understand that it can be extremely frustrating to invest time (and possibly money) on a new book and find that you cannot build the accompanying source code per the author's instructions. If you've tried unsuccessfully to fix a build or runtime error yourself and find yourself ready to throw your computer (or this book!) out of the nearest window, just send me an email (PracticalDesignBook@gmail.com). I'll do my best to get you up and running as quickly and as painlessly as possible.

Organization of the Source Code

The easiest way to explore the source code is through an IDE such as Qt Creator. However, this appendix is provided as a navigational guide to the source code tree. In addition to the source code files listed in the following tables, the source tree also contains CMake project files, a few assorted configuration files, and a few baseline files for regression tests.

The root level in the source code tree contains the root level `CMakeLists.txt` file and two directories, `src` and `test`, which contain the source code for pdCalc and the unit tests, respectively. Let's look at these directories separately.

B.1 The src Directory

The `src` directory subdivides into six directories: `3rdParty`, `app`, `utilities`, `backend`, `ui`, and `plugins`. The `3rdParty` directory contains the single instance of third-party code provided with pdCalc. The `app` directory is a folder for containing the `pdCalc`, `pdCalc-simple-cli`, and `pdCalc-simple-gui` directories. The `utilities` directory contains utility classes for pdCalc. The `backend` directory contains the stack module, the command dispatcher module, and all of the plugin management functionality. The `ui` directory is a folder for containing the user interface components, including both the CLI and the GUI. Finally, the `plugins` directory houses the single plugin included with pdCalc. Let's now look at the files contained in each directory.

© Adam Singer 2022
A. B. Singer, *Practical C++ Design*, https://doi.org/10.1007/978-1-4842-7407-1

B.1.1 The 3rdParty Directory

The 3rdParty directory contains the single third-party tool required by pdCalc, cppcoro's generator.hpp. While this file is only included in a single source file, Tokenizer.m.cpp in the utilities directory, it was placed in its own directory to clearly delineate code that is part of pdCalc versus code that is external to pdCalc.

B.1.2 The app/pdCalc Directory

The pdCalc directory contains the source code that compiles into the pdCalc executable. Notably, this directory contains the main() function located in main.cpp, which is the entry point into the application.

B.1.3 The app/pdCalc-simple-cli Directory

The pdCalc-simple-cli directory contains the source code that compiles into the simple CLI-only executable defined at the end of Chapter 5. This directory contains a single file, main.cpp.

B.1.4 The app/pdCalc-simple-gui Directory

The pdCalc-simple-gui directory contains the source code that compiles into the simple GUI-only executable defined at the end of Chapter 6. This directory contains a single file, main.cpp.

B.1.5 The utilities Directory

The utilities directory contains generic, reusable components, none of which are specifically associated with the calculator's logic. Table B-1 lists the files contained in the utilities directory.

Table B-1. *Source files in the* utilities *directory*

Module Interface Files

Exception.m.cpp

Observer.m.cpp

Publisher.m.cpp

Tokenizer.m.cpp

Utilities.m.cpp

B.1.6 The backend Directory

The backend directory contains all of the "business logic" for the calculator. From the model-view-controller perspective, this directory contains the model and the controller. The backend directory also contains all of the logic for loading and managing plugins as well as the observer intermediary classes. Table B-2 lists the files contained in the backend directory.

Table B-2. *Source files in the backend directory*

Module Interface Files	Implementation Files
AppObservers.m.cpp	Command.cpp
Command.m.cpp	CommandInterpreter.cpp
CommandDispatcher.m.cpp	PlatformFactory.cpp
CommandInterpreter.m.cpp	PosixFactory.cpp
CommandManager.m.cpp	StackPluginInterface.cpp

(continued)

Table B-2. (*continued*)

Module Interface Files	Implementation Files
CommandFactory.m.cpp	StoredProcedure.cpp
CoreCommands.m.cpp	WindowsFactory.cpp
DynamicLoader.m.cpp	
PlatformFactory.m.cpp	
Plugin.m.cpp	
PluginLoader.m.cpp	
PosixDynamicLoader.m.cpp	
PosixFactory.m.cpp	
Stack.m.cpp	
StackPluginInterface.m.cpp	
StoredProcedure.m.cpp	
WindowsDynamicLoader.m.cpp	
WindowsFactory.m.cpp	

B.1.7 The ui Directory

The ui directory contains the source code for the user interface module, including both the CLI and the GUI. Notably, this is the only directory in pdCalc that contains traditional header files (excluding the test suite). Table B-3 lists the source files found in the ui directory.

Table B-3. *Source files in the* ui *directory*

Header Files	Module Interface Files	Implementation Files
CommandButton.h	Cli.m.cpp	CommandButton.cpp
Display.h	UserInterface.m.cpp	Display.cpp
GuiModel.h		GuiModel.cpp
InputWidget.h		InputWidget.cpp
LookAndFeel.h		LookAndFeel.cpp
MainWindow.h		MainWindow.cpp
StoredProcedureDialog.h		StoredProcedureDialog.cpp

B.1.8 The plugins Directory

The plugins directory is a placeholder directory for the source code for plugins to pdCalc. It only includes one subdirectory, hyperbolicLnPlugin, which contains the source code for the hyperbolic functions and natural logarithm plugin developed in this book. The only source file in the hyperbolicLnPlugin directory is HyperbolicLnPlugin. cpp. The source code implementing plugin loading and plugin management is all contained in the backend directory.

B.2 The test Directory

The test directory is the home directory for all of the unit tests for pdCalc. This directory is simply a container for the following subdirectories, each of which tests the shared library corresponding to its name: utilitiesTest, backendTest, uiTest, and pluginsTest. The testDriver directory contains the code necessary to instantiate the tests, add them to the test manager, and execute the test suite. While I like to believe that I have been diligent in testing pdCalc thoroughly, I am certain of two things: I could have tested the code more, and bugs will be found after publication. We now detail the contents of each of the directories under test.

B.2.1 The testDriver Directory

The testDriver directory contains a single source file, main.cpp. This file sets up the QTest environment and registers all of the individual test modules. main.cpp compiles into the testPdCalc.exe executable, which is responsible for running all of the unit tests.

B.2.2 The utilitiesTest Directory

The utilitiesTest directory contains the files necessary for testing the utilities module. The files contained in this directory are listed in Table B-4.

Table B-4. *Source files in the utilitiesTest directory*

Header Files	Implementation Files
PublisherObserverTest.h	PublisherObserverTest.cpp
TokenizerTest.h	TokenizerTest.cpp

B.2.3 The backendTest Directory

The backendTest directory contains the source code for testing the backend shared library of pdCalc. The files contained in this directory can be found in Table B-5. In addition to the source code files, the directory also contains a hypotenuse file containing a test stored procedure and the files plugins.unix.pdp and plugins.unix.win, which are plugin loader files for the two respective operating systems.

Table B-5. *Source files in the backendTest directory*

Header Files	Implementation Files
CommandInterpreterTest.h	CommandInterpreterTest.cpp
CommandManagerTest.h	CommandManagerTest.cpp
CommandFactoryTest.h	CommandFactoryTest.cpp
CoreCommandsTest.h	CoreCommandsTest.cpp
PluginLoaderTest.h	PluginLoaderTest.cpp
StackTest.h	StackTest.cpp
StoredProcedureTest.h	StoredProcedureTest.cpp

B.2.4 The uiTest Directory

The uiTest directory contains the source code files necessary for testing the user interface. The files contained in this directory can be found in Table B-6. In addition to the source files, the uiTest directory contains a subdirectory, testCases. The testCases directory contains input files and output baselines used in testing the command line interface.

Table B-6. *Source files in the backendTest directory*

Header Files	Implementation Files
CliTest.h	CliTest.cpp
DisplayTest.h	DisplayTest.cpp

B.2.5 The pluginsTest Directory

The pluginsTest directory contains the source files for testing the single plugin included with pdCalc, the hyperbolic functions, and natural logarithm plugin. These tests are contained in the following two source files: HyperbolicLnPluginTest.h and HyperbolicLnPluginTest.cpp.

References

[1] Cmake. `https://cmake.org/`.

[2] fmtlib/fmt: A modern formatting library. `https://github.com/fmtlib/fmt`.

[3] vector<bool>{true, true, false}; The creations of a mad(dening) template specialization. `https://vector-of-bool.github.io/`.

[4] Alfred V. Aho, Moica S. Lam, Ravi Sethi, and Jeffrey D. Ullman. *Compilers: Principles, Techniques, and Tools.* Addison-Wesley, Boston, Massachusetts, second edition, 2007.

[5] Andrei Alexandrescu. *Modern C++ Design: Generic Programming and Design Patterns Applied.* Addison-Wesley, Boston, Massachusetts, 2001.

[6] Lewis Baker. Asymmetric transfer: Some thoughts on programming, C++, and other things. `https://lewissbaker.github.io/`.

[7] Lewis Baker. cppcoro: A library of C++ coroutine abstractions for the coroutines TS. `https://github.com/lewissbaker/cppcoro`.

[8] Grady Booch, Robert A. Maksimchuk, Michael W. Engel, Bobbi J. Young, Jim Conallen, and Kelli A. Houston. *Object-Oriented Analysis and Design with Applications.* Addison-Wesley, Boston, Massachusetts, third edition, 2007.

[9] Grady Booch, James Rumbaugh, and Ivar Jacobson. *The Unified Modeling Language User Guide.* Addison-Wesley, Boston, Massachusetts, 1999.

[10] Thomas H. Cormen, Charles E. Leiserson, Ronald L. Rivest, and Clifford Stein. *Introduction to Algorithms*. The MIT Press, Cambridge, Massachusetts, third edition, 2009.

[11] Erich Gamma, Richard Helm, Ralph Johnson, and John Vlissides. *Design Patterns: Elements of Reusable Object-Oriented Software*. Addison-Wesley, Boston, Massachusetts, 1995.

[12] Free Software Foundation, Inc. GNU Public Licence version 3, June 2007. `www.gnu.org/licenses/gpl.html`.

[13] Nicolai M. Josuttis. *The C++ Standard Library: A Tutorial and Reference*. Addison-Wesley, Upper Saddle River, New Jersey, second edition, 2012.

[14] Brian W. Kernighan and Rob Pike. *The Practice of Programming*. Addison-Wesley, Reading, Massachusetts, 1999.

[15] Donald E. Knuth. *The Art of Computer Programming: Volume 1, Fundamental Algorithms*. Addison-Wesley, Boston, Massachusetts, third edition, 1997.

[16] Donald E. Knuth. *The Art of Computer Programming: Volume 2, Seminumerical Algorithms*. Addison-Wesley, Boston, Massachusetts, third edition, 1998.

[17] Donald E. Knuth. *The Art of Computer Programming: Volume 3, Sorting and Searching*. Addison-Wesley, Boston, Massachusetts, third edition, 1998.

[18] Stanley B. Lippman. *Inside The C++ Object Model*. Addison-Wesley, Reading, Massachusetts, 1996.

[19] Stanley B. Lippman and Jos´ee Lajoie. *C++ Primer*. Addison-Wesley, Reading, Massachusetts, third edition, 1998.

[20] Steve McConnell. *Code Complete*. Microsoft Press, Redmond, Washington, second edition, 2004.

[21] Scott Meyers. *More Effective C++*. Addison-Wesley, Boston, Massachusetts, 1996.

[22] Scott Meyers. *Effective STL*. Addison-Wesley, Boston, Massachusetts, 2001.

[23] Scott Meyers. *Effective C++*. Addison-Wesley, Boston, Massachusetts, third edition, 2005.

[24] Scott Meyers. *Effective Modern C++: 42 Specific Ways to Improve Your Use of C++11 and C++14*. O'Reilly, Beijing, China, 2015.

[25] Eric Niebler. Range-v3: User Manual. `https://ericniebler. github.io/range-v3/`.

[26] Eric Niebler. Standard ranges. `https://ericniebler. com/2018/12/05/standard-ranges/`.

[27] Martin Reddy. *API Design For C++*. Morgan Kaufmann, Amsterdam, The Netherlands, 2011.

[28] Suzanne Robertson and James Robertson. *Mastering the Requirements Process*. Addison-Wesley, Upper Saddle River, New Jersey, second edition, 2006.

[29] Diomidis Spinellis. *Code Quality: The Open Source Perspective*. Addison-Wesley, Boston, Massachusetts, 2006.

[30] Bjarne Stroustrup. *The C++ Programming Language*. Addison-Wesley, Upper Saddle River, New Jersey, fourth edition, 2013.

[31] Herb Sutter. *Exceptional C++*. Addison-Wesley, Boston, Massachusetts, 2000.

[32] Herb Sutter. *More Exceptional C++*. Addison-Wesley, Boston, Massachusetts, 2002.

[33] Herb Sutter. *Exceptional C++ Style*. Addison-Wesley, Boston, Massachusetts, 2005.

[34] Herb Sutter and Andrei Alexandrescu. *C++ Coding Standards: 101 Rules, Guidelines, and Best Practices*. Addison-Wesley, Boston, Massachusetts, 2005.

[35] Alexander Tarliner. *Developer Testing: Building Quality into Software.* Addison-Wesley, Boston, Massachusetts, 2016.

[36] Karl E. Wiegers. *Software Requirements.* Microsoft Press, Redmond, Washington, 2003.

[37] Wikipedia. Liskov substitution principle. `https:// en.wikipedia.org/wiki/Liskov_substitution_principle`.

[38] Wikipedia. Model-view-controller. `https://en.wikipedia. org/wiki/Model-View-Controller`.

Index

© Adam Singer 2022
A. B. Singer, *Practical C++ Design*, https://doi.org/10.1007/978-1-4842-7407-1

Printed in the United States
by Baker & Taylor Publisher Services